"This is a finely written and well-researched life of a great British hero. Driven by her deep Quaker faith and her concept of duty, Elizabeth Fry made society care about prisoners. There were three hundred women in Newgate, half-naked and lice-ridden, in just two wards: Elizabeth Fry taught their children and set up a workshop. She loved the unlovable. A driven campaigner against capital punishment, transportation, and slavery – she changed things for the better, but at a great personal sacrifice." – *Kenneth Baker (The Rt Hon Lord Baker of Dorking C.H.)*

"I was moved to tears by some of the stories, and I was also moved in a profound way by her example as a woman with a vision, battling against social and religious norms, health and so much else.

"Jean Hatton's biography gives us a penetrating and profoundly moving insight into a woman of extraordinary vision, courage, ability and determination. Piecing together the intimate thoughts and events of Fry's life from her journals, Hatton brings to life a woman who overcame childhood fears and frailty to become one of the outstanding reformers and campaigners in British history. Hatton's vivid and beautifully written book establishes Elizabeth Fry as a more significant and influential figure than previously recognized, particularly for women, who owe her a huge debt for paving the way for women to play a part in public life." – *Christina Rees, writer and theologian, member of the General Synod of the Church of England, and Chair of WATCH – Women and the Church*

"Elizabeth Fry was a most remarkable woman, and Jean Hatton's book does her justice. This sympathetic portrait recognises the turmoil and pain of Elizabeth Fry's inner life, but it also explains her unique public position in 19th Century Britain.

"The prison conditions Eli▨▨▨▨ ▨▨ ▨▨▨▨▨▨▨▨▨▨ ▨▨ England and in Scotland were d▨▨▨▨▨▨▨▨▨▨▨▨▨ conditions are better now, but t▨▨▨▨▨▨▨▨▨▨▨▨▨ as punitive. Her Christian fait▨▨▨▨▨▨▨▨▨▨▨▨▨

D0487160

reforming: this book demonstrates the power and the understanding which she derived from it. Jean Hatton makes it clear that Elizabeth Fry's contribution to the civilising of Europe was exceptional: and much more exceptional still in the context of the contemporary attitudes to women." – *Andrew R C McLellan, HM Chief Inspector of Prisons for Scotland; formerly Moderator of the General Assembly of the Church of Scotland.*

"A biography in a grand tradition: a remarkable story of physical survival and personal courage. Elizabeth Fry worked in one of the darkest areas of the early 19th century – Britain's prisons. Newgate was the most notorious, a place where strangers were unwelcome, where drunkenness and sexual abuse flourished, and where extortion and fear predominated. The prison was a truly lawless place. In these surroundings, Elizabeth worked with no sentimentality and no self-pity. Against almost overwhelming odds, she succeeded in transforming the lives of those most rejected by society. And as anyone who reads this book must attest, she did it in magnificent fashion." – *Paul Cowley, Director: Caring for Ex-offenders, www.caringforexoffenders.org, Holy Trinity Brompton, London, SW7 1JA*

The author

Jean Hatton was born in London where she also attended art college. After some years as an art teacher and adult education tutor, she went on to complete a degree in history. During this period, while also working for the Christian charity, Bible*Lands*, she wrote her first book, *The Light Bearers*. *Betsy* is her second. She has two adult sons and lives in Buckinghamshire.

BETSY

The dramatic biography of
prison reformer Elizabeth Fry

Jean Hatton

MONARCH
BOOKS

Oxford, UK & Grand Rapids, Michigan, USA

Copyright © Jean Hatton 2005.
The right of Jean Hatton to be identified
as author of this work has been asserted by her in
accordance with the Copyright, Designs
and Patents Act 1988.

All rights reserved.
No part of this publication may be reproduced or
transmitted in any form or by any means, electronic
or mechanical, including photocopy, recording or any
information storage and retrieval system, without
permission in writing from the publisher.

First published in the UK in 2005 by Monarch Books
(a publishing imprint of Lion Hudson plc),
Mayfield House, 256 Banbury Road, Oxford OX2 7DH
Tel: +44 (0) 1865 302750   Fax: +44 (0) 1865 302757
Email: monarch@lionhudson.com
www.lionhudson.com

ISBN 1 85424 705 0 (UK)
ISBN 0 8254 6092 1 (USA)

Cover portrait by Samuel Drummond, National Portrait Gallery, London

Distributed by:
UK: Marston Book Services Ltd, PO Box 269,
Abingdon, Oxon OX14 4YN;
USA: Kregel Publications, PO Box 2607,
Grand Rapids, Michigan 49501.

Unless otherwise stated, Scripture quotations are
taken from the Holy Bible, New International Version,
© 1973, 1978, 1984 by the International Bible Society.
Used by permission of Hodder and Stoughton Ltd.
All rights reserved.

British Library Cataloguing Data
A catalogue record for this book is available
from the British Library.

Book design and production for the publishers by Lion Hudson plc.
Printed in Great Britain

For Daniel, Nicholas and Sanja

Elizabeth Fry (1780–1845)
*(From the watercolour by George Hammond, ca. 1830. Reproduced by
permission of the Religious Society of Friends, London)*

Preface

O may I join the choir invisible
Of those immortal dead who live again,
In minds made better by their presence, live
In pulses stirr'd to generosity,
In deeds of daring rectitude, in scorn
For miserable aims that end with self,
In thoughts sublime that pierce the night like stars,
And with their mild persistence urge men's search
To vaster issues.
    So to live is heaven:
To make undying music in the world.

George Eliot

*T*HESE WORDS BY GEORGE ELIOT appear at the front of the 1895 edition of Augustus Hare's book, *The Gurneys of Earlham*. I feel it is particularly appropriate to repeat them here, for as I learned more about Elizabeth Fry, and about many of her close family and their circle, it became increasingly clear to me that theirs was a heroic generation. Their vision was to transform the world in which they lived, and to leave it a better place than they found it. And to a very large extent, they succeeded.

Even among such illustrious contemporaries, Elizabeth Fry was unique in the scale of her achievements and the influence she exerted on her own generation. Indeed, in a letter of 1838, written home from North America, her brother Joseph John Gurney told his children that his way in that country was eased by the enormous reputation there of his sister, Elizabeth Fry.

Elizabeth is also unique in the legacy she left to history: the transformation of social attitudes towards offenders; the establishment of a professional prison service; educational and training provision within prisons; and rehabilitation services for discharged prisoners. She was also instrumental in changing attitudes towards the insane and the poor. The legacy she left to the many hundreds of thousands of women who since her time have found fulfilment and recognition in the world beyond the domestic sphere is immeasurable.

I was surprised to learn, as I read the contemporary accounts, that not only was Elizabeth Fry the most high-profile woman in Britain (apart from royalty), but her fame was spread across Europe as far as St Petersburg. When she travelled in the British Isles and on the continent, crowds in their thousands flocked to hear and see her. Yet it seems today, despite several previous biographies, and Elizabeth's face appearing on the British five-pound note, that this extraordinary woman, so crucial to our history in so many ways, somehow remains in the shadows.

When I began my research into Elizabeth's life, I knew little about her except that she was a Quaker and a prison reformer who lived at a historical period in which I was particularly interested. However, as I engaged on what became an extraordinary journey of discovery, the woman (whom I soon thought of as Betsy, the familiar name by which she was known to her family) not only began to seem very real to me, but also curiously modern. In the privacy of her journals Betsy confessed to thoughts, feelings and fears that today form part of our everyday debate: the stresses that arise for women when the role of wife and mother is in conflict with a career that promises great fulfilment; the tensions that emerge when a family does not share one member's interests or agree with deeply held convictions; the suffering brought about by depression, and the guilt induced by a weakness for the substances that bring comfort. For Betsy, however, these issues were uncharted and often forbidden territory. Yet she dared to think about them, and with the resources at her disposal she attempted to reach rational and moral conclusions. As I grew closer to her, I became increasingly filled with admiration for this heroic woman who, with few points of reference, struggled to take control of her own life and understand the forces that drove her.

I would like to thank many people who helped smooth my way on this extraordinary journey. Firstly, Heather Rowland, Josef Keith and Joanna Clark at the Library of the Religious Society of Friends, London, where I spent every Wednesday for over a year reading Elizabeth Fry's journals and the correspondence of her family and friends. Also the staff at the Norfolk Record Office in Norwich, who keep two journals and other documents relating especially to the Gurneys; at Johnson Matthey plc, London, who have one journal in their possession; and at the British Library, London, who have a collection of Fry and Gurney papers. The help of the staff at my local library in Chesham, Buckinghamshire, was invaluable, saving me hours of precious time by consistently and efficiently procuring an enormous number of books published in the nineteenth and early twentieth centuries, together with the reports of Parliamentary Select Committees to which Elizabeth Fry was called as an expert witness. I owe them an enormous debt of gratitude. I would also like to thank the staff at Earlham Hall, Norwich, who allowed me to wander around alone, open closed doors, and generally get a feel for the house where Elizabeth spent her youth. Finally, I would like to thank Jan Greenough at Monarch Books for her positive and insightful suggestions, Sue Howard and Liz Waumsley who also read the manuscript and provided valuable encouragement, and Judith Rand for her company on a day of exploration in Norwich.

I should also say that all Elizabeth's quotations in this book are taken from her original journals, except in a few very rare instances where the writing was illegible or too faded to read. In these cases I used the copy made by her daughters shortly after her death. Elizabeth's reflections throughout the book are generally given my own words, based on my understanding of her thoughts and feelings.

Finally, it is my hope that this book will play some part in making Elizabeth Fry known to a wider public than before, and that others, like me, will recognise how much we owe to her courage and her pioneering spirit. I hope too that they will be inspired by her vision that all people are valuable, and that no matter what their present condition, they can help shape their own destiny and also leave their own world a better place.

Jean Hatton
Chesham, Buckinghamshire.
January 2005

Contents

Genealogy

Gurney

John Gurney
1716–1770
of Keswick, Norfolk
m. Elizabeth Kett
d. 1788

Children:

- Richard Gurney
  1743–1810
  of Keswick, Norfolk

- John Gurney
  1849–1809
  of Magdalen
  Street, Norwich,
  later of Earlham
  Hall, Norwich
  m. Catherine Bell
  1754–1792
  of Stamford Hill,
  London

- Rachel Gurney
  b. 1750
  m. Robert Barclay

- Joseph Gurney
  1757–1830
  of The Grove,
  Norwich

Children of John Gurney (1849–1809) and Catherine Bell:

- Catherine
  1776–1850

- John
  1777–1778

- Rachel
  1778–1827

- Elizabeth
  1780–1845
  m. Joseph Fry

- John
  1781–1814
  m. Elizabeth
  Gurney of Keswick

- Richenda
  1782–1855
  m. Revd. Francis
  Cunningham

- Hannah
  1783–1872
  m. Thomas
  Fowell Buxton

- Louisa
  1784–1836
  m. Samuel Hoare

- Priscilla
  1785–1821

- Samuel
  1786–1856
  m. Elizabeth
  Sheppard

- Joseph John
  1788–1847
  m. 1. Jane Birkbeck
  2. Mary Fowler
  3. Eliza Kirkbride

- Daniel
  1791–1880
  m. Lady Harriet
  Hay

Genealogy
Fry

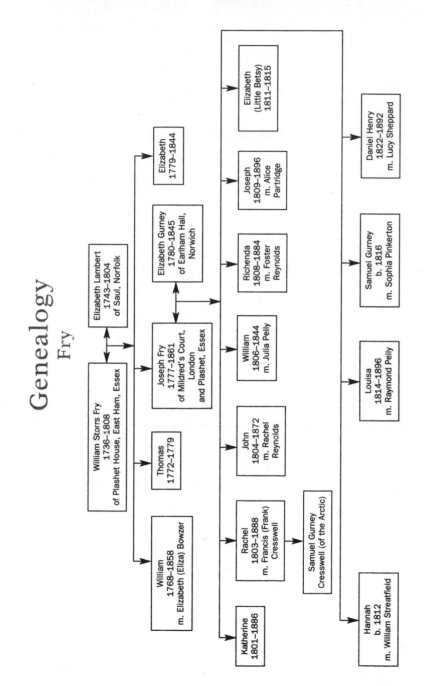

CHAPTER ONE

The child at Earlham

*B*ETSY GURNEY WAS AFRAID of the dark. By day she feared the shadows that lurked in shuttered empty rooms or prowled along gloomy corridors, while at night, as she lay in her narrow bed, listening to the nocturnal moans and shudders of the old house, she waited in terrified and rigid anticipation for stealthy footsteps and gliding apparitions. And as her family went heedlessly about their everyday lives, or slept, unaware of their danger, Betsy alone gazed into the darkness.

For Betsy, just twelve years old, Earlham Hall was alive with presence, and at times its air seemed thick with foreboding. On nights when cramps in her stomach and aches in her teeth kept her awake, when painful thoughts played a drearily repetitive tune in her mind, she became fearfully and exquisitely conscious of all the other beings that shared Earlham with the Gurneys. Half-spirit, half-human, they were creatures of nightmare, phantoms with substance, with contorted faces and twisted hearts. Unpredictable and malevolent, they meant everyone harm.

Betsy knew that all day they skulked in Earlham's deep cellars, until evening fell and the night hours began their weary progress, when they crawled from cobwebby hiding places to grope their way up blind, black staircases and along hushed corridors. Some reached out greedy hands to steal Gurney silver, the bowls and candlesticks that gleamed faintly in the darkness. Others poked pins into the keyholes of cabinets and bureaus, twisting and turning until locks gave way and grubby fingers reached into alcoves and drawers, scrabbling among rustling papers for money and jewels. Most terrifying of all among the intruders was one whose quest was more terrible than the theft of Gurney possessions, for its prey was not candlesticks or money boxes. Instead, it was searching for children to steal. Stealthily, it turned the handles of bedroom doors and slowly, slowly, opened them. Then, with its eyes gleaming in its pale face, it peered inside.

From her childhood until her death Betsy Gurney kept a series of journals. In them she recorded her everyday concerns, her innermost hopes and fears, and details of her spiritual progress. She also included copious references to the ill health that dogged her. However, in 1828, by which time she was widely regarded among her own generation as embodying Christian and female virtues, and was herself becoming aware that her life-story was also likely to interest future generations, she sought to remove from those journals anything that might cast a cloud over herself and her family. After her death, her attempt at concealment was aided by her two eldest daughters, who in 1847 composed an anodyne memoir based on a severely annotated version of their mother's original journals.

As well as the torn-out pages and obliterated paragraphs of her later journals, Betsy also made it clear that she burnt everything written before 1797, the year she became 17. What those books contained, she evidently considered too potentially damaging for the future to know, and as she attempted to draw a veil over her childhood and adolescence, she substituted a brief sketch of only four pages.[1]

Yet from this brief sketch, from fragments in the later journals that escaped her scissors and inky pen, from other hints and allusions in those copious journals, and from journals kept by her family, it is possible to catch a glimpse of the child and the adolescent she once was. As she emerges, this shy, fair-haired, blue-eyed girl, the picture she presents is an extraordinarily complex one. It would seem that she was a highly intelligent, intensely passionate, and exquisitely sensitive individual, yearning to please but hampered by low self-esteem, who often drove her immediate family to distraction. She was also often fearful, confused and lonely, and from a very early age suffered profound anxieties, physical illness and dark depressions.

From a careful reading of her original journals, it is possible to deduce that the origins of her distress lay in conflict, and that deep within her there were powerful forces at work, which as a child of her time, and of her particular background, could not on any level be recognised, admitted or named. And that it was in her struggle to suppress these forces; principally a fear of extinction, a potent sexuality, and a sense of inadequacy fuelling an enormous urge for self expression, that their resultant manifestations provoked serious emotional and physical illness.

At the same time, these same forces also impelled her to action. When combined with her fine intelligence and her ability to empathise with those most rejected in her society, they produced a chemistry that made her compellingly attractive; and because she lived at a great transitional moment in her nation's life, they eventually helped to propel her onto the stage of world history.

As she grew up, Betsy Gurney, the child who lay so fearfully awake at Earlham, the adolescent who suffered the torments of a savage melancholia, and who felt herself inferior to all those around her, was destined to become what no woman before her (who was not born into a royal house) had ever been: a woman who by her own efforts changed the world. In doing so, and at considerable cost to herself, she pushed open a door through which generations of her sisters have subsequently passed.

Betsy was born on 21 May 1780, at the Court House, her parents' home in Magdalen Street, Norwich. It was an elegant and imposing residence, situated right in the centre of the town's busy commerce, but set apart from it by a dignified distance, just like the Gurneys themselves.

It was Gurney business flair and commitment to the cloth trade, the town's principal industry, that by the 1770s had helped make Norwich one of the largest and richest towns in England. Over several generations, their factories and mills had flourished, and since 1775, their family banking business had prospered. A reputation for honest dealing and personal integrity had also earned them influence and respect. By the year of Betsy's birth, John Gurney, her father, a wool-stapler and spinner of worsted yarns, was among the wealthiest and most well-regarded men in the whole of East Anglia.

He had also been one of the most eligible, and his family had looked forward to a marriage linking another great fortune to their own. When he fell in love with Catherine Bell, the beautiful, intelligent daughter of an impoverished London merchant, the disappointment and opposition were intense. However, her devotion to John, her good nature and a winning charm finally overcame all hostility. And, while she brought them no fortune, Catherine brought to the Gurneys another prize: her great-grandfather's reputation.

Both families were members of the Society of Friends – the Quakers – and when John and Catherine married in May 1775, they united two great dynasties, both tracing their origins to the movement's foundation in the mid-seventeenth century. Catherine's great-grandfather, Robert Barclay, was the Society's great systematic theologian, who had also been an associate of its founder, George Fox. While less illustrious, John's own ancestor, an earlier John Gurney, had also been converted to Friends in the days when Fox first preached his radical message. Like the Barclays, he had added his name to the Society's swelling numbers and left membership of it as a legacy to his descendants.

John and Catherine Gurney of Norwich were an attractive and compelling couple. Both were warm-hearted and good-natured, and with his red hair, his ruddy complexion and an athletic physique, John was as handsome[2] as his wife was beautiful. He brought to their new home a Gurney fortune and his aptitude for business, while Catherine brought refinement, good taste and an impressive degree of knowledge, curiosity and conversation.

As a newly wedded pair, wealthy, attractive and cultivated, the Gurneys of Magdalen Street were at the centre of the city's most fashionable society, and appeared blessed with abundant good fortune. When they began their family, it seemed likely that each child would receive a rich inheritance, not only in wealth and material possessions, but also in good looks, intelligence, and an inclination towards industry and culture.

The first to arrive, in 1776, was Catherine, or Kitty, named after her mother; but a boy, born in 1777 and named for his father, died in infancy. Rachel followed in 1778, and then in 1780 came Elizabeth, whom the family fondly called Betsy. Another eight children followed, almost one every year until 1791: a second John in 1781, then four girls, Richenda, Hannah, Louisa and Priscilla, and finally, three more boys, Samuel, Joseph John and Daniel.

Catherine Gurney loved her children dearly and despite her regular pregnancies and the rapidity with which her growing brood changed from helpless infants into restless creatures full of curiosity and high spirits, she did her best to develop a special relationship with each child. "To enjoy each child individually" was Catherine's aim; to nurture their special gifts and abilities while uniting them with each other and their parents in a close family bond. Her own Quaker upbringing, with its emphasis on quiet discipline, education, good manners and service to others was the pattern she employed.

Beginning each day with a period of silent meditation, in those first quiet moments Catherine gathered her thoughts and brought her mind into "a state of silent waiting and worship, preparatory to the active employment of the day". Then, cool and composed, she made her way through the house to the rooms of her children, and after the cheerful commotion of washing, dressing and playfulness, if there was time before breakfast, she read to them a passage from the Bible. If there was not time beforehand, she said, "it should not be afterwards omitted."

John was not omitted either, and despite the demands of children and servants, breakfast and Bible, Catherine always found time for her husband before he left home for his business in the town. "Forget not the kindest attentions to my dearest companion before parting for the day,"[3] she reminded herself in her journal.

John and Catherine complemented each other. Both were devoted to their family, but while John also loved sporting days among the wild, wide landscapes of East Anglia with their reed-filled waterways and their hunting fields, his wife, quieter and more reflective, loved gardens and picturesque pastures. Family summers spent in the village of Bramerton, just a few miles from their Norwich home, were among her greatest joys. There, in the sprawling gardens of the Gurneys' country cottage, full of ancient fruit trees and rambling beds of English shrubs and wild flowers, Catherine brought stories from the Bible so much to life, that in later years Betsy always recalled the Bramerton gardens of her childhood whenever she thought of Paradise. She also remembered the long, sunny days when Catherine and her children, in their straw hats and carefree country clothes, explored Bramerton's common together, delighting in its abundant life. Leafy tangles of wild trees, brown streams drifting between mossy banks, and massive bramble clumps beneath clouds of hovering butterflies were all spurs for Catherine's bright imagination. Together with wild fruits and flowers, and the multitudes of creatures that crept and crawled among them, or buzzed and fluttered about them, they provided opportunities to draw her children's attention to the wonderfully ordered world of nature.

Catherine was intrigued by the natural world, and she loved it as much for its complexity and construction as she did for its beauty. She was also eager to share her fascination with her family, and to cultivate in them not only a basic knowledge of natural history, but a desire to understand the world and to discover more about it for themselves. She firmly believed that for all cultivated people, it was "our reasonable duty to improve our faculties, and by that means to render ourselves useful".

Catherine's quest for knowledge, and her eagerness to encourage her children in their "reasonable duty" towards improvement and usefulness, were shared by many of her contemporaries, and for people of her background, the second half of the eighteenth century was an exciting time to be alive. Europe was powerfully influenced by the radical thought of the Enlightenment, whose watchword was Reason: clear, logical, independent thinking. As Enlightenment philosophers, musicians, artists and writers moved freely between Edinburgh and Berlin, London and Vienna, Paris and St Petersburg, sometimes it seemed as if every branch of knowledge was alive with new ideas.

"Nature and nature's laws lay hid in night" wrote the poet Alexander Pope in 1730; "God said, Let Newton be! And all was light." Late in the seventeenth century, Isaac Newton had demonstrated that the heavens and the earth, previously so awesome and mysterious, were in reality governed by sets of laws which could be formulated clearly in the language of mathematics.

When he died in 1727, the world Sir Isaac left behind him had changed for ever. Most educated people had abandoned the medieval world view that human life and the natural world were entirely controlled by supernatural forces, and there was a confident belief that Reason, as demonstrated in science by the scientific method, would eventually probe all of "Nature" and bring all of "Nature's laws" to light.

Reason and order, light and clarity, it was believed, would be brought into regions where formerly there had been ignorance and darkness, and all over Europe there were people eager to take part in the great experiment. From the voyages of Captain Cook, who took with him to the South Seas in the late 1760s the men and instruments necessary to observe the transit of Venus, to the botanical rambles of obscure country clergymen in England, nature was everywhere investigated, "discovered", categorised and listed. The results were published in books and learned journals, and more informally in a growing number of periodicals such as the *Spectator* that were popular among those with education enough to read them and leisure enough to do so.

The Christian faith was subjected to the same scrutiny, and was found wanting. Most of the more influential Enlightenment thinkers considered its claims of revelation to be at odds with their own view of a world governed by natural laws, where scientific knowledge was superior to any knowledge based on authority, whether secular or divine. Belief in the incarnation, the miracles of Jesus, the resurrection, the authority of Scripture, or the leading of the Holy Spirit, were met with a scepticism that created widespread doubt. But, except for a few who became atheists, or who retained orthodox forms of Christianity, in the Enlightened nations of Europe, many educated people who were sceptical of Christianity were generally attracted to other forms of religious belief, particularly those influenced by Deism.

The universe, according to Deist theology, had been created by a good and wise God, a Supernatural Designer, who had regulated it with scientific laws which could be discerned by intelligent human beings, but who had then removed himself from his creation. According to Deists, God was a remote being who had never involved himself in human history, and never would. If humankind were to discern his will and purpose, they said, then it must be sought in the fabric of nature, in the universe at large, and in human nature itself. The true religion was the religion of nature, "natural religion", and its evidences, which were part of the order of nature itself, were as old as creation.

Deists were also scathing of anyone who thought otherwise, and their most severe condemnation was reserved for those they termed "enthusiasts" – Christians who were not only openly committed to their faith, but who talked about God as if they had a personal acquaintance with him, preached loudly about it in public and encouraged the conversion of others. So influential was the Deist view, that throughout fashionable society enthusiasts were viewed with distaste, their passion was regarded as vulgar, and their views as not only contrary to science, but an attempt to undermine progress and send humanity back into the ignorant darkness from which the Enlightenment had so recently rescued it.

Catherine Gurney herself was caught between both worlds. As an hereditary Quaker she was wedded to her Christian faith, but as an intelligent woman she was also attracted to some of the other belief-systems on offer, and in Norwich there were many to be found.

The town had a strong Dissenting tradition that dated back to a succession of European Puritan refugees who sought refuge there during the upheavals following the Reformation.[4] By the late eighteenth century, however, as well as continuing as a centre of Dissent, it was also well known for its political radicalism and religious scepticism.[5] Its wealthy elite were largely well educated and cosmopolitan, and were fond of philosophical and literary salons and radical political societies that advocated extension of the suffrage and annual parliaments. Many citizens were Deists, while many others were Unitarians, a rational, individualistic group who advocated democracy and maintained that Jesus Christ was a human religious leader to be followed as an example, but not worshipped. Some even proclaimed themselves atheists.

Under the influence of her favourite cousin, Betty Lindoc, for a time Catherine Gurney was drawn powerfully to Unitarianism. She was also, as a member of fashionable society, familiar with the Enlightenment expectation that people in her position should appear cool, detached and rational. Like many of her friends, she believed that living in harmony with nature's harmonious laws was superior to anything approaching emotional involvement or passion, and as she did her best to unite her Christian faith with modern beliefs, she tried to ensure that her children received a wide Christian education free of any taint of enthusiasm.

God has given us life, health and strength of body, she told them, and also an understanding mind. And since that mind "will shew us what is reasonable and right to do," she said, "then we should certainly consider whether it is not right to love and obey that excellent Being, who has certainly placed us here on earth and surrounded us with blessings and enjoyments, that we may become as He would have us, that is, good."

Catherine also believed that goodness, together with other qualities, could be promoted by education and example. It was part of the Enlightenment view that people were partly shaped by environment; and that nations, communities and families governed by Enlightenment principles would be regulated by peace, economic prosperity, the rule of law and religious and intellectual freedom. Through the continued application of Reason, it was argued, individuals and human society itself would ultimately be perfected.

Education, therefore, in Catherine's view, should be regulated according to the "ultimate design" envisaged. "It would be certainly wise," she said, "in those engaged in the important office of instructing youth, to consider, what would render the objects of their care perfect, when men or women; rather than what will render them pleasing as children."

For the ultimate perfection of her own children, Catherine was convinced that a broad educational curriculum was as necessary for her girls, educated at home, as it was for their brothers who would eventually be sent to tutors and boarding schools.

Together with their investigations into the natural world, Catherine ensured that her daughters studied Latin and French, their own English language, ancient and modern history, geography and mathematics. She also maintained that since women of their background would inevitably spend a great deal of time regulating the affairs of a family, even if not involved in the more mundane tasks themselves, they should nevertheless be familiar with all household tasks, from plain sewing and the cutting-out of clothes, to the customs of the table and the keeping of accounts. Finally, Catherine noted, "it should be here observed, that gentleness of manner is indispensably necessary in women; to say nothing of that polished behaviour that adds a charm to every qualification." To the latter, Catherine believed, "children may be led without vanity or affection, by amiable and judicious instruction."

Although Catherine endeavoured to provide that "amiable and judicious instruction" for all her daughters, and to enjoy each one individually, little Betsy was something of a favourite.

At just a few years old, there was a serenity about her, a sweet placid gentleness emphasised by her pale blond hair and blue eyes, that Catherine found restful after the boisterous high spirits of Kitty and Rachel. "My dove-like Betsy scarcely ever offends," she told her cousin Priscilla Hannah Gurney.[6]

And, while Catherine found Betsy's placid nature soothing, the child's obvious pleasure at accompanying her mother on charitable visits to poor neighbours in Norwich and Bramerton also secretly delighted her.

Central to Catherine's life, and something she emphasised strongly to her daughters, was her concept of duty. "Remember" she said in 1788, as she concluded a long entry in her journal relating to her family and their routine, "that these desultory remarks are designed first, to promote my duty to my Maker – secondly, my duty to my husband and children, relations, servants, and poor neighbours." Among her duties to her Maker, she reminded herself, were her thanks: "Forget not the excellent custom of grateful, pious acknowledgement for blessings received."

That the Gurneys were surrounded with more blessings than most, Catherine believed to be a sign that God commended their faith, their honesty and their charity. It was important, therefore, that her girls especially should continue her own custom of personally sharing those blessings with people less fortunate than themselves. However, whenever Catherine set out on her charitable excursions to some of her favourite neighbours – one-armed Betty at Bramerton, or Betty's neighbour, Greengrass, an old lady who kept strawberry beds around a little pond – she noticed how quick Kitty and Rachel were to skip away. Whereas Betsy liked to linger, close to her mother, quiet and unobtrusive, gazing with grave eyes as baskets of Gurney provisions, arranged neatly beneath clean white napkins, were received with smiles and little bobs of gratitude. Catherine noticed too how Betsy smiled shyly at the old women whenever they spoke to her, and how their own weather-beaten country faces lit up in return.

But despite Betsy's fondness for visiting poor neighbours, and her aura of tranquillity, there was something about her little daughter that troubled Catherine. She smiles at Betty and Greengrass, she told John, but when other adults looked at her or spoke to her, she often cried and clung to her mother's skirts. "I frequently cried when looked at," Betsy herself recalled later, "and used to say that my eyes were weak."[7] Wasn't Betsy always too good, Catherine asked her husband, too docile and unoffending? Shouldn't she display more of the noisy high spirits that characterised her brother and sisters?

John Gurney, however, was reassuring. In any large family, he told his uneasy wife, there was almost bound to be one child at least who was timid and delicate. He and Catherine must be thankful, he maintained, that only one infant had been lost, their first little John, and be grateful for such robust well-being in nearly all of the others. As for Betsy, he continued, her parents should watch her carefully for signs of sickness, respond quickly if they saw her ailing, and be prepared to indulge her a little if she became restless or fretful.

Almost as if John had foreseen it, as she grew older, the child who had once been so placid gradually did become restless and fretful. "I think I suffered much in my youth from the most tender nervous system," she recalled. And, as the fears that had driven her to hide behind Catherine's skirts grew in magnitude, eventually it seemed that the more she learned and saw of the world, the more her imagination conjured up horrors.

Darkness especially terrified her, and as daylight ebbed away, or when candles and rushlights were snuffed, she sobbed in fear and refused to be comforted. Later she commented how that early terror gave rise to so much that followed. "I ... suffered so acutely from being left alone without a light after I went to bed," she said, "that I believe my nervous system was injured in consequence of it."

Perhaps it was in the darkness of Betsy's childhood nights that a fear was born and took shape – a fear that was to haunt her whole life. Perhaps it was the result of an incautious remark or inadequate explanation about a mysterious older baby brother stolen away by a malign creature called death. It certainly appears to be the case that as her vivid imagination produced terrifying possibilities, more and more did she fear that the same creature would cause endless agony for herself and her family. "My childlike wish was," she recalled later, "that two large walls might crush us all together, that we might die at once, and thus avoid the misery of each other's death."

So great was her fear that her mother would be taken, that Betsy began watching her with a morbid intensity. As she did so, her sisters and little brother, fascinated and alarmed, saw her creep up regularly upon Catherine, who often dozed in the daytime when she was heavily pregnant, to ensure that her mother still breathed.

To John and Catherine's dismay, the outings and holidays they planned for their family with such optimism were also increasingly spoiled by Betsy's growing nervousness and fear. Once, to John's barely concealed exasperation, she held up the family carriage for so long by refusing to join her parents inside, that all thought of travel was finally abandoned. It was her father's sporting gun, she admitted later, left lying casually on the seat, that had convinced her that just as Abraham once planned to kill Isaac, so too did her own parents plan to sacrifice her. "On this account," she observed, "I think the utmost care needed, in representing religious truth to children."

The sea, too, especially the great grey expanse of water that lay off the Norfolk coast, held such dread for Betsy that she shuddered and wept at the very sight of it. When plunged beneath its surface she howled in terror. Her fear caused her parents enormous distress, for they were eager to indulge their children in the newly fashionable pleasure of seaside outings, and made frequent use of a country retreat near Cromer that was the property of John's older brother Richard. Anxious that their children should benefit from the cold salty water whose health-giving properties were so highly recommended by doctors, they frequently hired a bathing woman at the beach. Yet as they watched every other child squeal and splash with delight, they could only ask themselves uneasily just what it was that Betsy feared so much as the dark waters closed over her head.

In 1786, when Betsy was six years old, John Gurney felt rich and successful enough to move his family away from the city, and to live as a country gentleman, farming rich acres for pleasure, shooting and fishing in his own woods and rivers, and entertaining widely and lavishly. When he rented Earlham Hall, a seventeenth-century mansion of red brick and stone, two miles from Norwich, together with additional farmland nearby, he felt profoundly satisfied. When his family fell as much in love with it as he was himself, he was even more delighted.

Earlham, however, was easy to love. There was a picturesque grandeur to its russet walls, its tall chimneys and vine-swathed bay windows; while standing at its imposing south-facing doorway, and looking onto green lawns flanked by ancient mossy trees surrounded by carpets of long grasses and wild flowers, anyone could feel at peace with the world.

The Gurneys also loved Earlham for its sense of history, that seemed all the more real when their older relatives came to call. John's mother, Grandmother Kett, invariably dressed in the old-fashioned Quaker hood of black silk and a drab-coloured camlet gown;[8] while cousin Henrietta Gurney, who always sat on the sofa very formally, wore the stiff and stately silks of a bygone day. Though both women regularly brought with them finger cakes and sugar plums, to the Gurney children such visitors almost seemed like spirits who had emerged briefly from the distant past of their home.

In many other ways too, Earlham was a delight for children. Its attics, cupboards and powder-closets seemed made for hide-and-seek, while its wandering corridors and winding staircases sometimes encouraged abandoned climbing, running and chasing, and at others, induced a sober sense of stateliness and grandeur. In the park surrounding the house, the children raced on their ponies, rolled in the sweetly scented grass of summer and built snowmen in winter. In spring they gathered armfuls of bluebells and bunches of primroses from the woods. Sometimes they wandered the broad avenues and winding pathways that led away eventually into quiet farmlands, and best of all, they played beside the placid River Yare, sailing their boats and lingering on warm evenings among the shady groves that lined its banks.

For Betsy, Earlham was also a house of anxieties, for her imagination ran riot there. She was nervous of walking alone through the mansion's unused corridors or entering its empty rooms, and she worried continually about ghosts and about thieves. Often she felt that unseen eyes watched her, or that mysterious creaks and rustles were the tread of stealthy footsteps. When her family were gathered in Earlham's candlelit rooms, talking cheerfully around a fire, or with their heads bent over sewing or a book, Betsy sometimes wondered why they seemed so unaware of the other world that hovered beside them, just at the edge of vision, just beyond the boundary of consciousness.

She wondered too, why she never felt the otherness that was so evident at Earlham when she attended the Quaker Meeting House at Goat Lane in Norwich. Eventually, she supposed the reason to be that whatever it was that lived at Earlham would probably feel as restless and as bored at Meeting as she felt there herself.

John and Catherine Gurney were liberal in their Quaker observance and attended Meeting only once or twice each week. Even so, Betsy and her sisters hated it. At the time of their childhood, in the late eighteenth century, Quaker children were required to sit through long silent assemblies lasting two hours or more as noiselessly and as stilly as the adults around them. Sometimes Betsy thought her father hated it too, since whenever she peeped at him during the tedious hours when the Gurney children fidgeted and sighed and squinted through half-opened eyes at the hushed adults around them, she often saw a restless expression on John's ruddy face. It made her think that her father would rather be outside in the windy air, with his gun and his friends and his brown and cream dogs. When she looked at her mother, however, she always wondered what it was that made Catherine appear so serene.

By her thirtieth year, Catherine Gurney had lost her fascination with Unitarianism and had drawn more closely to her ancestral faith, and when Betsy asked about it, she tried to explain. We should love and adore God at all times, Catherine told her puzzled daughter, but our lives are so busy that we often quite forget that not only is it his due, but that it is also our own truest enjoyment. For that reason, she said, "it is necessary to retire with our friends and neighbours from hurry and business, that we may think of Him who delights to bless us, and will consider us as His children, if we love Him as a heavenly Father." Therefore, Catherine had instructed, in the peculiarly Quaker language she used with her family, "do not suffer thy thoughts to wander, or to dwell upon trifles, when thou art most immediately before Him, whom thou must strive to love, with all thy heart and soul."

Anxious to please, Betsy tried hard to keep her thoughts under control, but to her dismay, the harder she struggled, the further afield they wandered, until sometimes she found herself back in Bramerton again with one-armed Betty, or gazing with Greengrass at her scarlet strawberries nestling in their green beds. Then, guiltily, she remembered that she was before God, whom she was supposed to love and worship, and she wondered if he was watching her, and whether he was cross, and where exactly it was that he was.

The God who watched from his hiding place, and whose demands were so hard to meet, joined Betsy's anxieties. She knew he loved to bless those who truly loved him, for her mother had told her so, and also, that she should be grateful for everything the Gurneys had received at his hands. She also knew (and even thinking about it made her feel guilty) how much she and her sisters hated going to the meetings where God was, and that in private, they called them "dis" – disgusting!

Was it only Catherine Gurney, she sometimes speculated, who truly loved and worshipped God? Was it only Catherine whom God loved in return, and for whose sake he blessed the Gurneys? If so, what would happen if her mother died? Would God turn his face away from her family just as he had turned it away from Adam and Eve? Would the Gurneys be banished from Paradise?

As Betsy grew older, eight, nine, and ten, her worries became relentless, as ghosts, intruders, death and God all obsessed her. At night she often lay wakeful or tossed restlessly in a sleep disturbed by dreams. She was also bitterly ashamed of her fears. In her handsome, sociable father, her beautiful, gracious mother, and her boisterous sisters, she saw only self-assurance, and she felt herself to be somehow malformed and inferior. "I remember having a poor, not to say low, opinion of myself," she recalled, and in her shame she closed herself to the world and shut herself up in her own timid heart.

As she did so, bouts of great weariness also began to oppress her; "languor of mind as well as body", she recalled, that sometimes led to days when she could hardly bring herself to move, and when something like a dry fog settled in her mind to block every good thought and hinder all attempts at communication. It stopped her from learning, and her lessons suffered, and despite desperately wishing it were otherwise, she seemed to have no power to control it. "I used to think that I was so very inferior to my sisters," she recalled, and as she watched bright Kitty and pretty Rachel please everyone with their neat work and their clever conversation, she became miserably conscious of just how slow and stupid she was.

Catherine was endlessly patient, sitting beside Betsy at lessons and encouraging her stumbling efforts, but despite her mother's devotion, Betsy slowly and steadily became perverse. If her sisters or the governess claimed something was so, Betsy questioned or contradicted, pursuing arguments she even doubted herself, to the point where tempers were lost and tears were shed. At such times, only Catherine could soothe her, waiting quietly for the anger and tears to subside before taking her to a quiet corner of the house or garden where they could be comfortably alone. Sometimes they sat together in silence, while at others Catherine prayed aloud for her daughter, or read to her from the Gospels or the Psalms in a soft, tranquil voice that lulled Betsy into a placid, dreamlike state, where she almost felt that the God her mother worshipped was real and loving and very close.

Catherine also tried to restore the friendships with the other children that Betsy so often damaged, and she encouraged Rachel, the sister nearest in age, to become her special friend. She gave them a little room to themselves, a bright airy closet where they kept their books, and for it she bought a cabinet, similar to the one that held her own treasures, for the pretty stones and sea-shells she encouraged them to collect and display. The two girls also kept their own special tea sets there, and sometimes, tucked away in their sunny chamber, playing at house, Betsy found the confidence to hint at her anxieties and fears.

Other fears, more private, she kept for her journal. It was a passion she shared with her sisters, encouraged by Catherine's own example. In their journals, she told them, when she presented them with their first empty books, they could try out ideas, ask themselves questions, and record the daily passage of their lives. Betsy spent hours with hers. Sometimes, when she felt most languid, she sat with its pages open and empty. At others, she frowned over her words while her pen scratched and her ink blotched. The other Gurney girls loved to share their daily entries, but Betsy often refused. Was it because she had too many secrets to hide? her sisters teased. Or was it because she was ashamed of her dreadful writing and atrocious spelling?

Towards the end of 1790, Catherine became pregnant again, and in May 1791, little Daniel arrived. John and Catherine now had eleven living children, and nearly all had fulfilled the promise of the couple's early years. The only disappointment, apart from the John who had died, was Betsy, whose delicate health was increasingly becoming a problem.

By the age of eleven she was more obstinate than ever, and her failures at lessons had become a sullen unwillingness to learn, while besides the physical and mental languor, other symptoms had also appeared: inexplicable headaches, nagging toothaches and abdominal cramps. She also suffered from dark depressions that she referred to as her "valleys", that annoyed her brothers and sisters. "Poor Betsy", they called her, and as their taunts increased her distress, bringing on even more sulks and tears, Catherine Gurney vowed to renew her efforts to encourage and reassure her troubled daughter.

But, late in 1792 Catherine fell ill; her bedroom became a sickroom and her husband abandoned his business and his sport to sit at her side or to pace the winter lawn beyond her window with his anxious dogs trailing at his heels. For three long weeks, Earlham became a house of lowered voices and whispers where everyone trod softly and where John, his children, and the entire household prayed desperately for recovery. Yet, even as they did so, Catherine grew weaker. Finally, she became delirious and fought with her doctor and husband as she struggled constantly to kneel on her bed to pray for her children. Mostly she prayed for Kitty, and for two of the boys: John, the Gurney heir, and little Joseph John.

Hearing of it, Betsy began to believe herself forgotten. She was also frightened, not only of her mother's illness, and the brooding tensions it aroused in the house, but of strange new symptoms that were shaking her twelve-year-old body and mind. "I certainly felt symptoms of ill-health before my mother died," she recalled, "that I thought of speaking to her about, but never did, partly because I did not know how to explain them." Possibly these symptoms marked the onset of puberty, although with two older sisters, and in a household filled with female servants, it seems unlikely that the most obvious manifestations of approaching adulthood were unknown or unexpected. However, Betsy drew a veil over the details, leaving only the distressing image of a child struggling to find the right words and the courage to speak them; then, as her most tender sympathiser and greatest hope appeared to abandon her, feeling eventually that she had nowhere to turn. The thing she most dreaded was coming to pass.

"Peace, sweet is peace," Catherine Gurney whispered over and over again, her words growing fainter as the hours passed by. She died on 17 November 1792. After she had gone, as John Gurney and his children stood gazing at her silent body, Betsy saw on her mother's face the same expression of distant serenity that she had worn so often at Meeting.

Later that night, alone in her bed, Betsy was overwhelmed by a great and terrible desolation. And, as all the shadows that had haunted her childhood fell upon her and pressed her down, she had no power to resist them, for her body and her mind were both numb. Eventually the shadows bore her away with them into regions of profound gloom, of valleys steeply walled and wreathed in shade, where no light gleamed. As they did so, maybe she dimly remembered that her mother had trusted in God's love and mercy, and maybe she called on his name in the darkness. Though she may also have strained to hear his answer, it seems that the infinite darkness remained empty and profoundly silent.

CHAPTER TWO

❧ ❧

The briary thorny
wilderness

*B*ETSY TURNED HER BACK on God. She didn't trust him. First, he had allowed her mother, who loved him, to die, and then he had abandoned Betsy herself to darkness and despair.

The black depression that overtook her after Catherine Gurney's death had terrified her, and as it clung about her, stifling her breath and lying heavy on her limbs, she felt that she truly walked through the valley of the shadow of death. It was a terrible journey, and with a growing sense of hopelessness, she walked it alone.

Seemingly forsaken by God, and tormented by thoughts that her dying mother had forgotten her, in desperation Betsy reached out to her family. But they too were shaken by shock and numbed by grief, and in their confusion and despair they were unable to hear.

Before she died, Catherine had begged 16-year-old Kitty to become mother to the family, and in his desolation, John Gurney added his own entreaties. "Here then we were left," Kitty wrote, many years later, in a moment of bitterness for her lost youth, "I not 17, at the head, wholly ignorant of common life, from the retirement in which we had been educated, quite unprepared for filling an important station, and unaccustomed to act on independent principle."[1] As Kitty struggled to cope, as John Gurney grieved for his wife, and the other children endeavoured to fill the sudden void in their lives, Betsy, the troublesome child with the delicate health, was left to herself.

At night she dreamed vividly.

First comes the rush of the sea! Then the slow, sliding roar of the shingle as the falling waves clutch it, and drag it, slithering and gasping, down the steep shelf of the beach, and into the heaving water. Betsy's foot slipping; Betsy falling; her hands grabbing at pebbles. Betsy seized by the sea; sucked by it, together with the shingle, into its cold, salty grasp. The water closing over her head. No sight, no sound. Only a handful of pebbles. Betsy opening her hand, letting them go.

Always she woke violently, sweating and breathless, her heart pounding. And, alone in the darkness or the uncertain half-light of dawn, as she wept tears of longing for her lost mother, she listened fearfully to the receding roar of the waves and the echo of the wind.

It was a dream, Betsy said later, that from early adolescence to the age of 17 she dreamed almost every night, and although she always woke up before death finally took her away, she nevertheless experienced all the terrors of being drowned.[2] That she dreamed it so frequently, or certainly claims to have done so, does invest the dream with considerable significance, and perhaps it can be interpreted on two levels. On one level, the sea may represent Betsy's ongoing fear of death, as well as a memory of her unhappy experiences at Cromer. On another level, however, it may also stand for the chaos of the unconscious mind, so often represented as an ocean, which is home to the uninhibited forces and desires that have the potential to overwhelm and perhaps even destroy a fragile personality. For a young woman as sensitive as Betsy, the borderline between conscious and unconscious must have been a delicate and shifting boundary, and it seems likely that what she sought to repress in the daylight, as well as being reflected in emotional and physical distress, also returned to her at night in her dreams.

As she assimilated Catherine Gurney's death into the ongoing reality of life, for the sensitive child who had suffered the loss of her mother at such a critical time in her development, the wound remained jagged and raw. In time, her inexplicable childhood aches and depressions were joined by intense moods, whose rapid and unpredictable changes were bewildering and frustrating for a family burdened by grief. Casual remarks from a sister often drove her to spiteful words or hostile tears, while for no obvious reason, cheerful willingness became sulky silence or passionate fury. Sometimes a relentless and inappropriate gaiety seized her, whirling her in giddy dances, painting her cheeks with hectic colour, and setting the whole family's nerves on edge. At other times she slumped morosely. To her father's concern, she seemed driven to please him, fussing over him constantly and demanding his attention, until it drove him finally to exasperation, and then to regret, and Betsy to sullen tears. Later in life, Betsy also referred very briefly to convulsions and fainting fits that were a feature of her life for several years after her mother's death.[3]

From comments made in their journals, Betsy's older sisters obviously had their disturbed days too, but unlike Betsy, they seemed more able to shake off low spirits and smooth the wounded feelings that followed their quarrels. For them, for John, the Gurney heir, for the next four girls, and for the little boys, life at Earlham eventually resumed an outwardly well-ordered and comfortable progress. Two of the family's most loyal servants – Hannah Judd, the Quaker housekeeper, and Sarah Williman, the nurse – both mothered the little ones, while Kitty concealed her sorrow at the unfairness of fate, and stood alongside her father as head of the family.

In her old age, she recalled them as they were when she assumed the role and title of Mrs Catherine Gurney. Rachel, the second sister, Kitty said, was a beauty, with curling flaxen hair, dark blue eyes and a lively personality. She was also thoughtful and kind, hardworking and persevering. Betsy, who came next, was quite different. Though as pretty as Rachel, she lacked her vivid colouring, while her timidity was in great contrast to Rachel's vivacious good-humour. Her obstinacy, Kitty remembered, was also annoying to others, while her aversion to learning was a disadvantage to herself. Nevertheless, Kitty added generously, "she was gentle in look and manner, and pleasing in person."

John, the oldest boy, who showed very early the promise of future good looks, was also affectionate and kind. He was already away at school in Wandsworth when his mother died, and Kitty remembered little of his childhood years. She was far more familiar with the girls known as "the four", as it was she who helped mother them and brought them up. Richenda, the oldest, was easy-tempered, active and happy, she said, while Hannah was another beauty who combined playfulness with a sweet nature and common sense. Louisa, she maintained, was the most talented of them all, while Priscilla, a fastidious child, was an example of tact and taste.

Of her three youngest brothers, Kitty remembered Sam as a sturdy, determined boy, who far preferred Earlham's farmyards and workshops to its parlour and schoolroom. It was a partiality which led John Gurney to send him to the Wandsworth school when he was just eight years old, and Kitty often recalled how resolutely he climbed to his rooftop seat on the London-bound coach. His brother, Joseph John, was another contrast, a quiet sensitive child who enjoyed the company and pastimes of his sisters. Like Betsy, he was timid and suffered from nightmares, but unlike her, he was an eager student and at school he rose rapidly to the top of each class. Daniel was virtually a baby when his mother died, and was brought up almost entirely by his nurse.

Nevertheless, in his old age, Daniel still remembered life at Earlham under Kitty's regime. It was both disciplined and regular, he said, well-seasoned with pleasures, and very much followed the pattern established by Catherine Gurney.[4] Like her mother, Kitty began the day early, well before six, and she encouraged the young ones to complete as many lessons as possible by mid-morning. After that there was needlework, done to the accompaniment of one sister reading aloud. In August 1796, their book was Livy's *Roman History*. Following the midday meal there were more lessons, and more needlework, while after tea, it was time to walk with Kitty in the park. In his mind's eye, Daniel could see them still, the four playing without their bonnets in the fresh air, with their red-gold hair, and the scarlet cloaks that were a present from their father, a bright splash of colour in his memory.

There were also music lessons, drawing lessons from Mr Crome,[5] the Norfolk painter retained by John Gurney, and French conversation. In the evenings, under Kitty's supervision, all the girls wrote up their journals until supper.

"Everything we know, and all the little good we can boast of," said Priscilla of Kitty, "we owe almost entirely to her."[6]

Despite her role as teacher and surrogate mother, Kitty relied on her two oldest sisters for support. Together they held frequent family conferences in Kitty's cosy sitting room, and in Kitty's leisure time, Rachel and Betsy were her company. On summer days, when even Betsy's moods grew sunny, they sometimes rode together into Norwich, where they strolled the fashionable streets, gazed at tempting goods displayed in bow-fronted shop-windows, and listened to open-air concerts performed by military bands. They also surreptitiously eyed the good-looking officers in shining boots and red coats, who mingled so picturesquely with the crowd that it was often hard to remember just why they were there.

In 1795, when Kitty was 19, Rachel 17, and Betsy barely 15, Britain had been at war with revolutionary France for two years. The declaration by France, in February 1793, had followed her invasion of Austria the previous year, and as Britain's forces in Europe struggled to contain the French armies, there was a constant fear of invasion.

Six years earlier, in 1789, thousands of people in Britain had supported the French Revolution, seeing in its aim of replacing old corrupt orders with others based on rationalism and liberty, an expression of Enlightenment ideals and a hope for future generations. Though many supporters had subsequently been disillusioned when the Terror began in 1793, it remained the British government's constant fear that an invading French army would find a welcome in Britain. Norwich, with its radical views, that had greeted the Revolution with joy,[7] was regarded as particularly susceptible, and the army, quartered throughout East Anglia, was as ready to quell violence from British republicans, as it was to repel foreign invasion.

The war, events in revolutionary France, politics, philosophy and religion were all subjects discussed frequently at Earlham, where independent thought and conversation were both encouraged. Kitty herself had a particularly inquiring mind and she read widely and regularly attended lectures on radical themes. However, despite the war, and the ever-present threat from across the sea, on sunny days in Norwich the Gurney girls found it hard be serious. Especially when their pretty faces, and their slender figures shown off by the scarlet riding habits that were also John Gurney's special gift, so obviously turned the heads of the red-coated young men.

To her own astonishment and the wonder of her family, towards the end of 1795, when she was still just 15, Betsy also turned the head of a young Quaker. His name was James Lloyd, he was the son of a Birmingham-based banking family as rich and influential as the Gurneys,[8] and during an extended visit to Earlham he had been powerfully drawn to the fair-haired girl with the lovely smile, who so often seemed lost in her own thoughts. Sadly, it seems likely that among the documents she later destroyed, Betsy included much that related to James Lloyd. What remains, however, makes it clear that there was a formal engagement. Given James's reputed good looks, the Lloyds' wealth, and that Betsy was the first of her sisters to be chosen, it would also seem likely that Betsy would hardly have believed her good fortune. It also indicates that even at 15, she exerted a powerful attraction on the opposite sex.

Something, however, the details long gone, happened to bring the engagement to an end. Since a formal engagement most definitely implied a future marriage, and would almost certainly have induced the two hugely wealthy families at least to discuss financial settlements, the ending must have been embarrassing for all concerned, and cataclysmic for a very young woman in love. "He has I suppose done me hurt in his time," Betsy said of James in February 1798, thus suggesting that it was he who broke off the relationship. But, in August that year she also lamented her conduct towards him, "which I fear he never understood."

From other remarks, hints and allusions made by Betsy and by others, it appears that she suffered an emotional breakdown at this time, and that its effects continued throughout the year. With no firm evidence it is impossible to say whether it was concern over her physical and mental stability that precipitated the end of the engagement, or whether the collapse in her health followed it. In her later journals she refers intermittently to having visited London at this time, the memory of which continually distressed her. There is a hint that the visit was to a physician. Her sisters also refer to her being away, and that her behaviour beforehand had been particularly disturbing. Anticipating her return, they evidently waited nervously. "I do not know what we shall do when Betsy comes home," Louisa wrote in April 1796, "for we are all afraid of her now, which is very shocking."[9] Almost immediately, however, she was overcome with remorse, and struggled to make amends. "Dearest Betsy!" she said, "she seems to have no one for her *friend*, for none of us are intimate with her."

Betsy's reserve, her unpredictable moods and her irritability under pressure were not only barriers to close fellowship, they also roused hostility. "I hate Betsy's management of our lessons," said Louisa, after a particularly fraught day in August 1796, "now that Kitty is away at Northrepps,[10] Betsy does it, and is quite disagreeable, she is so soon worried."

Betsy also had an unerring knack of attracting attention and upsetting her sisters in the process. "I had a good drawing morning," said Richenda, "but in the course of it gave way to passion with both Crome and Betsy – Crome because he would attend to Betsy and not to me, and Betsy because she was so provoking."[11]

But, it was the attention she received from John Gurney, for her pains, her insomnia and her depression, that provoked her sisters most of all, and at times they could hardly help paying her back. And they knew exactly where it hurt. "Stupid," they sometimes hinted.

Betsy hated herself for her educational failures, but despite all attempts to fill the gaps in her knowledge she remained unable to learn, and she failed at nearly every subject. At

French, the language considered so vital for fashionable young ladies, she was hopeless, while her handwriting and her spelling continued to be a source of family amusement. "I think, having the name of being stupid, really tended to make me so,"[12] she remembered much later.

Despite Betsy's sickness, her melancholy moods and her family battles, it was hard for her to remain totally isolated for long. The Gurneys were a large, energetic family, while Earlham itself was not only always busy, but was at the heart of a huge, interwoven community. Closely surrounding the family, their house and their household lay a complex of stables, coach-houses and workshops, together with a bake-house, brewery and laundry, while away in every direction stretched the estate, a region of woodlands, pastures, cultivated fields, cottages, cowsheds and barns. Everyone from John Gurney to the humblest farm-labourer knew each other, and although they also knew their place in the Gurney scheme, they were all aware of how much they needed each other. It was impossible to walk far without meeting a familiar face and exchanging family information, or views on subjects of common interest.

Beyond the estate lay the country around Norwich that had been home to the Gurney family for generations. It was filled with aunts, uncles and cousins close and removed, all of whom visited each other with intimate regularity: for dinner at three, at six to drink tea, and in the evenings for family parties. All of them were also the objects of tireless gossip and fascination.

John Gurney's older brother Richard, always called Uncle Gurney, lived on the family estate at Keswick, just a few miles from Earlham. The Earlham girls called it Kiswick, and the old white family house full of cousins, and the pretty bathing house at the end of a long garden walk to the River Yare, were among their favourite haunts. Nearer still, at Lakenham Grove, always called "The Grove", was John Gurney's younger brother, Uncle Joseph, his wife, Aunt Jane, and still more cousins.

There were also endless opportunities to be out and about in Norwich in support of any relative involved in the town's public affairs or in England's wider politics. It was a tradition that dated back to an earlier John Gurney, who pleaded the

cause of the woollen manufacturers of Norwich before a
House of Lords committee,[13] and when Uncle Gurney's oldest
son, Hudson, stood at the election of 1796, his cousins rallied
to his cause. "Norwich was in the greatest bustle," Louisa
remembered, "we had blue cockades, and I bawled out of the
window at a fine rate – 'Gurney for ever!'"

Hudson was a regular guest at Earlham, and despite being
older than his cousins, and rather sophisticated, he was never
too dignified to join in their games. When the younger girls
locked him in the pantry one day, and subjected his cheerful
good nature to their childish tricks, Kitty found it hard to scold
them.

Even Kitty herself was not above mischief at times. One
summer day she was even persuaded, for a lark, to join her six
sisters, and to stand with them, their arms linked, in a laughing line across the gently rising road near Earlham to bring the
Norwich mail to a shuddering, chaotic halt. After they did so,
and as the great horses stamped and steamed and jangled their
bits, and the passengers laughed and admired the girls for
their pluck, the coach-driver swore he was going straight to
John Gurney to complain. But he never did, and even if he
had, it was unlikely that the girls would have received anything
more than a mild admonishment from their father.

John Gurney had never recovered from Catherine's death, and
he lived in fear that any emotion on his part would set loose an
inconsolable grief. "When I see my children delighting themselves in those pursuits in which my dear Catherine led them,
and wherein she was chief companion, my feelings are truly
mournful," he wrote to his friend and cousin, Joseph Gurney
Bevan. "I feel the necessity of checking an indulgence of emotion which may become injurious, and I am always so afraid
of throwing a damp on my dear Kitty and the elder children,
that I endeavour, as well as I can, to keep up the countenance
of comfort."[14]

Part of that endeavour, he believed, was to make up to his
children for their loss, and when he saw them engaged in innocent pleasures, it convinced him that he was succeeding.

On the lazy summer afternoons his daughters devoted to picnics with cousins and friends, he often lingered by Earlham's windows, gazing nostalgically at the pretty picture he saw on the grass; the girls in gauzy high-waisted gowns tied with coloured ribbons, and the young men, so eager to be useful, hovering anxiously around them. How Catherine would have loved it, he often reflected to himself.

The musical evenings organised by Kitty were also a special joy to him, since those were the times when Betsy was most likely to forget her interminable aches, and throw herself into the gaiety. He especially loved hearing her sing, for there was a quality to her voice that moved him, and when she joined Rachel in pretty duets, the most enthusiastic applause in the room always came from their father.

"Betsy had an exquisite voice," Kitty remembered, "and threw into it all the expression that the heart can give."

Betsy threw all the expression of her heart into dancing too, and she relished the informal evenings when a good-natured crowd of neighbours filled one of Earlham's great rooms and local musicians were hired to play. A special favourite was a blind fiddler, whose lively country tunes raised the lowest spirits, encouraged a carefree merriment and brought everyone to their feet. *"Dear, darling, elating fiddle,"* Louisa wrote ecstatically, "I really am fit to jump out of my skin at the sound of it."

Betsy was also fit to jump out of her skin, and when she abandoned herself to the music, her sisters wondered whether she could really be the same girl that provoked them with her temper and spent so many hours moping in bed. Bathed in candlelight and moving in perfect time, with her tall slender grace, her profusion of soft flaxen hair, and her bright face and shining eyes, Betsy turned everyone's head. On such occasions, she seemed as happy and healthy as her sisters, and it gave her father much pleasure to see it.

Looking on his family at such happy times, delighting in their laughter and bright faces, John Gurney was reassured that his motherless brood were contented, and that even if he did indulge them a little, it was no more than they deserved.

He was also reassured that he was bringing up his family in

accordance with the convictions of the Society of Friends. He was proud of his Quaker lineage and connections, and regarded himself as a good man: an honest businessman and a father who provided well for his motherless children. The details of religion, however, held little interest for him. He ensured that his family attended Meeting regularly each week, but he saw no reason to insist on a lifestyle that would deny his daughters their pretty gowns, Earlham its joyful dances, and himself his company and country sports. He was also perfectly aware that many Quakers in Norwich, and throughout Britain, shared his views.

Uncle Joseph Gurney of The Grove, however, was not one of them. Unlike his brother, he was rigorous in his view of faith, and he was intensely troubled by John's casual attitude. Though he saw it was partly the result of an indulgent personality, he also believed that the scepticism of the age, and the emphasis on material rather than spiritual things, had led many Quakers to regard much in their faith as irrelevant, and to succumb to the temptations of the world. In his view such Friends were foolhardy, for he was unshaken in his belief that the world remained the "briary thorny wilderness" that George Fox had named it when he founded the Quaker movement, and that still waited to trap and deceive the unwary and frustrate their path to salvation.

George Fox was born in 1624, in the Puritan village of Fenny Drayton, Leicestershire. He grew to manhood during the years of the English Civil War, a time when religion and politics were intimately linked, and when many people believed that the end of days was at hand.

Early in life he had been seized by an inner restlessness that drove him to grapple with spiritual questions, to search the scriptures relentlessly, and to ask endless questions of religious men. Finally, however, frustrated and disappointed, he was forced to admit that no human agency could answer his need. At that moment, he said later, deep within his being a transformation took place, that he likened to being brought out of an ocean of darkness and death into an infinite ocean of light and love.[15] That light, he believed, was the boundless love of God, and it became central to his understanding, both of the experience itself, and of God. It was also the core of the message he preached. It did not matter what a person's previous life had been, Fox said, nor what their present condition might be, nor how lost or how depraved they were. By turning to the light of God that was Christ Jesus, that was in all people and available to all people, and by encountering and knowing the Spirit of Truth in the inward parts, all lives could be redeemed and transformed. He called the experience "convincement", and with the certainty that the millennium was approaching, he believed he was called to convince the whole world and to return the church, devoid of the encumbrances it had gathered over a thousand and a half years, to the principles of primitive Christianity.

Thousands who heard him agreed with him and then followed him. Together they called themselves Friends, although since they were so often seen trembling at the power of God, others named them Quakers. As they proclaimed the coming Kingdom and urged people everywhere to turn from darkness to the light, the new Friends also declared the world to be a briary, thorny wilderness, whose corruptions were to be confronted, overcome, and finally swept away.

Determined to live their lives as witnesses to the light and to God's Kingdom, and with a reliance on the inner promptings of the Holy Spirit, and on the Bible, as their guides, Friends made clear their rejection of the existing world order. In an atmosphere charged with Millennial expectations, however, their refusal to accept any authority but God, and their proclamation of the equality of all people beneath him, convinced the leaders of church and state that Quakers were disruptive and dangerous. Their distinctive and uncompromising customs and manners also alienated many people. Instead of joining in the familiar and ordered prayers and communion service of the established church, led by a priest, Quakers met in their aggressively plain Meeting Houses and sat in silent contemplation that might last several hours. The silence could also be broken by any individual who felt moved by the Holy

Spirit to speak out in prayer, in prophecy, in personal testimony or in lengthy extempore sermons known as ministry. Their plain, unadorned costumes and their use of the familiar "thee" and "thou" were also regarded by many as an uncomfortable and unwanted rebuke to their own worldly ways. As hostility mounted, Meeting Houses were demolished, preachers were beaten and abused, and thousands of Friends suffered imprisonment. Some died in prison while others were transported as criminals to Britain's colonies in America.

Throughout the years of persecution, as Friends continued to preach their fiery message and sang hymns in their prison cells, their organisation solidified and their numbers grew. Then, ironically, with the growth of political and religious toleration that came at the end of the 1680s, when belief in the millennium had also faded, they began to fall. By 1715 there were just 39,000 Quakers in England and Wales,[16] and as calls for convincements fell on indifferent ears, the movement was forced to reassess itself. As it did so, although the doctrine of the light remained central to Friends' beliefs, and they themselves continued to maintain they were a people specially chosen by God, their attitude to the briary, thorny wilderness changed. For no longer did they fight great social and spiritual battles in its midst, instead they began increasingly to isolate themselves from it.

Like all non-Anglicans, Friends were excluded from English universities and the professions, but whereas other Dissenting groups established academies and paid ministries in order to sustain and pass on their faith, Quakers depended increasingly on birthright and tradition. They also encouraged their young people to take up business, and a reputation for honesty and integrity saw them prosper. A policy of intermarriage also created an intimate network of wealthy Quaker families, while a penalty of disownment for children who married out, and for parents who allowed them to do so, ensured that they became gradually more insular. It was an insularity that grew more profound after Friends turned increasingly to the theology of Catherine Gurney's great-grandfather, Robert Barclay, whose emphasis on the inner work of the Holy Spirit eventually led them into quietism.

By the mid-eighteenth century, the Quaker focus was on social exclusivity, on passive contemplation, and a denial of what was outward and "creaturely". The distinctive plain dress, speech and manners that had once seemed so vital a witness became regulated by strict codes, and Quaker opposition to the world was often expressed in a rejection of music, dancing, novels and plays. Anxieties also increased over distinguishing the divine from the creaturely voice, so that in time, the Meetings that had once also been a platform for spoken prayer and testimony became ever more silent. Sometimes several weeks of Meetings might pass without a word being spoken.

While for some Quakers, the combination of passive and plain was intensely fulfilling, for others it was a constraint that produced boredom, frustration and guilt, and by late in the century, a gulf had widened between "Plain" Friends like Joseph Gurney, and "Gay" Friends like his brother John.

The very thought of passive and plain made the Earlham girls shudder. "Oh, how I long to get a great broom and *bang* all the old Quakers, who do look so triumphant and disagreeable," Richenda wrote after a particularly dreary Sunday at Goat Lane.

"I spent *four* hours at Meeting! I never, never wish to see that nasty hole again," she complained after another.

Though they took a perverse delight in always wearing their most fashionable and expensive clothes to Meeting, and revelled in the frowns of their Plain brethren, Goats, nevertheless, always made the girls feel "goatified and cross".

"Goats was *dis*," was a regular feature of their journals, and Betsy, in particular, seemed to have an extraordinary capacity to be ill whenever Meeting loomed.

To increase Uncle Joseph's distress, as much as they loathed Meeting, the Gurney girls also appeared to be following in their mother's footsteps as they explored a wide variety of belief systems. Peggy Lindoc, with her Unitarian views, was still a regular visitor to Earlham, and when the older girls, especially Kitty, began making friends in Norwich society, they discovered many more like her, all eager to discuss the latest ideas in philosophy and literature, radical politics and religious belief.

One of them was Dr Enfield, a local Unitarian Minister. Kitty had been first to meet him when she attended his public lectures before Catherine's death, and very quickly a close bond had developed between their two families. For a while, young John Gurney had been a pupil with the doctor, and while Kitty and Rachel had rapidly become firm friends with all the Enfield children, it was the good-looking Henry and his sister Anna to whom they were particularly close.

Kitty remembered them as a delightful pair, charming, gifted and cultivated, and together the young people shared a romantic pleasure in the beauties of nature, in conversations ranging from natural religion to poetry, in singing and in books. One of the books, Kitty remembered, was a volume by the radical French philosopher, Jean Jacques Rousseau. "And I need not say," she said later, when her ideas had much changed, "how undermining this was to truth, both in theory and practice."

Amelia Alderson and her widowed physician father were good friends of the Gurneys, too. The doctor, who provided a free medical service for the Norwich poor, belonged to one of Britain's Corresponding Societies, whose object was to urge democratic values and encourage parliamentary reform. As a republican, he had also supported the American Revolutionary War and the French Revolution; his house was a centre of radical opinion and full of progressive books that included volumes by the arch-sceptic and iconoclast, Voltaire, as well as *The Rights of Man* by Tom Paine.

Dr Alderson had brought up his daughter to be independent and free-thinking, and when the 19-year-old Amelia created a sensation in the streets of revolutionary Paris by singing "Fall, Tyrants Fall",[17] Dr Alderson had been intensely proud. He was equally proud of her literary career that brought her into contact with progressive artists, writers and philosophers. One of them, the philosopher William Godwin, had once been her admirer and remained a close friend. His wife was the writer

Mary Wollstonecraft, who had lived in revolutionary France, and later lived openly with Godwin before marriage. She had also published, in 1792, a book that had a profound effect on anyone who came across it. It was called *A Vindication of the Rights of Women*, and it argued for true liberty and political rights for women and a complete transformation in the social relations between the sexes.

John Pitchford was as challenging in his way as the Enfields and the Aldersons were in theirs, except that John was a committed Christian. Although making no secret of his particular admiration for Rachel, he was a good friend to all the girls, and he spent long hours in their company, reading poetry around the fire, acting in pantomimes, and accompanying Rachel and Betsy as they sang. When he joined them in "Come, ye Lads and Lassies Fair", the Epithalamium written by Joseph Gurney Bevan for John and Catherine's wedding,[18] he couldn't help thinking that although the Gurney sisters were also fair, their ignorance of religion and their casual acceptance of sceptical arguments was quite shocking. He made it his business to explain Christianity to them, and although he was careful never to press the claims of his own Roman Catholic Church, he described how his personal prayer life gave him great joy and how the Bible could become the basis for a moral and rewarding life.

He was also careful to intersperse his allusions to Christianity and pleas for faith with more secular pleasures, and in July, 1797, he left an example in his journal.

> This is a day which I shall ever remember with delight. I have spent 17 hours with my seven most enchanting friends. I rose at 4 a.m. and walked slowly to Earlham, as I did not wish to disturb them too soon. I had partly made up my mind not to throw pebbles at their windows (the preconcerted signal of my arrival) till six, but I found them already risen. The morning was clear and brilliant. Rachel saw me first and knocked at the window. Then Richenda and Louisa came down, and soon all the rest except Betsy, who does not rise so soon on account of her health. After a

short walk, the four were sent to the schoolroom to do their lessons. Kitty, Rachel, and I seated ourselves in the shade. I had brought *Peregrinus Porteus* in my pocket, and read the beautiful description of the farm at Pitane, and the glowing language in which the Christian preacher enlarges on the character and manner of our Blessed Saviour: they completely enjoyed it ... "

We enjoyed a charming breakfast together, Betsy having joined us, and then we went into the kitchen-garden to eat fruit. After this, we selected a shady spot on the lawn, where the whole party reclined upon a haycock, while I read to them part of my journal, omitting certain passages which avowed my attachment to Rachel. Three or four times, however, I stumbled on passages of this kind, and was obliged to interrupt myself. I am not clear whether the sharp-sighted Rachel did not suspect the truth, but her behaviour during the rest of the day was full as kind as ever. They were all interested with my journal. "Now we really know you," they exclaimed, "let us join hands and vow an eternal friendship." This we did with rapturous feelings and glowing hearts. Rachel now read some of Henry Enfield's journal, which he regularly sends her, and Betsy read part of her journal, in which she acknowledges all her faults with the most charming candour. Finally, Kitty read part of her journal.

After dinner we went to the pianoforte and Rachel and I practised some songs. I taught her the "Stabat Mater" which she much liked. We then went in the boat, and had some most interesting conversation, and after tea chose a delightful spot in the garden facing the setting sun, where Kitty read the poetry of "The Monk", and I "The Deserted Village". Then we went to the village church, where I read Gray's "Elegy" by twilight with great effect. Kitty said, "We will be your seven sisters." When we got to the river-side, we again had enchanting singing, finishing by "Poor John is dead", and, as we returned, promised each other that any of us in danger of death should be visited by the rest. Then we extended our views beyond the grave, and enthusiastically sang till we reached the house "In Heaven for ever dwell". It was with difficulty that I tore myself away after supper. It was a day ever to be remembered with transport.[19]

As Betsy entered the second part of her sixteenth year, she continued to struggle with the dark depressions that had coloured almost all her adolescence. "My mind is in so dark a state, that I see everything through a black medium," she wrote early in 1797.[20] Yet she could not help being increasingly intrigued by what she heard from Cousin Betty, from the Enfields, the Aldersons and John Pitchford, as well as from many other individuals who spoke at public meetings at Norwich or frequented the dinner table at Earlham. For, she was desperate to find an explanation for a peculiar restlessness that had overtaken her, that was sometimes so intense that it felt like an aching within, or a powerful yearning for something she was disconcertingly unable to name.

She considered discussing philosophy and religious ideas with Amelia and John Pitchford, but eventually she rejected it. Although she liked to listen, she could never quite forget her stupidity, and on the rare occasions when she did speak, her words frequently seemed foolish to her. If people responded encouragingly, she often imagined it was born merely of a desire to be kind, whereas if they were at all critical, then something inside her shrivelled, and she felt like a child again, clinging to Catherine Gurney's skirts.

Sometimes she thought of talking to Uncle Joseph, but she was often tongue-tied in his company and never quite certain whether he and Aunt Jane really liked her. If she spoke, she feared she would be rebuffed.

After pondering alone on all she had heard, she was drawn first to Unitarianism, because her mother had been drawn to it, and then to republicanism because of Amelia. In the end, however, she rejected them both. John Pitchford sometimes offered her books on Christianity, but she spurned those too. When she felt the need of faith, she told him awkwardly, she would judge clearly for herself by reading the New Testament. As for his suggestion that God was a loving father who entered into personal relationships with his children and responded to prayer, Betsy knew better. She knew there was nothing in the universe, in the great silent darkness, that responded to the desperate pleadings of a small human voice.

In the end she decided that in all probability the Deists were right. "It was my lot, in very early life," she remembered later, "to be much in company with Deists, and to be rather a warm advocate for their doctrines." There was a God, she maintained, to anyone who asked her, a God who had designed and created the universe, wound it up like a clock, set it in motion, abandoned it for ever, and could not be reached.

Yet it failed to satisfy. The restlessness within her was not assuaged. It remained, doggedly insistent, like a question demanding an answer.

CHAPTER THREE

The light

"*I* AM 17 TO-DAY, AM I A happier or a better creature than I was this time twelvemonths?" Betsy asked herself on her birthday.

The day, 21 May 1797, had dawned fair, with a radiant sky, a carol of birdsong and an early morning warmth that woke all the scents of the earth. Standing before her window, Betsy felt unexpectedly confident. "I know I am happier, I think I am better," she assured herself, and opening the window wide, she leaned into a morning that seemed breathless with anticipation. "I hope I shall be much better this day year than I am now," she continued optimistically, "I hope to be quite an altered person, to have more knowledge, to have my mind in greater order, and my heart too, that, wants to be put in order as much, if not more, than any part of me, it is in such a fly-away state."

Betsy's search for answers to her inner restlessness had led her to a quest for Virtue, an Enlightenment concept that implied moral perfection in all things, and whose pursuit involved detailed and regular self-examination. But, as she soon discovered, Virtue was elusive.

"I have the oddest feeling when I do as I think right," she said, "I always feel so silly. I wonder why?" She was also painfully conscious that although she struggled so hard for Virtue, somehow she seemed inexorably drawn towards her vices.

"Why do I wish so much for the Prince to come?" she had asked herself in April. "Pride, alas! is the cause," she had concluded.

John Gurney had met Prince William Frederick of Gloucester, a nephew of King George III, just a few months earlier, and had cordially invited the affable young man to Earlham. The Prince, quartered nearby with his regiment, had been charmed by the invitation and by John Gurney's beautiful house, but far more by his seven pretty daughters, and together with his fellow officers he became the family's regular guest. "Red coats and fine ladies glittered before my eyes," Richenda wrote ecstatically of the elegant dinner parties and dances, that as the girls grew older, were replacing the informal occasions of former years.

Uncle Joseph, however, was shocked that his brother had succumbed to the vanity of royal connections, for in his view, the advent of Prince William was yet another example of just how far worldly pleasures were seducing John's family from the paths of righteousness. The older girls especially concerned him, for just as he had already seen them intrigued by sceptical philosophies, now he saw them seized by an enormous appetite for pleasure. When his remonstrations were met, particularly from Rachel, with nothing but protestations and tears, he decided that the time had come to speak earnestly to his brother. Should any of the young men who buzzed around his daughters capture a Gurney heart, he warned, the result could be disownment from the Society of Friends, the severance of family and business connections and possible ruin for the other children.

Contritely, John agreed to be more pious.

"I am sorry to see him grow so Quakerly," Louisa said unsympathetically. Her sisters agreed that she spoke for them all.

While Betsy shared her sisters' passion for parties, unlike them, her quest for Virtue was also leading her to question the carefree life of Earlham. "I feel by experience how much entering into the world hurts me," she confided to the intimate journal that she now called "the little friend of my heart".

"Worldly company," she said, "I think, materially injures; it excites a false stimulus, such as love of pomp, pride, vanity, jealousy, and ambition." Furthermore, she continued, it encouraged frivolous thoughts about dress, and a passion for novels and scandal.

Even as she wrote the words, however, she knew she was not immune. "I have lately been given up a good deal to worldly passions," she confessed after a merry evening with the Prince. But she also observed something curious. "My mind feels very flat after this storm of pleasure," she said.

Fearing herself incapable of withstanding worldly temptations, she also worried about the effects of her weakness on others. "I believe by not governing myself in little things," she said, "I may by degrees become a despicable character, and a curse to society; therefore my doing wrong is of consequence to others, as well as to myself."

Eager for Virtue, she examined herself relentlessly. "I have known my faults, and not corrected them," she admitted, "and now I am determined I will once more try, with redoubled ardour, to overcome my wicked inclinations." Unflinchingly, she listed them. "I must not flirt; be out of temper with the children; contradict without a cause; I must not mump when my sisters are liked and I am not; ... be angry; ... exaggerate; ... give way to luxury; ... be idle in mind." She also included her embarrassing tendency to chatter nervously, as well as the sarcastic remarks that sometimes slipped from her tongue before she could catch them.

Yet though she was determined to continue her quest, it was hard to struggle alone.

"I am at this present time in an odd state," she wrote just after her birthday, "I am like a ship put out to sea without a pilot. I feel my heart and mind so overburdened, I want someone to lean on."

Like all true seekers after Virtue, Betsy was anxious to acknowledge her good impulses as well as her faults. "I love to feel for the sorrows of others, to pour wine and oil into the wounds of the afflicted," she wrote dramatically. She also wondered whether the trials of her past might hold a clue to her future. "May what I have suffered be a lesson to me," she said, "to feel for those who are ill, and alleviate their sorrows as far as lies in my power."

In July, she recalled the previous year, that had been marked by so much depressive illness. "Look back at this time last year," she wrote, "how ill I was, how miserable." She also reflected that although God had inflicted suffering upon her, he had nevertheless enabled her to bear it. If she were devotional, she said, she would fall to her knees in gratitude. But, although a God who interacted with his creation was beginning to intrude on her Deist consciousness, her acquaintance with sceptics, and her commitment to the view she had chosen, ensured he was kept at a distance. "I love to 'look through Nature up to Nature's God'," she wrote, quoting Alexander Pope, "I have no more religion than that, and in the little I have I am not the least devotional."

Almost imperceptibly, although she instructed herself to ensure that her happiness was governed by Reason alone, by the end of July she was considering whether Virtue and faith could somehow be combined. "My idea of religion," she said, "is not for it to unfit us for the duties of life, like a nun who leaves them for prayer and thanksgiving; but I think it should stimulate and capacitate us to perform those duties properly."

Among her own duties she believed, and constantly reiterated, was her continuing need to please John Gurney. "I do love my father from the bottom of my heart," she said, "I would do anything to make him happy."

Since his brother's warning, John Gurney had valiantly attempted to curb his daughters' worldly excesses, but in the face of seven pretty girls determined to enjoy life to the full, his indulgent nature had frequently admitted defeat. In August 1797, anxious to please him by conforming to his more Quakerly aspirations, Betsy resolved to forgo a long-awaited delight. "I had very much set my mind on going to the Oratorio," she said virtuously, "the Prince is to be there, and by all accounts it will be quite a grand sight, and there will be the finest music; but if my father does not like me to go, much as I wish it, I will give it up with pleasure." The temptation, however, was too great. "I went to the Oratorio," she admitted ruefully, "I enjoyed it, but spoke sadly at random; what a bad habit!"

Days later, religion was occupying her again. "I do not know if I shall not soon be rather religious," she said, "because I have thought lately what a support it is through life, it seems so delightful to depend upon a superior power, for all that is good." But, even as her heart warmed towards it, her scepticism revolted. "I fear being religious," she decided flatly, "in case I should be enthusiastic."

Shamefully, she attempted to banish the subject from her mind.

Just as John Gurney had been reluctant to enforce a ban on the Oratorio, he also found it hard to resist when his daughters pleaded for parties. As the summer of 1797 became autumn, an almost continuous procession of elegant vehicles swept gaily along Earlham's carriage-drive to bring the Prince, Amelia, or the young Enfields to the Gurneys' front door. In return, John Gurney's carriage travelled just as gaily into Norwich, delivering the girls, in their prettiest gowns, to tea-parties, dinner-parties, and sparklingly bright dances.

"Betsy went to the assembly last night, and danced a great deal," Louisa recorded in November. "How most droll! Quite a new excursion!"

But, as November grew gloomier, and the last leaves dropped from Earlham's trees into puddles fed by drizzling rain, a tragedy begun to unfold. At its heart were Rachel and Henry Enfield, who had fallen passionately in love almost at their first meeting, and whose romance had been kept secret by Rachel's sisters. When he discovered it, John Gurney was distraught; furious for not seeing what was under his nose, bitter at being duped, tormented by guilt for the freedoms he had allowed, and overcome with grief at bearing such things alone. As he contemplated the awful possibility of Rachel's disownment, his indulgence turned to harshness, and Henry and the whole Enfield family were banished from Earlham. So terrible was Rachel's grief, however, that her father finally agreed that after two years a meeting might take place, and also that if she and Henry were still so much in love, the possibility of a marriage might then be discussed. Meanwhile, Rachel's sisters also suffered from the absence of the Enfields. "This was to us all a blow of no common pain and trial," Kitty recalled later, "and hard did we feel it to be kept in such constraint, separated from our dearest friends."

In dark December, as Christmas passed by, Betsy also felt herself drifting away from what she had earlier gained. "I think I am by degrees, losing many excellent qualities," she said sadly, "I am more cross, more proud, more vain, more extravagant. I lay it to my great love of gaiety and the world." Briefly, she returned to the subject of faith. "A thought passed my mind," she said, "that if I had some religion, I should be superior to what I am, it would be a bias to better actions."

Still, the world was hard to resist; especially when Prince William and his comrades arrived for a New Year party at the beginning of January 1798. All afternoon the revels grew boisterous, until finally, after the girls' mocking descriptions of Goats had reduced their guests to helpless laughter, the Prince insisted that Rachel preach him a sermon. Rachel, who blamed Uncle Joseph and his Plain Quakers for her separation from her lover, was delighted to oblige. "I never saw anything so droll," Richenda said, "as it was to see the Prince and all of us locked up in Betsy's room, and Rachel preaching to him, which she did in her most capital manner, giving him a good lesson in the Quaker strain, and imitating William Crotch to perfection."[1]

The party continued into the early evening. "Betsy had an *offer* from one of the officers," Richenda said breathlessly, "I never knew anything so droll!"

Richenda's sisters also found it droll, and most bewildering, that the withdrawn, moody young woman who was often confined to bed with sickness, and who recently had appeared more lost in thought than usual, should so constantly attract young men. Yet there was no doubt that she exerted a powerful fascination, for it was not only James Lloyd and Prince William's young officer that had been captivated by her; her sisters were also aware of a large number of neighbours and friends who made no secret of their admiration.

After the Prince left, and as more guests arrived, Earlham resounded to the sound of fiddles and dancing feet. So infectious was it, that everyone joined in; single and married, old and young, the distinguished and the humble alike.

The festivities continued all week. On the next day, Wednesday, there was another dance, on Thursday another, and still another on Friday. On Saturday, the party was hosted by Dr Alderson and the dancing went on from seven until midnight. "I had no idea that gay company could be as pleasant as it was," Richenda said afterwards.

Neither could Betsy, and as she danced her way through the cold winter nights, partnering one admirer after another, her scepticism took firmer hold. "I am sorry to say," she said, on 13 January 1798, "I have no real faith in any sort of religion."

Three days later, however, she was less certain. "My mind is in a state of fermentation," she said, "I believe I am going to be religious, or some such thing." Two days after that, she despaired. "I am a bubble, without reason, without beauty of mind or person," she lamented. "I am a fool. I daily fall lower in my own estimation ... I am now 17, and if some kind, and great circumstance does not happen to me, I shall have my talents devoured by moth and rust."

Uncle Joseph, however, had no intention of allowing Betsy's talents to be devoured either by moth or by rust. For, there was a quality to her that stirred something in his Quaker soul. He could not overlook the fact that she was difficult: her obstinacy and moodiness had antagonized most of her relatives over the years. Yet for all her prickly exterior, he sensed that deep within his troubled niece there was something original seeking nourishment, and an independent spirit struggling to be free. The insight had persuaded him that she should be encouraged to follow a religious path, but despite many attempts to coax her to Meeting, he was constantly rebuffed. Just a mention of Goats brought on a headache. Even the un-Quakerly bustling that overtook the Friends of Norwich in December 1797, which became quite a commotion in January 1798, failed to intrigue her. Neither did the promise of a preacher quite extraordinary.

The Gurney sisters had heard visiting preachers before, and although according to Kitty, they made "a little change", despite the novelty of a strange face and different voice, none of them had ever shaken the girls' scepticism, dispelled their boredom or relieved their loathing of Goats. That the expected visitor was an American, provoked mildly more interest than an Englishman might have done, but apart from encouraging them to reflect on life across the Atlantic, the girls expected the stranger's visit to be quite unremarkable and to leave nothing in its wake.

Sunday, 4 February 1798 dawned icy and bleak. A black, bitter wind from the north blew discouragingly over the flat Norfolk landscape, and at Earlham, Betsy was ill. Her stomach ached, she had been wakeful all night, and she was determined to stay home by the fire.

Her father was disappointed and cross. His brother had been particularly insistent that Betsy should be at Goats to hear the American, and John was keen to comply. Anxiously, he pressed his daughter to change her mind.

"Every Quaker in Norwich will be there," he told her. But it had little effect. Taking up the previous week's *Norfolk Chronicle*, he quoted from its pages. "A celebrated preacher from America," he read, "of prepossessing appearance and address."[2] Betsy stared at the fire, her jaw set and her face expressionless. His desperation growing by the minute, John Gurney attempted to remember everything Joseph had told him about William Savery.

Born in Philadelphia in 1750, in his American homeland Savery was widely regarded as a man of principle and peace. As a passionate opponent of slavery, in 1783, together with other American Quakers, he had petitioned the United States Congress to use its influence for the abolition of the slave trade.[3] Later, in 1794, as an equally passionate supporter of the rights of Native Americans, he was invited by the Haudenosaunee, the Six Nations of the Iroquois Confederacy based in New York State, to lead a Quaker delegation charged with safeguarding their interests during negotiation of the Treaty of Canandaigua.[4]

In the following year he had felt a powerful concern to make religious journeys to the European nations most disturbed by revolution and scepticism, and also to visit Britain.[5]

As such, Savery was continuing the Quaker tradition of itinerant preaching that had begun with George Fox, and which by the eighteenth century was referred to as the travelling ministry. Its beginning was usually a powerful inner concern which, although an individual might not know the precise reason for his destination, told him clearly that he was being called to visit a certain locality. Having discussed it with his local Meeting, and having been endorsed by them with a certificate, the aim of the visit was generally to strengthen and encourage groups of Friends elsewhere.[6] In some cases, as in that of William Savery, the aim of the traveller might also include emphasising the Christian message generally, and sometimes standing alongside others to oppose injustice or promote human welfare.

Betsy agreed that Savery seemed an interesting and inspiring man.

He had also heard, John said cautiously, that William Savery had not always been a Plain Friend. Once he had been just like the Gurneys, worldly and disbelieving, until a powerful spiritual experience had shaken him and utterly transformed his life.[7] Finally, Betsy was captivated. To her father's relief she agreed to go with him to Goats.

Privately, though it troubled her conscience a little, she thought that if large crowds really were expected, then she would rather like to show off her new boots.

Immediately on entering Goats, Betsy saw that John Gurney had been right, and that on the benches that were usually so empty, over 200 people now sat so closely crammed together that there was scarcely an empty seat.

Settling herself beside her sisters, on their bench among the women, near the minister's gallery, she was conscious of an air of expectancy pervading the Meeting. Rather than the usual fidgets and bored expressions of those who attended only from obligation, there were eager rustles of anticipation and faces alight with interest. She noticed too, with a mixture of unease and pleasure, that the Gurneys were not alone in the extravagance of their clothes. For scattered liberally throughout the assembly, and quite outnumbering the sober-hued Plain Quakers, were men in the most fashionably-cut coats and women costumed in rainbow brilliance; in unabashed reds, luscious greens and scintillating blues. There were also, she saw, some luxurious furs, some elegant feathers and some perfectly exquisite bonnets. In fact, the colour and prodigality, the immodest aroma of scent, and the atmosphere of general excitement, Betsy decided, made Goats seem almost like a playhouse.

Intrigued by the novelty of the crowd, at first she gazed into its many faces, but eventually she realised that almost every pair of eyes in the room was staring quite unashamedly at a middle-aged man who sat among the elders and ministers.[8] Finally she too turned her attention towards him.

He himself appeared entirely oblivious of the interest he aroused, and continued to sit solid, silent and still, with his eyes closed, deep in his own quiet waiting. Intrigued, Betsy examined him. He was well built, she saw, probably quite tall when he stood up, and although he was dressed in Plain Quaker fashion, in a coat without collar or lapels, his clothes were well cut and hung pleasingly upon his frame. His face, faintly lined on the forehead and about the eyes, wore an expression of self-sufficient tranquillity. Staring at him intently, she sensed an overwhelming gravity about him that suddenly made the silken rustles in the room seem shamefully frivolous.

Time passed, and William Savery sat on in a silence that lengthened, and then grew longer still.

Finally, Betsy sighed and wished she hadn't come. Despite all that had been said, it was to be another *dis* Goats. Dispiritedly, she turned her attention to her boots; she was completely in love with their shiny purple leather and bright scarlet laces,[9] and as she turned them this way and that, examining them from every angle, she was conscious that the air of expectancy that had filled Goats earlier was dissolving, and that the shuffling of feet and the clearing of many disappointed throats was becoming uncomfortably insistent. If it grew any louder, she thought, it would be quite a commotion.

Suddenly there was silence. Betsy looked up. William Savery had risen to his feet and was looking hard at the English crowd that sat in rows before him. Startled, the crowd stared back. The atmosphere was tense.

When he began to speak, although his voice was not loud, it filled the room. There was also a warm tone to it, and a lengthening of vowels that was unsettlingly foreign but compellingly attractive, and as he spoke, he smiled occasionally. His words, however, were not meant to charm; they were sorrowful, harsh and unnerving.

He was grieved, William Savery said, by the gaiety he saw in Norwich, especially among Friends at Goat Lane. And he was grieved too at the state of England, where true religion had been abandoned for a religion of nature, even for unbelief, and where far too often, even among Quakers, the paths of virtue were abandoned for the ways of self-centeredness, indifference and greed.

The Goats crowd drew in its collective breath.

In Christian England, Savery continued, people thought more of wealth than of their immortal souls, and even though Jesus Christ himself urged them to store up treasure not on earth but in heaven, they wrapped themselves in luxury and thought only of today. Did they imagine they would live for ever?[10] Had their fathers done so? How many years would it be, he asked his audience, before it was finally too late to turn from their sinful ways?

He reminded them of the message of Jesus, that spoke of God's love for humanity and his free gift of salvation, but that was also a message of warning. For if we are not saved, he said, we are surely heading for a destruction more final and more terrible than anything we can imagine; an ocean of darkness and death.

Do not turn from the light that is Christ Jesus, he urged. That light is salvation; salvation that redeems people in this world and fills their earthly lives with energy, purpose and virtue, and also promises everlasting life in the next.

No lives are so unlovely, nor so unworthy, nor so lost, he said, that they are beyond the reach of the light. And those who turn to it and are saved will carry its message to other lost souls, and bring them too, to the light. Even you, he said to the room in general, can be saved and created anew; and even you can also bring others to that same saving light.

Then, as suddenly as he had stood up, he sat down. In the silence that followed, no one moved. Goats sat hushed.

When she finally tore her eyes away from William Savery's face, Betsy saw that her hands were clutched to her heart and that they were wet with her tears.

Outside Goats, the glowing disc of the sun hung low in the winter sky. Narrowing her eyes, Betsy peered into its dazzle, and as the light flared over the icy roofs of Norwich, through the black branches of seemingly lifeless trees, and onto the frozen grass of the meeting-house garden, for a moment she saw the desolate landscape before her transformed into a radiant glory.

In Uncle Joseph's grand-parlour, however, she shrank back to the shadows. William Savery's presence there unsettled her, and though she struggled hard to resist, she felt herself inexorably drawn to him. She glanced continually in his direction, at his dark head that about the temples was fretted with grey, yet, when for a moment her eyes met his, she became confused, and she felt herself to be once again the child who clung to Catherine Gurney's skirts. Also, for the first time in her life, she was ashamed of her fashionable clothes. Such discomfort made her resentful. "There was a *soft*, pleasing manner in friend Savery," she said, "but I thought he had something of the *hoteur* of Quakers about him."

Joseph Gurney had watched Betsy carefully for most of the morning, and seeing the tears, he believed he knew what they meant. Determined, therefore, that she should profit further from the American's visit, and blind to her discomfort, he arranged for her to travel alone with him in Joseph's own carriage to the second meeting of the day.

It was an uncomfortable journey, full of uneasy silences and halting conversations. Not very "concerning", Betsy recalled later. She imagined it to be her fault.

William Savery's thoughts, however, were elsewhere. "I thought it the gayest meeting of Friends I ever sat in," he wrote later, describing the morning's events, "and was grieved to see it."[11] He also recounted how his original plan to pass the entire meeting in silence had been violently overturned when a powerful inner voice had bid him speak.

His visit to The Grove had also increased his concerns, particularly his introduction to some of Joseph Gurney's relations. "Several Gay Girls, Daughters of John Gurney, and their father with them, gave us their Company,"[12] he said.

He found it all intensely depressing. "There seem to be but few upright standard-bearers left among the members in this place," he observed, and even though he saw some potential in the young, he held out little hope. "Several of the younger branches," he said, "though they are enabled, through divine grace, to see what the Truth leads to, yet it is uncertain whether, with all the alluring things of this world around them, they will choose the simple, safe path of self-denial."[13]

Two thousand people packed the Gildencroft, the larger of Norwich's two Quaker Meeting Houses, to hear William Savery preach the simple, safe path of self-denial. They were rich and poor, royalist and republican, Deist and Unitarian, and Christian high and low, and many of them anticipated that the preacher's message would reflect a growing public conflict between scepticism and a resurgent Protestant Christianity.

The beginnings of the conflict, together with the epithet "enthusiast", lay in the emergence of Evangelicalism in the 1730s, and in the preaching tours in England and America of John Wesley and George Whitefield. Ignoring the missiles of stones and rotting vegetables, as well as verbal abuse, the two men had challenged scepticism, indifference, and Christians whose religion had become lukewarm. They had emphasised "justification, the forgiving of our sins through the atoning death of Christ; and the new birth, the renewing of our fallen human nature at the time of conversion."[14] Behind them, in towns and villages by the score, and in many Christian denominations, Wesley, Whitefield and those who came after them left Christians newly converted, Christians revived and renewed, and men and women ready to take up the challenge of a living, vital faith and to go out and preach it to others. William Savery was such a one.[15]

"The name of the speaker was Savery," John Pitchford recorded in his journal, "and his sermon the best I have ever heard among Quakers, so full of candour and liberality."[16]

A week later, in its issue of 10 February 1798, the *Norfolk Chronicle* reported the meeting for its readers.

> On Sunday evening last Mr Savery, from America, commanded the attention of a very crowded and respectable audience, at the Quakers' Meeting, for above two hours. The subject was generally interesting, founded upon the maxim that the society which did not revert to first principles was liable to decay, which he with considerable address and seriousness applied to the individual professors of religion, observing that the innovation of creeds and articles, framed and imposed by human authority or cunning, had produced much infidelity, and arose from a want of adherence to first principles. That the creed of the great founder of Christianity was simple, being directed to promote "Peace on earth and good will towards men"; he expressed his hope that the turnings and overturnings of the present time would end in restoring the primitive union of Christian fellowship, and that countries assuming the appellation of Christians would no more delight in War, adding, he could not think it an acceptable service to thank God for victory over an enemy.[17] He related with great advantage and perspicuity the advantage he had enjoyed in finding amongst what are called Heathens, men of piety and goodness, who, though they were destitute of a written law, were a law unto themselves, and favoured with the assistance of the spirit of the Almighty; very happily illustrating that the salvation published by the Gospel would be participated by numbers in the extensive nations of the earth, who never possessed the means of knowing it, while those who rejected its great advantages would be exposed to just condemnation.[18]

It was an emotionally charged evening, and among the vast audience were many who found that William Savery's words roused painful memories or provoked disturbing reactions. Betsy herself was reminded constantly of the past. "I thought how near *my mother* was to me in the burying ground, which led me to think about death," she said, "and then a lady went into hysterics, and it did so remind me of my old feelings."

In the closeness of the carriage back to The Grove, she found herself telling it to William Savery. He was unexpectedly sympathetic, and later, she remembered how he had listened to her carefully, answered her questions as best he could, and then prayed for her. It had been something like an unconventional Quaker Meeting, she recalled. Later, in Uncle Joseph's parlour there was another Quaker Meeting, of a more regular sort.

By the time she arrived home to Earlham, after midnight and almost too tired to climb into bed, her mind reeled with impressions: the fashionable crowds at Goats; William Savery and the light; Uncle Joseph's parlour; William Savery at the Gildencroft; Catherine Gurney's grave; William Savery in the carriage; William Savery's insight and concern. When she finally closed her eyes, her sleep was restless. "I had a painful night," she said, "and dreamed nor thought of anything but this man and what had passed."

Next morning, on his way back to London, he called at Earlham, where he shared a family breakfast, admired John Gurney's library, charmed Betsy's sisters and was especially attentive to the young woman who had briefly opened her heart to him. In the morning light, he also seemed different: no longer the powerful preacher, or the minister who spoke intimately to God, but a kind, affectionate and very approachable man. Later, she stared after his carriage until it had entirely disappeared from her view. "I hope he will *come again*," she confided to her journal.

"I have had a faint light spread over my mind," Betsy wrote next day, as she reflected on Sunday's events. "At least, I believe it is something of that kind," she continued, "owing to having been much with, and heard much *excellence* from, one who appears to me, a *true Christian*."

But almost as the words reached the page, she had misgivings. Was the light real? her sceptical past enquired. And even if it was, would it last? Could anything good come from a Plain Quaker? asked her love of music and dancing. Her well-bred Gurney cultivation also raised the horrid spectre of enthusiasm. For certainly, it pointed out, there was nothing worse than enthusiasm and folly. Unless it was "growing the Quaker", added her loathing of Goats.

Anxiously, Betsy tried to put her thoughts in order. We had much serious conversation, she reflected, recalling William Savery's words as best she could. She also tried to describe how they had felt to her. "In short," she said, "what he said and what I felt, was like a refreshing shower, falling upon earth that had been dried up for ages."

Was this extraordinary feeling of nourishment and light what was meant by enthusiasm, she wondered. For if it was, then it seemed to answer a deep inner need. "I wish the state of enthusiasm I am now in may last," she decided eventually, "for today I have felt *that there is a God and immortality*."

God, it seemed, had finally entered Betsy's life, together with William Savery. It was so overwhelming a combination that she could hardly stop talking about either of them.

Her sisters found it hugely amusing and they teased her relentlessly, both for her new-found enthusiasm, and for the man they claimed was responsible. They also alluded to a neighbour, young Robert, who they knew admired her, and harnessing his name to that of William Savery, they accused her of being a flirt.

Although Betsy strove to ignore them, the sisterly taunts were disturbing. Was she in love with William Savery, as her sisters claimed? "I felt a sort of adoration for him," she admitted. She also felt an unsettling urge to be with him. Had he asked, she said, "I should have gone to America." About love, though, she tried to be cautious. "I have no doubt it was partly the mystery that always is about such sort of people," she reassured herself. Yet she remained uneasy. Her feelings were, she said, "unintelligible."

Two days after the momentous Sunday, Betsy rode alone towards Norwich. She was desperate to escape Earlham and

her sisters and to find time and space for solitude and reflection. But, within hours, all her good intentions had collapsed:
first of all, an encounter with young Robert himself brought
on worldly feelings, while later, the undisguised admiration of
a bold group of redcoats brought on vanity.

"I rode home as full of the world as I had ridden to town full
of heaven," she said ruefully.

It was no better next day, especially when she left Earlham
with her six sisters for an evening at The Grove. Inside the carriage, as it bowled gaily along behind John Gurney's sleek
black horses, Rachel sang most beautifully, while outside, the
frosty roofs of Norwich sparkled and the sky glittered with
stars. "We went over Castle Hill,"[19] said Betsy, "and for a
moment my feelings were open to anything. I looked at the sky
and thought of God, I looked at the hill and thought of redcoats, and my feelings were jumping around most drolly. A
fine military band went past the carriage, I could have flown
after it."

"The more I reason upon it, the more I get into a labyrinth of
uncertainty," Betsy wrote disconsolately, a week after William
Savery's visit to Norwich. She was tormented by doubts and
unable to stop asking questions.

Was enthusiasm acceptable? Or was it better to be a sceptic? Was it wrong to be worldly? Could a person be worldly and
also virtuous? Could they be virtuous without being religious?

She talked about it to her sisters until they begged her to
stop, for they were no longer quite so amused. "And don't ever
think of becoming a Plain Quaker," they warned.

She talked about it to her cousin Hudson, and was
rewarded with some long, appraising stares that made her
blush.

She talked about it to John Gurney, until he lost his temper,
and then demanded, for the sake of harmony in the family,
that she curb her wretched enthusiasm.

But, Betsy was unable to curb it. The parched earth that
had been watered by William Savery was growing increasingly
desperate for a great shower of rain.

Finally, risking John Gurney's anger, but counting on his indulgence, she begged to visit London. It was important to her, she pleaded, to truly understand what she would be giving up if she were to become a religious person like Uncle Joseph. In the capital, she said, the great city where the world lay exposed in all its hedonistic extravagance, she would soon see if the world, or religion, called to her most strongly. In London, though she avoided mentioning it to her father, she would also be almost certain to see William Savery.

It is perhaps worth emphasising that although Betsy was evidently powerfully infatuated with the man who had arrived in her life only months after she had confessed her need for a pilot, and for someone to lean on, and who perhaps significantly was exactly the same age as John Gurney, something within her that was both rational and steadying nevertheless urged caution. "I may be led away," she warned herself. "Beware! My feelings are far more risen at the thought of seeing him than all the play-houses and gaieties in the world." At 17, however, caution frequently exists alongside the most extraordinary optimism, and when just as she had suspected, and after only the briefest resistance, John Gurney acquiesced to her request, she was ecstatic.

"My mind is in a whirl," she wrote on 15 February, underlining her words more forcefully than usual, "I shall go to London. *Many, many* are the sensations I feel about it."

CHAPTER FOUR

A minister of Christ

*T*HE LAST LIGHT OF THE SHORT February afternoon drained swiftly away, and as darkness settled on London, Betsy grew increasingly fearful. In the street outside, beneath the window of the room where she sat alone, a succession of footsteps passed by. Some were accompanied by a brief blaze of light, as a link-boy led someone home, but others, especially those attended by muffled voices, seemed threatening. Straining to hear them, when she thought that they lingered, she was uncomfortably conscious of the thudding of her heart. She also heard, echoing in streets and alleys nearby, aggressive shouts and drunken laughter, and once or twice she heard a woman shriek.

"I do love being so independent," she had written boldly, just after John Gurney left her, with one female attendant from Earlham, in the grand Brick Lane house of her Hanbury relatives. How unwise that was, she commented later in life, to allow a young impressionable girl to spend so much time alone in London with only a servant for her constant company! Yet in 1798, when she was just 17, it had all seemed so different. Even with the family away, she had assured her nervous father, as he hesitated at the door, she felt perfectly safe within London's Quaker community of Spitalfields.

Later, surrounded by the dark, and the night-time music of a great city, her confidence drained away. Peering nervously into the shadowy corners of the unfamiliar room, the looming shapes made her think of thieves and kidnappers, and the highwaymen who haunted the long lonely road from Norwich.

Crossing Newmarket Heath the previous night, the apprehensive driver of the London Mail had whipped up his horses to a gallop. With the coach swaying, the horn wailing and lantern beams careering wildly over twisted trees and stunted hillocks, Betsy had collapsed in a fit of sickness and fear. She was revived at a wayside inn with watered brandy and laudanum, and though she slept the rest of the journey, on reaching London her nervous father sent for a physician. Though her journal at this point is unclear, she implies that the doctor had been in some way involved with the treatment she received at the end of her engagement to James Lloyd. "I *cannot* say *how* odd I felt at meeting him," Betsy said, "it renewed all my old feelings when I was in town last time." Perhaps it was in recalling those feelings, together with her fear of intruders, that an old sorrow stirred. "I am not such a tempting morsel as for anybody to wish to run away with me," she said. Presently, she moved closer to the comfort of the fire. "I won't call anyone yet," she said, "but try to overcome my weakness."

In the daylight of Sunday morning, London was a different city, and after jumping out of bed and rushing her breakfast, Betsy set off dutifully for Gracechurch Street Meeting. Her way led her through a tangle of narrow streets topped by a jumble of rooftops and spires, where sometimes the turning of a corner produced an unexpected view. Often, it was the dully gleaming river, or far-off green fields, but occasionally it was Christopher Wren's cathedral, and the sunlight and cloud shadows that played on the dome that towered reassuringly into the sky.

Whenever she paused to stare, Betsy also became conscious of the morning air. It reeked powerfully of London: smoky and sooty from the city's industry and thousands of fires; putrid from the refuse fouling the Thames; and flavoured with the aromas of coffee houses and chop-houses and the bales of tea and spices that packed innumerable gigantic warehouses.

She also gazed wide-eyed at the passing throng. There were gentle-folk heading to church, costermongers heading to market, and water-carriers, sandmen and milkmaids all going about their trades, while garbed in tawdry finery, a few early-morning prostitutes worked the street corners. On the road-ways, a ceaseless procession of carriages and carts rumbled and screeched, while on the walkways, divided from the road by painted posts, burly sedan-chairmen buffeted aside anyone who dared impede their progress.

Already home to a million people,[1] each year London attracted thousands more. They came seeking fortunes in busi-ness, advancement in the professions, humble ordinary jobs of work, or shelter within anonymous streets. As they did so, the city continued the remorseless expansion away from its ancient square mile that had begun over a hundred years ear-lier.

To the west, beyond St Paul's, lay the elegant terraces of the West End, whose enormously wealthy community was served by sumptuous shops, skilled craftsmen and vast armies of ser-vants. Eastwards, on low-lying land past the Tower, stretched a region of dismal slums, housing a rapidly swelling popula-tion who performed poorly paid jobs in noxious industries. To the north, reaching out towards Islington, Camden and Pentonville, jumbles of poorly constructed terraces and cot-tages clustered around factories and workshops, untidy con-glomerations of builders' yards, breweries, warehouses, stables and taverns.

In such a metropolis, there were many diversions.

At the apex of London's social life, as the eighteenth century drew to a close, was the dazzling high society that revolved around the wayward and charming Prince of Wales.[2] Rife with gossip and sexual intrigue, its exquisite manners masked loose morals, while its ornate and extravagant display cloaked a con-tent that was shallow. Its exclusive membership, including many of the wealthiest and most influential individuals in the land, devoted hours to dress and display and then followed them with nights of partying in grand houses, carousing at exclusive drinking clubs, or gambling at Boodles or Whites, the gaming clubs in St James's where casually staked fortunes were won or lost in an evening.

Less exalted Londoners also frequently drank to excess, but

in more mundane drinking clubs and taverns, while their gambling took place at cockfights, around pits where bears and bulls were baited with dogs, or at boxing matches between men and between women.

For rich and poor alike, there were also thousands of prostitutes, many of them children. The most successful advertised in directories, while others worked theatres, taverns and chophouses, or walked the parks and streets.

For visitors like Betsy who sought more innocent pleasures, there were theatres and exhibition rooms by the score, the pleasure gardens of Vauxhall and Ranelagh, and a multitude of dancing rooms, supper rooms, waxworks, puppet shows and freak shows, as well as carriage rides in Hyde Park and boat trips on the Thames.

Anxious to savour them all, on the Monday after her arrival, when she moved from Brick Lane to her Barclay relatives at Clapham, Betsy threw herself into London life. But, on her very first night, to her great consternation, she felt she saw all the world's snares displayed together in the spectacle of Drury Lane Theatre. Hardly knowing where to look next, she had stared in amazement at the rapidly changing scenes on the candle-lit stage, the dalliances of the foppish men-about-town in the pit, the wide eyes of the awestruck citizens in the first gallery, the vulgarity of the mobs of footmen in the second, who yelled at the actors and threw orange peel, and the unashamed buying and selling taking place in the boxes between prostitutes and their clients. "To be sure the house is grand and dazzling," she said, "but I had no other feeling whilst there than that of wishing it over." She also wondered what William Savery would think of her going to a play. "I fear I should not like his knowing," she said.

On Tuesday, after an evening at Covent Garden, she remained disillusioned with the theatre. On Wednesday, during a morning of social calls, she felt awkward and out of place, while in the evening, at a dance, she was lonely. Despite her concerns over worldly pleasures, she had secretly hoped to sparkle a little, and for someone, at least, to find her attractive. Instead, she was ignored by the London Quakers, whose for-

mal manners and sophisticated conversation far exceeded anything she had experienced before. "I am not a quarter of the
consequence I am at Earlham, or in gay circles at Norwich,"
she lamented, "how I longed for an agreeable heart to be with."

By Thursday, she was completely dispirited. In the evening
she saw Hamlet and Bluebeard,[3] and while she admitted that
the acting, the music and the scenery were all equally spectacular, she still thought them shallow and empty. Her elaborately
powdered hairstyle also made her feel like a monkey. "London
is not the place for *heart felt* pleasures," she said, "so I must not
expect to find them."

She did, however, expect to find William Savery, and by
Friday, the urge to see him was so powerful that she set out
deliberately to find him. "Walked about the streets of London
and hated everything until I happened to see the Rock of
William Savery," she said innocently.

In the artificial and transient world she had entered, the
man whose words had brought about her conversion represented certainty. Perhaps it was also a certainty which Betsy
found reassuring when compared to John Gurney, whose faith
was ambiguous and who could so easily be coaxed into indul-
gences. Betsy also knew Savery to be an insightful and compassionate man, with an agreeable heart, and as she sought for
solid ground in the strange world of London, and in the shifting
seas of her new-found faith, relentlessly she began to seek out
her rock. As she did so, she had the extraordinary impression
that he answered her questions before they were fully formed,
and sympathised with feelings she still struggled to name.

"The Deist, and those who did not feel devotion," he said, at
Westminster Meeting House early in March, "looked at nature,
admired the thunder, the lightening and earthquakes as
curiosities. But they looked not up through them to nature's
God."[4] As she listened, Betsy felt things falling into place. She
suddenly saw where Deism was limited, and as William Savery
gave expression to the spiritual dimension she had always
sensed in the world around her, she was ready to cry, not only
with relief, but with something approaching ecstasy.

Eagerly she pressed her Barclay cousins to share the revelations and the rapture, but she received instead a lecture on enthusiasm and about William Savery in particular, together with the realisation that communications were passing to Clapham from Earlham. It annoyed her intensely. "I think I am very enthusiastic about him," she agreed. But she was also unrepentant. "If I can," she said stubbornly of her efforts to meet him, "I will. Through thick and thin!"

Sometimes thick and thin meant secrecy, slipping from the house when she thought no one watched, to snatch a few precious minutes at a meeting house, before arriving home breathless but secretly triumphant. Sometimes it meant inviting herself to the house where William stayed with his English Savery relatives,[5] and on one occasion, after arriving so early that the family were all still in bed, she waited alone in the parlour while a bemused housemaid lit the fire. "Then came my friend," she said, "it was delightful to see him. I always feel quite a palpitation at my heart at the sound of his voice. He seemed at first rather low but when he and I were left alone, he said it did *him good* to have me come. He is wonderful."

Quite forgetting the caution she had warned herself against, so desperate was she to see him, that one Sunday in mid-March, she publicly defied her Uncle Barclay. It followed a furious argument, where her exasperated relative refused her permission to seek out William Savery at Ratcliff Meeting after he failed to appear at Gracechurch Street. Finally, leaving behind her a group of open-mouthed cousins, and an uncle threatening to send her back to Earlham on the next available coach, Betsy stubbornly set off alone for the mean streets east of the City. Later, uncomfortably aware of possible family retribution, but having heard William once more, "to my inexpressible joy", she persuaded a poor Quaker family to give her a bed in their cramped grubby nursery where she talked until three in the morning with the daughters of the house. "My most odd adventure," she called it later.

Eventually family conflict and the force of her feelings brought on stomach cramps and insomnia, and when she heard that William Savery was soon leaving London, the thought of losing her rock confined her to bed. "A most bad night," she wrote, "I am so *very* low. I cannot bear the thought of William Savery's going."

In her mood of desolation and uncertainty, it was a relief to leave Clapham behind and to spend a day with Amelia Alderson, where she could talk openly of William Savery, and also hear the latest news of Amelia's forthcoming wedding.

It had not been easy, even for an unconventional woman like Amelia, to accept an offer from John Opie,[6] for although he was a successful painter whose fame had brought him a fortune, his Cornish accent, peasant ancestry and divorced first wife were obstacles not lightly dismissed. The discovery that the new Mrs Opie would be at the heart of a brilliant circle of artists, writers and musicians, however, had finally laid Amelia's doubts to rest, and now, as the wedding approached, she introduced that dazzling world to her innocent young friend from Norwich.

Sadly Mrs Siddons, the most famous actress of the age, was not at home when they called, but in Amelia's company, it was difficult to remain downhearted for long. With her, even dressing up almost became fun.

"I was painted a little," Betsy said, before a night at the opera, "I had my hair dressed, and did look quite pretty, for me." Later, in the company of Amelia and John, and their clever, witty friends, the theatre also took on a different hue, and for one night, even William Savery dissolved in a dazzle of light and colour. "I own, I do love grand company," Betsy admitted, "the Prince of Wales was there; and I must say, I felt more pleasure in looking at him, than in seeing the rest of the company, or hearing the music. I did nothing but admire his Royal Highness, but I had a very pleasant evening indeed."

She had a pleasant time too with her wealthy Hoare relatives in the fashionable village of Hampstead, where she spent the next ten days. It was a break from the tensions of London, and in their house by Hampstead Heath, that was more informal than the homes of London Quakers, the cheerful gatherings of young people reminded her of the Earlham she was beginning to miss. However, she also missed William Savery, and, curiously, the high life of London, which over the previous weeks had become less strange to her. She found it all very disconcerting.

Back once more at Clapham she wrote to William, telling him she felt drawn to the Plain Quaker path. Then she begged Uncle Barclay for a visit to the opera. "I was most merry," she said afterwards, "I just saw the Prince of Wales."

She had no idea what to tell John Gurney about whether religion or the world called her more strongly. And when he arrived at the beginning of April to fetch her home, she was so glad to see him that she felt like a child. "This morning my dearest dad came to London," she said, "and we larked about all the morning."

Earlham in April was alive to the spring. Every tree in the park was a haze of tender green, and the lawns were lush with new grass. Shafts of clear sunshine warmed the rooms of the old house.

"Betsy is come back," Richenda wrote, "... she has seen a good deal of William Savery, whose soul seems formed and made for true religion and perfect faith. From the workings of her own mind and her acquaintance with him, Betsy seems to be changed from a complete sceptic to a person who has entire faith in a Supreme Being and a future state, and I should suppose she feels all the delight which such a belief must bring with it."

For Betsy, however, it was not quite so simple. Struggling towards faith, she had also encountered sin, and with horrifying clarity she had seen the obvious explanation for the weaknesses, the failures and the transgressions that she listed so unflinchingly in her journals. Perhaps she also caught glimpses of those disturbing forces which she so ruthlessly attempted to bury in the recesses of her mind, but which inevitably, and quite without warning, sometimes rose to the surface to embarrass and confuse her.

Fuelled by insecurity, she also worried endlessly about salvation, and about the destruction that waited for sinners in the ocean of darkness and death. How very appropriate Fox's metaphor must have seemed! Once back at Earlham, she also became painfully aware of just how rapidly the extraordinary assurance she felt in William Savery's company faded when she was alone, when her sceptical past returned to haunt her. Before very long she was desperate for guidance.

On 20 April a letter arrived from William Savery, a reply to one she had sent him from Clapham.

"My attachment has not been more cordial or agreeable to any young Friend in England," he wrote, "and my heart leaped with joy to find thou art willing to acknowledge a state of hunger and thirst after righteousness, which if thou cherish and dwell in, thou never need to doubt, my dear friend, will eventually be crowned with the enjoyment of the heavenly promise, 'thou shalt be filled'."

It was a long and compassionate letter (Appendix 1) and its emphasis on the satisfactions achieved by a dutiful Christian life, and of hard, relentless struggle and constant vigilance as the sure way to salvation and the promise of eternal reward, reminded Betsy of her mother's belief that blessings waited for those who did God's will. That, and the confidence that William Savery so obviously had in her, prompted her to renew her quest for Virtue. "I want to set myself in good order," she wrote early in May, "for much time is lost and many evils committed by not having some regular plan of conduct." Eagerly, she mapped it out. "Never lose any time," she began, "never err the least in truth, … never say an ill thing of a person, … never be irritable or unkind, … never indulge myself in luxuries that are not necessary … "

But, such ideals were hard to maintain in a household where company and indulgence were a way of life. "I drank rather too much Madeira and got into high spirits," she confessed, less than a week after formulating her plan. Dismayed, she resolved to do better.

She was more successful, she felt, when she directed herself outwards. To the surprise of Friends she had previously mocked, she became regular in her attendance at Goat Lane, and though her mind wandered erratically through the long silences, she became determined to persevere. And, though it had been hard at first to enter a cottage where the stench of sickness was overpowering, she was also determined to persevere with poor Bob. She had known him since childhood, when he rode beside her to steady her pony, and now that it was obvious to the whole estate that the young servant was dying, Betsy was eager to comfort him. With the certainty of her newly acquired faith to support her, she assured Bob that she was so convinced of the blessings of immortality, that it was impossible for her to pity him. It was a curious speech to make to a dying man, she admitted later, but she fully intended to be with him at the end.

When John Gurney heard about it, however, he was angry and afraid. Blaming religious enthusiasm, when Betsy developed a feverish cough he demanded that the visits be stopped. Betsy, however, had no intention of abandoning Bob, and just as she had earlier defied Uncle Barclay, to her surprise, she now discovered that she was equally prepared to defy her father. Through thick and thin, Betsy was determined to lead the dutiful Christian life encouraged by William Savery.

It was at this time too, that she experienced a dramatic change in the pattern of her dreams. For now when the sea came to wash her away, she said, she was saved by clinging to a large rock. Whether the rock stood for William Savery, for God, or for faith, or for a confusing mixture of all three, is not clear. Later, however, in notes added to her first surviving journals, she elaborated and revealed that something else was at work. She was riding a horse, she said, along a rocky promontory 300 yards high but only one foot wide. "Dangerous as it appeared," she went on, "I thought while I continued without fear I was safe, though going at full gallop, and turning my horse round, the waves were mountainous high and came over my head but did not touch me. One time I thought I feared I doubted my power and fell, but though I fell, I said I have power of my own to rise."

Even allowing for changes in emphasis taking place over the years between the dream itself and the written account, it does appear to encapsulate the forces that drove her, her fear of death, her powerful sexuality and an urge for self-expression. It also very evidently marked a transition between her old life and the new, and suggests that in some way she had reassured herself that henceforward, rather than being completely at the mercy of chaotic forces, she would endeavour to overcome them and take control of her life.

As well as maintaining her visits to Bob, Betsy also increased her charitable visits to the local poor, and after discovering that it cost John Gurney £40 a year to keep her, and that her weekly washing bill would maintain a poor family, she began using some of her allowance to help her poor neighbours. For one woman there was a shift, for another, nine shillings' worth of cloth for a bed. Then, late in May, after giving half-a-crown to help send a poor boy to school, an idea began taking shape in her mind.

Days later, she paid a visit to Mrs Coslington, a poor woman in the nearby village of Colney, and offered to teach her son Billy. "I have some thoughts of by degrees increasing my plan for Sunday evening," she said, "and of having several poor children, at least, to read in the Testament and religious books for an hour. I have begun with Billy, but I hope to continue and increase one by one."

She also read the Bible aloud to Mrs Coslington, to Nurse Norman, Joseph John's old wet-nurse, and to their various families. She also encouraged those among them who could read to study the scriptures for themselves, just as she now did herself, and had done every morning since returning from London. To her own reading she was also gradually adding other books, especially the Apology written by her great-great-grandfather Barclay,[7] and although her lack of education made it hard, she laboured with a dictionary over each unknown word, and repeated the sentences until they made sense.

"Really the parson read so badly it quite vexed me!" Betsy said after Bob's funeral. The clergyman's carelessness, which had seemed like an insult to Bob, had added to her anguish. For, at the last, she had been unable to face his death, and later, the sight of the corpse shook her so badly that with all thoughts of the blessings of immortality driven violently from her mind, she had collapsed, fearful and weeping. At night, the memory of Bob's dead face haunted her imagination.

Nevertheless she was anxious to overcome her fear. "The alteration is so great," she reasoned, "I am sure there must be a soul to enlighten the body. ... Silly girl, to let the sight of a dead body make me so miserable, but I will not be miserable, but look up to the only true support."

As she struggled to do so, she also wondered if the faintness and palpitations that followed Bob's death were another aspect of the nervous disorder that had plagued her for so many years. What was it, she asked herself, that made her head ache, her limbs tremble, and her spirits to be "now low, now high"? Why was she sleepless so often? Why did she sometimes collapse unconscious to the ground? "I feel such a fear of falling down, and frightening other people," she said of what she called her "faintings", "but I seldom fear them when I am alone." Was it some disease of the head or brain, she asked, that caused such symptoms? And would more activity improve her health?

Apart from a brief comment made by her doctor much later in life, there is no record of what the physicians retained by the Gurneys made of Betsy's physical and mental state, except that it was treated with the remedies to hand, alcohol and opium. No doubt later in the nineteenth century she would have been labelled an hysteric and treated accordingly. Freud and his twentieth-century followers would surely have found her fascinating had they read her journals. Today, in the twenty-first century, she would almost certainly be diagnosed as suffering from a depressive illness, and as well as receiving drug treatments would probably be in therapy. Given her own life-long fascination with her malady she might well have eventually outstripped the therapists and herself become an analyst.

In the summer of 1798, however, she recalled that William Savery in his letter suggested that afflictions were often mercies in disguise, working eventually for the good of those who loved God, so she resolved to accept her infirmity in that light, and to cultivate patience. But perhaps it was Reason that was behind her decision to walk more often in the fresh air.

Watching Betsy struggle with her new Christian life, her sisters grew increasingly alarmed. "We all feel about it alike," said Richenda, "and are truly sorry that one of us seven should separate herself in principles, actions and appearance from the rest." They themselves had no intention of changing, and the sight of Betsy going eagerly to Meeting and dressing each day with more simplicity distressed them almost more than they could bear.

So too did Betsy's inconsistency, as one day she joined their dances and duets, while on another, she rejected them as worldly. They found it painfully reminiscent of her contrary childhood. Betsy herself was miserably aware of the problems she caused. "This evening I have got myself rather into a scrape," she wrote in June. "I have been helping them to beg my father for us to go to the Guild-dinner, and I don't know whether it is quite what I approve of."

Often she felt that she walked in a labyrinth, and as she thought of William Savery, her rock, she imagined herself, safely guided, ministering at his side. "If he came to Norwich," she wrote wishfully, after a rumour suggested he might, "I think I may go with him till he leaves England."

John Gurney also longed to be away from Norfolk. The events of the past few years had wearied him: first Rachel's love affair, and then Betsy's religious enthusiasm. The time had come, he decided, for a family holiday.

Betsy, however, was in no mood to leave Norwich, where there were her poor to be visited, and more boys already joining Billy at school. When her father forbade her journal book, claiming she was far too obsessive about it, she became even more frustrated. Her feelings were relieved only when she learned from a young house-guest that William Savery still lodged in London. "J. Fry has been telling me he saw W. Savery not a week ago," she recorded, "my heart leapt at the remembrance of him and dear London."

She did see William Savery in London, at the very beginning of the Gurney holiday, but it was to say goodbye. For the inner voice that had brought him to Europe was finally send-

ing William home, and at almost every Meeting he was surrounded by Friends eager to wish him well. On the few occasions she was alone with him, there was more to say than the
moments could hold. She could hardly bear the finality.
"William Savery is, I think, only five miles off *me this night*,
perhaps we never again shall be so near each other," she confided to the secret notebook that replaced the forbidden journal. "But I *firmly believe we shall*," she added hopefully.

She gave him a pocket book as a keepsake and longed to
know how he liked it. But on the following day she was on her
way to Farnham with the other Gurneys, and William Savery
was on his way to the wife waiting patiently for him in
Philadelphia.

Farnham, Winchester, Ringwood in the New Forest,
Weymouth; the Gurneys and their retinue of servants visited
them all as they made their way across southern England,
staying sometimes at inns, sometimes at Quaker houses. And
everywhere they went, they saw the sights. Tourism was the
latest fashion, part of an exciting new spirit of romanticism in
the air, where emotional responses to the picturesque and a
passion for untrammeled nature were replacing the eighteenth
century's quest for detachment and harmony.

For Betsy, however, long walks to quaint villages and ruined
castles were boring and frustrating. Her heart was on the
Atlantic with William Savery, her thoughts were in Norfolk
with her little boys, and in contrast the world around her
appeared drab and lacking in sensation. Her nights were also
invariably restless, and despite having a tooth out at Clifton,
she suffered continually from toothache. Some of the excursions also frightened her. "If the least accident were to happen," she said of a boat trip at Weymouth, "I should be
drowned."

She also drowned in dilemmas, as the growing gulf between
herself and her family became ever more stark. At Weymouth
she prevaricated over an invitation to a ball, aware that if she
accepted, she courted temptation among the snares of the
world, while if she refused, not only would her sisters and her
brother John take it as a personal slight, but John Gurney

would be distressed by the inevitable quarrel. "If I had been Plain I should not have been tempted," she observed after a dance at Dawlish.

There was more tension at Plymouth, when the memory of William Savery speaking out against war at the Gildencroft kept her from touring a man-of-war, fully rigged and ready to sail against the French foe, and the centre of an admiring and patriotic crowd. Her reluctance to support war also kept her from a military review, where she knew there would be cheering crowds, waving flags, marching sailors and triumphant music.

Later, when she glimpsed the streets that clustered around the dockyard, she was shocked. The houses were mean, the women and children were ragged and dirty, and away from the fine ships and martial sounds, the sailors seemed somehow shrunken – sallow ill-fed ordinary men, rather than the heroes who had earlier charmed the crowds. She was dismayed too by the throngs of prostitutes who lined the streets and filled every tavern. "I longed to do them good," she wrote, "to try one day to help make them sensible of the evil that they are in."

Betsy also wished she could make her family sensible of the joys of Quaker meetings, for their reluctance to share her passion for them was upsetting. "How little they appeared to consider my pleasure," she lamented, after Kitty and Rachel flatly refused to enter another Meeting House. "If only they had said they were sorry I was disappointed, I should not have minded, but they all appeared totally to forget my wish."

But despite her sisters' aversion to Meeting, Betsy spent as much time with Quakers as she could. At Abergavenny, early in August, listening to Plain Friends speak in their lilting Welsh voices, she began to think seriously about how to address people. William Savery always said "thee" and "thou", and so did Uncle Joseph, but the Earlham Gurneys used the form only when away from their worldly friends. Wasn't that hypocritical? she asked. Wasn't Plain speech a defence against the world and its snares? "Our virtue is hard to maintain without some fortress to support it," she decided.

At Aberystwth, other issues joined her concerns. Dancing, in particular, worried her, and after a merry evening at the local assembly rooms she felt she could no longer prevaricate. "Is dancing wrong?" she asked herself sternly. In a family context, she decided eventually, it could be innocent enough, but when she recalled some of her more abandoned public moments, flirting among a sensuous throng of bodies and provocatively glancing eyes, she was forced to admit it hardly seemed virtuous.

At Carnarvon, singing and music in general also began to worry her. She recalled how often she had been "off her centre", as she called it, whenever she had surrendered her rational self to words and rhythms that aroused a mass of passions and summoned her to follow in their wake. Looking back, she felt ashamed of how often she had allowed her emotions to take control.

The more she pondered on music, dancing and plain speech, the more it began to seem to Betsy that the Plain Quaker path was being offered to her by God as the fortress she needed to defend her through life. She was certain that the thoughts that were now crowding her mind, and the inner promptings that seemed to be driving her towards good actions, could not possibly originate with her own sinful self. With a pleasant shock of surprise, she also realised that she no longer felt silly when striving to do what she believed to be right. "I have such happiness when I overcome my worldly self," she said, "and when I give way to it, I feel uneasy." All these manifestations, she concluded, were proof that a divine agency was at work.

Nevertheless she was troubled. Despite the growing conviction that the Quaker path was meant for her, her old scepticism all too often crept into her mind and caused her to doubt. By the time the Gurneys crossed the English border, a nagging fear that faith could never be combined with Reason was keeping her awake through nights crowded with questions. Anxiously, she hoped there might be answers waiting for her at Coalbrookdale.

Ninety years earlier, in 1707, Abraham Darby I, a Quaker brass manufacturer from Bristol, had also arrived in the valley on the East Shropshire coalfield, and after reopening a derelict blast furnace, he had set himself up as an iron founder. When he devised a new method of smelting iron, that created much higher temperatures in the furnaces, it was the beginning of the revolution that was rapidly transforming Britain into the world's first industrial power.

Throughout the years that followed Abraham's success, continual innovation and growth had made Coalbrookdale a centre of industrial activity; its iron utensils supplied Britain's markets; its iron parts for steam engines kept British furnaces in blast and British mines free of water; its iron rims strengthened wheels that ran on iron rails; and its iron screw presses fuelled Britain's new hardware trades. In 1779, Abraham's grandson, Abraham Darby III, built across the River Severn, the world's first iron bridge, that was also one of its greatest industrial wonders.

On the hills overlooking the Dale, the Darbys planted gardens for their workers and built fine houses for themselves. At two of the most gracious, Sunniside and the White House, four Quaker women lived in harmony and directed the Coalbrook Dale Company. Three of them – Mary Rathbone, Deborah Darby and Rebecca Darby – were widows, while Sarah Darby, a grand-daughter of Abraham I, had never married. Deborah also followed the tradition of her mother-in-law, Abiah Darby, as a Quaker minister, and in the early 1790s she had travelled in America, visiting New York and Philadelphia, crossing the wild Allegheny Mountains, and supporting American Friends in their opposition to slavery.

Though not entirely on an equal footing with men, and often focussing on the relief of the poor and domestic issues, female Friends were free to enter the Quaker ministry. In this they were virtually unique among Christian denominations, most of whom believed that by apparently only choosing men as his disciples, Jesus had therefore prohibited women from undertaking public ministry in his church. The words of St Paul in his first letter to the Corinthians,[8] forbidding women to speak in churches, were also regarded by most Christians as implying a ban on the public ministry of women. That

Deborah Darby was not only a minister, however, but had also followed a concern to cross the Atlantic, marked her out as unique even within an organisation that was exceptionally tolerant towards an active religious role for women.

Also at Coalbrookdale was Catherine Gurney's cousin, Priscilla Hannah Gurney, who since 1791 had lived at Dale House with Quaker philanthropist Richard Reynolds and his wife Rebecca, who both regarded her as a daughter.

But while Coalbrookdale was familiar to Priscilla, to Betsy it was almost indescribably strange, and in her cousin's pretty sitting room, surrounded by elegant furniture and vases full of scented flowers, she listened in awe to the roar of the bellows, and stared in wonder at the glare of furnaces reflecting red in the pools and waterways that wound through the dale. She found the Darby women equally fascinating: silent and still at Meeting, yet later, as if it were the most natural thing in the world, discussing furnaces and forges, coal mines and steam engines, and the iron goods that went in ships down the Severn to Bristol and then into the wide world beyond.

It was late summer in Coalbrookdale, the days were warm and the nights balmy, and on Monday 3 September Betsy woke late from a restful night and made her way downstairs where Deborah Darby had already arrived for breakfast. She was greatly in awe of the older woman, so well-travelled and so competent, and who had told Betsy with a smile how highly William Savery had spoken of her during a recent visit to the Dale. As the meal progressed, Betsy found her glance constantly resting on Deborah's face. Finally, after the servants carried the empty dishes away, the company at table fell silent and in the long, following pause, Betsy became conscious of the wild beating of her heart.

Then, in the stillness, Deborah spoke.

"God will visit us all," she said, "God who is father to the fatherless and mother to the motherless." Turning to Betsy, she continued. "You are *sick of the world*," she said, "so you look higher, and you who are to be dedicated to God, will have peace in this world and glory everlasting in the world to come."[9]

Could anything more be wished for? Betsy asked herself

later. Following Deborah's words, in the privacy of Sunniside's garden she had wept for joy, conscious of an inner encouragement like nothing she had experienced before. It made her feel that all things were possible.

That night, in Priscilla's sitting room, she poured out all her frustrations: the struggles for virtue that seemed to achieve so little, and the family opposition to her religious quest. It was reassuring to discover that Priscilla understood, and that similar struggles had brought her to Coalbrookdale. Eventually, after studying her cousin's serene face, Betsy decided that the placid radiance she saw there was the reward for struggles overcome. "A Plain Friend I believe I *must* be," she wrote, before finally laying down her pen for the night.

She became more certain of it on the following evening, when she joined the Darby women, the Reynolds's and Cousin Priscilla in Deborah's parlour, and marvelled at how Plain principles, even among the enormously wealthy Coalbrookdale community, seemed to produce a spirit of unity and peace. She felt extraordinarily happy, and as the evening grew late, and the candlelight mellowed, she became gradually conscious of an overpowering sense of presence. "My heart began to feel as silenced before God," she said, "and without looking at the others, I felt myself under the shadow of his wing."

As the silence lengthened and grew deeper, once again, Deborah Darby spoke.

"A light to the blind, speech to the dumb and feet to the lame," she said, and as silence resumed, the prophecy hung shimmering in the air.

Betsy and Priscilla walked home to Dale House by starlight. In the valley beneath them, the furnaces roared and lit up the night with radiant bursts of fire, while on the cool hillside, among the trees, a night breeze brushed Betsy's face. With Deborah's words echoing in her mind, she lifted her eyes and looked through Nature up to Nature's God. "Can it be," she asked the starry heavens, "she seems to express as if she thought I was to be a minister *of Christ*. Can I ever be one? If *I am obedient* I believe I shall."

CHAPTER FIVE

Joseph Fry

"*T*HERE IS A MOUNTAIN for me to climb over," Betsy wrote in her book, on leaving Coalbrookdale. "There is a sacrifice for me to make, before I am favoured with faith, virtue and assurance of immortality." She almost relished the struggle and was anxious to begin.

Her first step was to embrace the Plain speech and say "thee" instead of "you". At first it made her feel awkward with her family, the servants at Earlham, and with friends in Norwich, but when she realised how much it made her think before speaking, she appreciated its value. "It will be a guard upon my tongue," she said.

She also replaced pagan names for the days and months with numbers, and as she wrote 1st day and 9th month in her journal, and on the letters she sent, she felt that it set another positive seal on her new life.

With the encouragement of Deborah Darby's prophecy, Betsy also redoubled her efforts for the poor. Visits to cramped cottages on the Earlham estate and the meaner streets of Norwich grew more frequent, while she often spent long Earlham afternoons cutting out linen cloth and stitching simple shirts and pinafores for ragged children.

She also befriended a mad woman. At first, she found it hard coping with the bizarre thought patterns and erratic conversations, but eventually she learned to observe quietly, to sympathise appropriately, and to act in ways that produced order and calm. Late at night, when she said her prayers, she always asked God to bless her sad friend.

When reports of sudden misfortune reached her, Betsy sometimes personally delivered baskets of provisions similar to those Catherine Gurney once took to one-armed Betty and Greengrass. Years later, a widow in Norwich told the story of the day, long before, when she was a young woman of limited means and had just given birth to her first child while her husband was away with the army. After a jangling at the doorbell, she said, her servant had hurried up the stairs with a neatly packed basket in her hand. It had been left by a beautiful lady, riding a fine horse and wearing a scarlet riding habit.[1]

Yet, somehow it all failed to satisfy Betsy. Maybe at this point it is worth considering the low self-image she describes in her brief sketch, that would certainly contribute to her sense that nothing she did was quite good enough, and which constantly drove her to achieve more. For while she had so much to be thankful for, she confessed, she felt she did little in return. "May I one day be capable of virtue," she said, "may I really be able to lessen the sorrows of the afflicted."

She was also anxious to improve the standards of her school where, by November 1798, 20 other poor boys sat alongside Billy. *"Dear little boys,"* she wrote, "I do really love them and feel deeply interested in their welfare." But, before they could advance beyond simple letters, she knew that improvements were needed in her own spelling and grammar, which still caused such family amusement. When she looked back through her journals, she was certain she saw mistakes. "Whent"? "Soshal beings"? "My schollers"? She glanced at her holiday notebook. "Is dansing rong I have just been dansing." None of it seemed quite right, and she resolved to work even harder with the dictionary.

She was also determined to set an example to the boys in other ways, and when one of them handed her a lizard one day, and the others waited breathlessly for her reaction, she steeled herself not to let her repulsion show. To her delight, however, as she took it in her hand, she discovered that the pattern of its scales was intriguing, and that its belly had the texture of silk. After calling her boys one by one to observe and to touch for themselves, she saw them eyeing her with a new respect. How curious it was, she reflected later, that when teaching her own younger sisters she had so often become flustered, whereas with these rough boys from the estate she began to feel herself in control.

By forcing herself to take up the lizard, Betsy reflected, she had also overcome groundless fears, and it encouraged her to face others that lurked within her mind. When John Gurney heard about her activities, however, that she spent long night hours alone in the empty upper chambers of Earlham beneath the roof, with not even a candle to relieve the blackness, he began fearing once again for her health. The memory of her earlier nervous collapse was still raw in his mind, and again blaming religious enthusiasm, he demanded that she stop. But, just as she had when he insisted she abandon poor Bob, Betsy stubbornly refused.

Though she trembled as the wind howled in the chimneys and moaned along empty corridors, and though she flinched at the apparitions conjured by slanting moonbeams from sheets draping long-discarded treasures, Betsy was determined to persist. Her rather confused account in her journal, however, indicates that several anxieties lay behind her nocturnal activities. "There is a strange propensity in the human mind to fear in the dark," she said, "there is a fear of something supernatural. I tried to overcome that by considering that as far as I believed in ghosts, so far I must believe in a state after death and it must confirm my belief in the Spirit of God, therefore if I try to act right, I have no need to fear the directions of Infinite Wisdom." Though Betsy was evidently attempting to overcome her fear of the dark and of ghosts – months earlier she began sleeping without a rushlight – she also implies that her new faith was not as solid as she would wish. For someone who remained terrified of death, and who was also struggling hard to achieve the "assurance of immortality", any doubts were seriously undermining. "What has been believed for all ages, and among all nations," she said in desperation weeks later, "*must* have some deep foundation in the mind of man."

Although her main purpose had been to investigate life

beyond death, she admitted that she was also attempting to overcome her fear of human intruders. In her journal she recounts how after waking one night in fear of them, she got up to bolt her bedroom door, then later unbolted it, and then, later still, bolted it again. Making her way along Earlham's dark passages as she set out to confront ghosts, she had also often wondered just what she would do if she encountered a thief. "God can equally protect us from man as from spirits," she told herself reassuringly.

Sometimes, however, she wished that God would more strenuously protect her from her family's frustrations. For as she struggled to follow a religious path, their opposition to her increased. "I have been told of my enthusiasm and all the rest of it till *I am tired of the sound*," she said. "I wish for their opinion to have much weight with me, but I wish to judge for myself."

It was not only Betsy's faith that distressed the Gurneys. It was also her continuing inconsistency, especially, when despite her Plain speech, her passion for Meeting, and weeks spent refusing to make up the numbers for the complex dances her sisters loved, she would sometimes burst into a crowded room and throw herself without warning into the gaiety.

"Quite the old Betsy came once more upon the stage," she wrote remorsefully in October 1798, after dancing the night away at a grand Earlham party.

How she hated her failures. Sometimes it seemed that no matter how hard she tried to live up to her ideals, she was completely unable to escape the uncontrollable passions that waited to trip her, ensnare her, and impede her progress. Even when she had them under control, she reflected, it seemed they could still thwart her.

Giving up singing had been particularly hard – partly because she loved it so, and partly because she knew how much John Gurney loved to hear her. Yet she also knew that once she began, an ecstasy took hold of her that unbalanced her and left her prey to disturbingly capricious emotions. Such reasoning, however, made little sense to her father, and her decision to withhold her beautiful voice hurt him profoundly.

For without it, Earlham's musical parties lost something of their charm, as well as the sense of harmony that had always so enchanted him and reassured him that all was well.

Betsy's growing inclination to wear cheerless brown and slate-grey gowns, in such drab contrast to the pretty colours her sisters chose, hurt her father too. On the day she informed him that the scarlet riding habit had been finally laid away, he had been almost ready to weep. When she donned the Quaker cap in April 1799, although its simple white shape gave her face a look of sweet gravity that touched his heart, he knew that although she prevaricated still, it was another step on the path to separation.

"I first put on my cap," Betsy said, recalling the decisive event, "then I feared I was mistaken and I took my cap off." Over and over again she had arranged the cap on her head, before doubtfully taking it off again. She had also consulted Rachel, who was staying with her at the Hoare's home in Hampstead. Ultimately, however, Betsy knew the decision was hers, and as she sat before her looking-glass, alternating between Quaker cap and her fashionable turban, she grew increasingly conscious of the faint hum of conversation drifting upwards from a large party gathering downstairs. If she wore the cap before the company, she knew her fate was sealed. "After much uncertainty," she said later, "I felt most easy to appear like a Quaker, and wear my cap, which I did."

In July of the same year, John Gurney planned to escape the tensions of Earlham by taking Betsy, Priscilla, and little Sam with him on an extended trip to Northumberland, to the estate near Alnwick where the Gurneys reared sheep for the wool trade. But just days before the planned departure, an unexpected visitor was ushered into his study. It surprised John Gurney to see him, for he had no idea what could possibly have brought Joseph Fry to Earlham but as he observed the young man's flushed face and anxious eyes, he was overcome by the uncomfortable certainty that once again his life was about to be disrupted by romance.

"At present things are most interesting," Betsy wrote

breathlessly in her journal, on a page more covered with blots than usual, "I shall mention them. I am most occupied with an affair of consequence as the present happiness of an individual seems much concerned." Despite her rather self-important words, however, she hardly knew what to think. All she knew about Joseph Fry was that he was the son of wealthy Plain Quaker parents, and all she could remember of him was the moment the previous summer when he had mentioned William Savery. Anything more was completely lost to her, and she was as bewildered as John Gurney had been earlier when Joseph had requested his permission to propose to his daughter. Later, she spent the evening with Joseph, explaining that as she barely knew him, and didn't love him, she must therefore reject him. "Left poor Joe Fry behind," she wrote on the following day, after setting off with her father for Northumberland.

In Yorkshire, near Pontefract, John Gurney broke his journey at Ackworth School.[2] It was founded in 1779 to provide education for the children of poor Quakers, and any interested Friend was invited to its Annual General Meeting, and to join the delegations examining its educational, religious and domestic arrangements. Just as John Gurney had suspected, Betsy was eager to participate.

As part of a women's delegation, she toured the classrooms where little girls bent studiously over their books, workrooms where they knitted, sewed and spun, and the bustling dining rooms and neat dormitories where they ate and slept. When asked to inspect the grammar school, however, she was apprehensive. "I did not say I had only a slight knowledge of grammar," she admitted later. To her surprise, she discovered that the experience of her own little school had given her confidence, and that she was able to talk comfortably to the children and make some assessment of their progress.

When the delegations gathered to make their final reports, she discovered more unexpected reserves of confidence.

"What do our young people think?" asked Hannah Barnard, an American Friend eager to encourage youthful participation. A long and awkward silence followed, as everyone feared being first to speak. Eventually, Betsy could bear it no longer. "*I took courage, (as I thought it more right than wrong)*, to speak," she said, "and said what I thought of the grammar and cyphering, and felt glad I had done it, though I trembled at *doing it not a little*."

Her reward was the attention of the Meeting and a host of further questions. Later, many of the older delegates smiled and nodded to her as they passed, while some among them stopped her to talk. Their interest was nourishing, and each night, contented and fulfilled, she slept well. "I sighed upon my pillow," she said, "for I overflowed with love for what was good."

At York, the Gurneys visited The Retreat, the Quaker refuge for the insane that had opened its doors two years earlier.[3] There, as she observed the humane treatment of the inmates, Betsy reflected on how much her disturbed friend in Norwich would benefit from such a regime.

Still, no matter where she went, or what she saw – schools, asylums, or the dramatic landscapes of Yorkshire and Northumberland – somewhere at the back of her mind Joseph Fry hovered restlessly. As she thought about him, her thoughts inevitably returned to the black months that followed the break with James Lloyd, when for a time she had seen almost every eligible young man as a potential suitor. But when none of those she really favoured returned her interest, and at the same time her depressive illness grew steadily worse, the idea of marriage had begun to seem remote. "Perhaps one day when I least expect it I may be married," she had said, "if not, I do not doubt I shall be a happy old maid." Yet now she was less certain. Her cousin, Anna Barclay, who was also her close friend, was shortly to be married, and as Betsy thought about Anna, and experienced an unsettling mixture of jealousy and longing, she wondered if an old maid was quite what she wanted to be.

Back home, she remained unsettled. Part of her couldn't stop thinking about Joseph Fry, while another was desperate for the religious intensity she had experienced with William Savery and Deborah Darby. Meanwhile the quarrels over enthusiasm wore her down, especially when Kitty demanded she stop discussing her views with the younger girls. She also hankered for the sense of purpose she had encountered at Ackworth. There, she reflected, where it was so busy, she had felt happy and well, while at Earlham, where time often hung heavily, she seemed plagued by illness.

Why did she suffer so? she asked herself yet again. Why was she tired, sometimes as soon as she woke, and why was the world so often wreathed in gloom? What was it that made her heart race so violently and caused such breathlessness? Why did she still sometimes collapse unconscious to the ground? And why, despite visits to the dentist, more extractions, and leeches to the gums, was there still no respite from the pain in her teeth? She also wondered whether the wine prescribed for sound health and strength, and the laudanum for stomach cramps, was really very helpful, although she was afraid to abandon them in case she became worse.

She also felt herself plagued by company – the endless round, day after day, week after week, for dinner at three, to drink tea at six, that she had once enjoyed, but which lately had seemed so pointless. "The latter part of the day was spent with company," she fumed in October 1799, "such days are so full of nothingness they turn out to so little account."

Even her school was not sacrosanct: she was expected to cancel lessons at short notice to join family gatherings, or entertain the visitors her sisters thought would be amused by the curious spectacle. Both Ackworth and her own experience had taught her that children needed routine, and she began a campaign to persuade the family to take her enterprise more seriously. At the same time, she drew up a list of rules for the boys. That she herself needed rules and a purpose in life, was becoming increasingly obvious to her, but she saw little prospect. "Day after day passes away!" she wrote despairingly, "and what do I do? How very little."

Yet despite her frustrations, there were consolations. Earlier in the year, when she took Kitty's friend, Mary Anne Galton,[4] on a tour of Norwich, she had been shamed by her ignorance of English history, but having added it to her reading list, she was discovering what delights could be found in the past. Although her tutor, Monsieur Le Sage, always pressed up so close she was constantly moving away from him, she was at last seeing success with her French. There were also her visits to Nobbs, the school for little girls she founded in Norwich,[5] and her own dressmaking classes at Earlham. "I have been principally occupied in teaching a poor girl to make her gown," she wrote, when she first began, "rather droll, as I don't know how to make one myself."

In October, the Friends at Goat Lane elected her representative to Norwich Monthly Meeting, the assembly where business administration and decision-making took place for Quakers in the Norwich area. William Crotch, the minister once mocked so unkindly by Rachel, had become her firm friend, and she often talked to him about her religious life. She also talked to Uncle Joseph and Aunt Jane, whose kindness and eagerness to befriend her had been a revelation. Their obvious regard, and the warmth of her welcome into the Quaker fold, added to her confidence. In November, although "in a manner so unconnected and trembling I believe they could but just understand me," she spoke at Monthly Meeting for the first time.

She talked about it later to Hannah Judd, Earlham's Quaker housekeeper, who, after 15 years of working alongside him, had finally married John Scarnell, John Gurney's loyal butler. She had recently produced their first child, and while nursing the baby, "a job I rather liked", Betsy's thoughts turned to Joseph Fry.

By refusing him, she knew she had lost an opportunity to marry well that might not come her way again. What would she do, she wondered, if as she suspected, Joseph were to propose again? If she turned him down a second time, there was a chance she might never marry at all.

Later that month, the consequences of missed opportunities were forced upon her with painful clarity.

On the last day of November, at the end of their enforced separation, Henry Enfield arrived unexpectedly to speak to Rachel. When he rode away, he left her in tears. "I have seldom seen more agitation," Betsy said, "Harry left Rachel in about two hours and my father told me the affair *was given up*." Rachel herself was distraught. She sobbed uncontrollably and all of Earlham was overshadowed by her grief.

Less than two weeks later a letter arrived from Joseph Fry. Just as Betsy had anticipated, in it he asked permission to visit Earlham again. In the face of Rachel's despair, the moment seemed unfortunate, although Betsy could hardly help reflecting that once again, of the three older sisters, she was the one being courted.

By this time, however, Betsy was no longer the overwrought young woman surprised by an unexpected lover; and during the intervening months she had had time to marshall her thoughts. "If I have any *active duties to perform in the church*," she said, "are they not rather *uncomfortable with the duties of a wife and mother*?" Marriage, she decided, must wait, at least until her course in life was clear.

Then she changed her mind. On the other hand, she said, if her religious feelings were to indicate that she should marry, then she would try to accept what came to her. She would perform all her duties well, she hoped, but should she ever be a mother, then she prayed that the duties sent to her would centre on her children and her husband. Let Joe Fry come to Earlham, she told John Gurney, let him have "one more *fair chance*."

He arrived just before Christmas, and this time Betsy studied him closely. He was a rather awkward young man, with a high pale forehead and light eyes, with none of the Gurney confidence and good looks that made her own brothers so attractive. When she walked with him in the park, however, beneath the stark trees and colourless winter sky, she discovered that she rather enjoyed his company. "I like him better than I did," she decided.

But it wasn't enough. "I love and like many so *far* better," she said. One of them was her cousin Hudson, for whom she had developed a passion since meeting him in London the previous year, far away from their family circle. Often, Hudson stalked her dreams.

Betsy's sisters didn't like Joe Fry at all, and when they made fun of his loud laugh, his lisp and his lack of sophistication, she noticed it too, and was embarrassed by him. Her reaction confused her, for the Frys were Plain, and generally she admired Plain Quakers and felt comfortable in their company. To her shame, when they went to Keswick, Hudson's home, for tea with Uncle Gurney and the family, sensing that she might be mocked if she seemed too friendly towards Joseph, instead she made sure she was unkind.

Joseph bore it stoically, both the critical eyes of the Gurneys and Betsy's discouraging behaviour, but once again she refused him. He was, however, given leave to return, and when he left, Betsy's thoughts followed him.

As the century turned, Earlham was surrounded by a cold dark fog, and close before the fire Betsy re-read her old journals and worried about John Gurney. "My father does not seem well or comfortable," she wrote anxiously, "which made me so low last night that I had quite a crying bout." She was also conscious of a strange and unnamable yearning that left her feeling desolate. She didn't think the cause could possibly be Joseph Fry. "At *this time*," she said, "I am not inclined to marry anybody, and *am not in love with any person*."

Rachel, by contrast, was still in love with Harry, and though no one knew exactly what had passed between them, her sisters knew that when she wrote to him in February 1800, she offered to be his if he chose to have her. To Rachel's horror, as soon as the letter left Earlham, a rumour arrived saying Harry was engaged to someone else. In desperation, she sent John Scarnell to the Enfield home at Nottingham with another letter, that if the rumour were true, contradicted the first.

"John Scarnell came home *from Nottingham*," Betsy recorded at the end of February 1800, "the report *was true*."

With her hopes in ruins, Rachel turned to Kitty for consolation. Betsy sometimes caught herself watching them, Kitty, whose prospects had vanished with Catherine Gurney's death, and Rachel, whose expectations had been so violently shattered. Both of them, she realised, were unlikely ever to leave Earlham.

As Henry Enfield was condemned, the Gurneys slowly changed their minds about Joseph Fry. Uncle Joseph, who knew Joe's family, encouraged his cause, while Uncle Gurney wrote personally to Betsy urging her to accept him. At Earlham, the discovery by Betsy's sisters that Joe loved music and had a fine singing voice had made his clumsy manners seem quite trivial in comparison. "They *all now* seem to *wish* for the connection," Betsy said in surprise. "I think I *also wish for it*," she added, " but I am not, I believe, the governor of my own heart, and therefore the more I leave the affair for the present the better."

John Gurney, however, had decided to pursue it.

One dark evening late in February 1800, he brought two friends to Betsy's school. After constant complaints of noisy boots on the stairs, she had transferred it from an attic in the house to an outbuilding sometimes used as a laundry, and as the three men came in from the cold night, with them came a rush of cold air that set the candle flames flickering and the shadows dancing.

Without stopping, and observed in respectful silence by her visitors, Betsy had continued her reading. When she finally fell silent, John Kirkman, a Friend from Norwich, knelt down in prayer for the little school and its scholars. "It was a very solemn time," said Betsy.

It was also a time of revelation as in the old outhouse, its shabby cobwebby spaces illuminated by a lantern on Betsy's desk and smoking rushlights on the walls, John Gurney saw his daughter in a new light.

Watching her, tall and grave in her plain dress and Quaker cap, he reflected on the determination that over almost two years had produced the class of 50 ragged scholars sitting on rough wooden benches before her. During that time he had seen her consistently prepare lessons and make up and mark workbooks, and though it was only by hearsay, he knew that his timid daughter had a reputation for facing down bullies and blasphemers until they agreed to behave.

Staring at the lantern-lit scene, John Gurney saw with great clarity that the convictions and passions that drove Betsy were real, and that she was unlikely now to abandon her Plain Quaker path. He also knew that within her there still lingered a troubled child, whose fears and nervous anxiety often caused her mental and physical suffering. Who better to care for her, he realised, than Plain Joe Fry, so steady, so rich, and so desperately in love.

In March, Joe wrote again to John Gurney. Two rejections had unnerved him, but he was desperate for one last chance. For ever since the evening he had walked beside her in the summer woods near Earlham, he had carried with him the memory of a shy girl in a brown silk gown, with a black lace veil wound turban-like around her head, and whose eyes were candid and blue. He still recalled her blush at the name of William Savery, and how she had eventually confessed, timidly at first, but with growing animation, how she too longed to reach out in love to lost souls. He had been amazed that such intensity could dwell in someone so apparently reserved. Before meeting her, he had never thought much beyond everyday life and its pleasures, but after Betsy Gurney opened her heart to him, he had been seized by a desire to possess her, to protect her, and to absorb some of her passion into himself.

Reluctantly, John Gurney advised restraint. Under the conventions that applied, he pointed out, if a third visit were also to prove inconclusive, then Betsy would be forced to take a line of absolute prohibition over any further friendly meetings. And since absolute prohibition was not what either man wanted, when Joseph learned that Betsy would soon visit London, he decided to see as much of her there as he could, while John Gurney hoped the opportunities would bear fruit.

Betsy went to London in March, feeling particularly well and in good spirits, and with the certain knowledge that her father favoured Joseph Fry. "I think that has now brought me to see the affair in a better light," she said.

She always dressed Plain now, and even on grand occasions she rejected the flimsy high-waisted dresses, with short sleeves and low necklines that were the height of fashion. Instead, she chose simple silk gowns with a natural waist, while a white handkerchief folded softly around her throat set off her Quaker cap. The sight of it encouraged Joe Fry as doggedly he resumed his courtship.

"It agitated me seeing him again," Betsy confessed, after their first London encounter.

She also confessed to feeling odd and changeable towards him, and that rather than the indifference she had felt at first, she now felt strongly, one minute really liking him, and the next finding him quite disagreeable. She also felt unable to describe her emotions clearly, except to say that she often found the remembrance of Joe Fry very pleasing.

Whether she wanted to spend her life with him was another matter. His devotion sometimes annoyed her, especially when he arrived early and left late, and she also wondered what it was about him that made her treat him as she sometimes did, "satirical and unkind", as if she deliberately wanted to hurt him. "I could hardly make myself out," she confessed. "I believe I have given him absolute pain today by his own account, and yet I appear to others to give him encouragement by letting him come."

Some of the others, especially her Hoare relatives at Hampstead, began to insist that Betsy make up her mind. It was unjust, they told her, to keep the young man in suspense.

She almost made it up in April, after an enjoyable supper together was followed by an equally enjoyable dream. "I mention that," she said, "because I think dreaming agreeably or disagreeably of a person has its effects in such a tossed about mind as mine." Thinking of dreams, she recalled her old dream of the sea, that had eventually been replaced by the dream of a rock standing firm among thrashing waves. Was Joseph Fry a rock? she wondered.

On 15 April, the morning after her dream of Joseph, she was almost ready to agree to the marriage. Their relations, including Joseph's older brother William, and his wife Eliza, thought she would soon do so too, and invitations began arriving for Betsy and Joseph as a couple. After one intimate family supper, after which they shared a snug quiet evening together, she felt even more inclined. Then, immediately afterwards, she panicked. The thought of leaving Goat Lane, her poor, and her little boys frightened her, for she had no idea what could possibly take their place. "I *do pray* as much as I can," she said, "if it is wrong, it may come to an end, as it is not now too late to refuse him."

Joseph saw it all quite differently. Once Betsy became his wife, he had no doubt she would be happy. Their families were part of the same Quaker aristocracy, business interests in the tea trade had made the Frys as rich as the Gurneys, and their country estate at Plashet, at East Ham in Essex, was as large and as grand as Earlham. Although he promised eagerly that he would always support her, and never stand in the way of whatever religious path she chose to follow, he was convinced that once they were married their future together would follow the same cheerfully placid progress as that of his own parents.

He encouraged his father, William Storrs Fry, to invite John Gurney to Plashet, and the visit, at the end of April, was a huge success. The two men discussed the complex financial details of a great Quaker union, Kitty and Rachel gossiped with Joseph's mother and admired her beautiful home, and both families became even more persuaded that Joseph and Betsy should wed. Then, this time with both Gurneys and Frys behind him, Joseph paid his third visit to Earlham. It was the moment of decision, he told himself, and he took with him to Norfolk a gold watch and placed it on a white garden seat. If Betsy took up the watch, he said, and kept it, it was a sign of their engagement. "I did not feel at liberty to return the watch," she said, "I cried heartily. Joseph felt much for me."

Although Betsy agreed to marry Joe Fry, the doubts that were continually confided to her journal make it clear she was uncertain that her decision had been wise. The pressures on her to accept him, however, seem to have been huge. Not only was there her failed engagement to James Lloyd, there was also the gloomy example of Rachel and what happened to those unable or unwilling to seize an opportunity that might not come again. Joe Fry was also persistent, and so too, were Betsy's family, who might well all have agreed that marriage to a steady young man was the very best thing for this unstable young woman. It was the intervention of her father, however, that seems to have been critical, and is likely to have been the deciding factor. It is also possible that in Joe Fry's easy-going and indulgent nature there was something that on a deep level reminded Betsy of John Gurney.

With uncertainty provoking anxiety, as the drowsy summer days of her engagement passed by, Betsy continued to be troubled. Why did she wilfully hurt Joseph and then feel a great rush of relief when he forgave her? Was it her own vanity, rather than affection, that made her long for his company? She did long for it now. In his absence, she missed him, and when he arrived, she was ecstatic. "I *almost* follow him about," she admitted. Yet too much of him still annoyed her, and she often felt her time could be better spent with her poor people or her school. "I had an idle afternoon with Joseph which was not pleasant," she wrote irritably at the end of May. "He seemed to me to have stayed long enough this time."

An almost constant toothache made her irritable too; so did her fears of leaving Norwich, and of becoming mistress of her own household. Her dreams grew more vivid: one night she dreamed she was already married to Joseph; on another she dreamed of William Savery. At Meeting, she struggled to control her thoughts. "It must be difficult to keep the heart devoted to things spiritual when it is much in love, for it tends the feelings so much to what I believe is sentimental and worldly," she observed unromantically.

Her sisters thought her quite unromantic too, and finally, early in June, Kitty lost her temper and reprimanded Betsy for her behaviour towards Joseph that was not sufficiently respectful, and far too dictatorial. Betsy vowed to mend her ways, but days later Joseph vexed her for not doing as he was told. "I did not think him quite so compliant as he should have been," she complained. Joseph, however, was oblivious to her bossiness, and he watched with delight as fine fabrics and clothes for her trousseau were delivered to Earlham.

Wasn't such finery inconsistent with Plain Quaker principles? Kitty asked acidly one day. Even though she tried, she was unable to overcome her bitterness at the fate that had denied her a lover of her own. Absorbed in her own concerns and her own dilemmas, Betsy was completely oblivious to her sister's distress. "Kitty made a remark about my wedding clothes that rather vexed me," she said crossly, "she said she thought them inconsistent with the rest of my things."

Even with wedding clothes arriving, and Uncle Gurney and Uncle Joseph fetching documents to be witnessed, Betsy could hardly believe that she would very soon be married. It became a little more real when her Norwich poor cried as she said goodbye, and even more so when she met her little boys for the last time. Leading the sad troupe to the summer-house for their final farewell, she realised to her surprise that they now numbered 86. After they left, she sat down and sobbed.

The approaching marriage also became more real as Joseph's increasingly urgent desire roused her own. "I seem as if I should not be able to know exactly how far personal attentions should be admitted before marriage," she wrote anxiously, as one part of her tried to set limits, while another, prey to unsettling nightly longings, was expectant with anticipation.

Early in August, Joseph escorted Betsy to Meeting, and for the first time he saw her speak in public. He was so proud of her that he could barely contain his excitement, but as he spoke to anyone who would listen, the sound of his loud voice and nervous laughter set Betsy's nerves on edge. "His spirits seemed to go almost painfully beyond mine," she said, suddenly embarrassed by him again. For Joe Fry, however, nothing could go beyond the love and admiration he felt for the pretty girl in the Quaker bonnet who was so soon to become his wife.

The marriage was set for Sunday 19 August at Goat Lane. Betsy woke before it was light, gripped by a chill of uncertainty, but by the time she reached Meeting it had passed, and though her hands were cold and her heart beat uncomfortably, she felt at peace, and that God was giving her his blessing. When the time came, she made her promise in a firm voice. "Friends," she said, "in the fear of the Lord, and before this assembly, I take this my friend, Joseph Fry, to be my husband, promising, through divine assistance, to be unto him a loving and faithful wife, until it shall please the Lord by death to separate us."

All around her the familiar old building was filled with the people who had crowded her past: Gurneys, Barclays and Hoares; Dr Alderson and Amelia; John Pitchford and William Crotch, as well as the entire Earlham household and many friends from Norwich. Over them all lay a hazy shimmer of sunshine, and as Betsy gazed upon the scene, and breathed the scent of sun-warmed wood and flowers, she reflected on how much had passed since William Savery bid her turn to the light. What lay ahead of her now, she wondered, as she began her new life as Mrs Elizabeth Fry?

CHAPTER SIX

I appear to have taken my flight from spiritual things

*T*HE HUGE HOUSE IN St Mildred's Court, at
the heart of the City of London and the centre of the Fry business empire, was in utter confusion. As Betsy looked at the
muddle she wanted to weep. Her sister-in-law, Eliza, appeared
to have abandoned any attempt to complete her own family's
removal, and except where it blocked doorways, her furniture
still occupied every room; her furnishings, except where they
lay in haphazard piles, still draped windows and beds; and her
pictures, looking-glasses and candlesticks, except those littering corridors or protruding from half-filled packing cases,
remained firmly fixed to the walls or were strewn indiscriminately across a range of Eliza's tables, sideboards and sofas,
that were themselves scattered throughout the whole house.
As she wondered what had become of her own new household
possessions, Betsy almost expected to see William and Eliza
Fry appear before her wearing the dismayed expressions that
always greet unwanted and unwelcome guests.

It was all a bitter disappointment, and very far from the joyful arrival at her first married home she had been picturing for
months. Imagining resentment to be the cause of Eliza's tardiness, she became immediately convinced that it was shared by
the entire household.

The conviction made her nervous of her servants who
waited silently in line for her to speak first. She felt that they
sensed her shyness and lack of experience, and that in their

hostility, they urged her to stumble. Desperately, she willed her husband to take charge, but Joseph, too, seemed ill at ease. As the tension mounted, in a voice that seemed uncomfortably loud Betsy eventually asked that a lower room used as a bedroom be transformed into a sitting room. Jane King, the housekeeper, issued the order immediately, and as she did so, Betsy knew that the unsmiling and efficient woman had made a comparison between her old mistress and the new, and that Betsy was found wanting.

In the haven of her new sitting room, Betsy thought back over the past ten weeks of her honeymoon, where she had felt so adrift in the unfamiliar territory of marriage.

"I did not much feel *myself a bride* all day," she had confided sadly to her journal as her wedding day drew to a close. The sense of disappointment had undermined her, and when the time finally came to leave Earlham, she had clung desperately to John Gurney and wept like a child.

But in the following weeks, as the newly wed couple stayed in turn with a host of their relatives, she had been surprised and pleased to discover that in their new intimacy, she felt more loving towards Joseph than before. Despite it, however, she also found the closeness stifling. "Hardly ever alone," she complained, "not even in my mind."

It had also unsettled her to discover that Joseph craved her attention and sympathy in areas where previously she had been accustomed to receive them for herself. And rather than patiently indulging his sick headaches and his tendency to feel himself a little poorly, her response was often a frustrated annoyance.

Over his casual attitude towards business, however, she was aware of more serious concerns. "I am more tried with what appears weakness in his habits," she said, when during their long visit to Plashet, her young husband showed a reluctance to leave his bed and set off early each day for the Frys' London office. Such behaviour was in stark contrast to the diligence of the Gurneys, and eventually, late in September, she resolved to take Joseph in hand. Determined to set an example, she rose early herself, accompanied him to London, shared breakfast at his side, and then left him with encouraging words at the counting-house door. It was the beginning, she hoped, of better things.

As the irritations and disappointments caused tensions, uneasily she attempted to rationalise their results. "The sweetest of tempers," she said, "will not, indeed, cannot, live harmoniously together without bickering."

That there could also be difficulties with her in-laws was equally disturbing. As Joseph's betrothed she had received nothing but kindness, but as Joseph's wife, she was left in no doubt that the Plain Frys frowned on the Gurneys of Earlham, and that despite her efforts to be Plain, they regarded Betsy as almost fatally tarnished by the dances, the musical evenings, and the sophisticated sceptical company of her home.

At close quarters she also found the Plain Frys disconcerting: not in their religious observance, their dress or their speech, but in their habits, interests and behaviour. Father Fry, especially, with his loud laugh and blunt references to her family sometimes seemed to Betsy bad-mannered and offensive. In return, her own tendency to dissemble, resulting from her shyness and desperation to be liked, left her in-laws impatient and angry. So too did "that polished behaviour, that adds a charm to every qualification", so beloved of Catherine Gurney. When Joseph informed her that "my manners had too much of the courtier about them", Betsy became miserably self-conscious of every word and action.

Forlornly, she reflected on how hard it was to please. To the Frys she was too worldly, to the Gurneys she was almost impossibly Plain, and though she tried hard, it seemed she could neither enter totally into one life, nor leave the other completely behind.

She was also bored at Plashet. "I wish to begin some useful employment," she wrote in frustration, but beyond domestic occupations, there was nothing to do, or to talk about. "We talked about common subjects a good deal," she said of the days she spent sewing with Mother Fry, where, guiltily, she often dwelt on the stimulating discussions of Earlham.

She also wondered what her clever, witty sisters would say

about the Frys' enthusiasm for animal magnetism. The procedure, a form of faith-healing using magnets,[1] Betsy regarded as
suspect, and an offence both to Reason and to her Christian
faith. "Rather a try'd state with some of the family," she said
after her first experience of it, "partly because they persuaded
my husband to magnetise my mother."

It had been a relief, as the honeymoon neared its end, to
escape back to Earlham. But, it was there, late in October, in
the familiar surroundings of the music room, that the pain and
potential tragedy of childbirth first began to haunt her. "I
begin to suspect myself of being in the way," she said anxiously, "I have an almost continued pain in my back."

When William Fry arrived uninvited to dinner, moments after
she emerged from her new sitting room, Betsy knew that her
sense of him somehow continuing to occupy Mildred's Court[2]
had been justified. Even for their first meal in their first home
together, she and Joseph were not to be left alone. William,
however, was oblivious to her feelings; he worked at the Court
overseeing the Fry business, and although he had followed
family tradition by relinquishing the London house when his
younger brother married, he saw no reason to forgo his previous habits.

When he finally departed, having all the time ordered the
servants and talked to Joseph exclusively of business, Betsy
consoled herself that at least during the evenings and on
Sundays, she and Joseph could share the quiet intimacy where
their relationship seemed most to thrive. "My Joseph and I had
a truly snug and comfortable tea," she said contentedly, as the
day drew to a close, "I believe both feeling the real comfort,
and may I say blessings, at being at last quiet in our own
house."

Three days later, on 3 November, Betsy and Joseph set out
from the quiet of their own house for Gracechurch Street
Meeting. It was their first appearance there as a married couple and they were anxious to make a good impression. "We
were very punctual to the time," Betsy recorded proudly. She
was particularly pleased to be welcomed there by her father's

cousin, Joseph Gurney Bevan, and his wife Mary, and the warmth of their greeting and their offer of immediate friendship, made her so happy that she cried.

It was a happiness, however, that was short-lived. So too was any anticipation of a quiet Sunday. "I felt low when I got home," she recalled painfully, "and seeing the freedom of the family in the house was rather a trial to me. I think they could not be freer if it were their own, and also there was such a state of muddle."

Not only was Mildred's Court expected to provide regular weekday dinners for William, Betsy discovered, but it was also regarded as the informal London headquarters of the entire Fry family. Without referring to the new mistress, Mother and Father Fry had settled themselves cosily in the parlour, where they called for more coals on the fire and re-ordered the menu for dinner, while William and Eliza, blithely disregarding their still-unmoved belongings, gossiped with Jane King, and entered every room to comment on Betsy's newly installed possessions.

Returning alone the following day from Gracechurch Street, where she had thought of nothing except the muddle at home, the behaviour of her in-laws, and whether she was pregnant, "I think I may truly say," Betsy said, "the world lived and the spirit died." Ruefully, she reflected that it had been the same ever since her wedding, when religion, and even its influence, seemed to have disappeared entirely from her life.

Sensing dark thoughts edging their way into her mind, she left her journal-book and moved to the window that looked out into the November-afternoon dark of Mildred's Court. Ranged along one side, the black bulk of the tea warehouse loomed massively, while beneath her, she saw a dim glow where candle-light from the counting-house windows struggled to pierce the gloom. Where was the dazzling ecstasy that had followed William Savery's preaching, she wondered, or the knowledge of God so powerfully present in the company of Deborah Darby? Glancing towards the court's narrow entrance, where the beams from a great iron lantern lit the cobbles and cast a golden shimmer on the wall of St Mildred's Church, Betsy begged God to send more of his servants to guide her steps back to the light.

With her husband and in-laws, Betsy found it impossible to object to a way of life they regarded as normal. When George Dilwyn, a Friend from Philadelphia travelling in the ministry, arrived a week after her entrance as a bride to spend six weeks based at her home, she found it equally impossible to contravene the traditions of Quaker hospitality.

Sharing her new home, still littered with Eliza's belongings, with a stranger, was far more unsettling than family intrusions, while Dilwyn's standing in the Society of Friends, and his abrupt manners, both seriously intimidated her. "I feel almost overcome with my own weakness when with such people," she confessed.

Convinced she had seen Dilwyn frown over her new furnishings, her discomfort reflected her own misgivings. During her shopping trips with Joseph for new furniture, she had become painfully aware that her own carefully nurtured attachment to expensive good taste sat very uncomfortably with the household expectations of Plain Joseph Fry. Although finally they had compromised on furniture that while handsome, was still relatively Plain, Betsy still shrank under what she felt was the American's stern gaze.

A disparaging reaction from George Dilwyn, as well as from William Fry, was almost certain, Betsy concluded, when, one gloomy November morning she felt a powerful urge to read the Bible aloud to her little household. "I feared doing it," she recalled later, "particularly as William was here and not liking the appearance of us *young people* appearing to profess more than they did who were here before us."

Anxious to avoid a confrontation, she struggled to ignore the inner prompting, but so relentless was it, that it drove her to confide in Joseph, who in turn consulted George Dilwyn. When Dilwyn proved enthusiastic, Betsy was astonished, for although Catherine Gurney had read the Bible aloud to her children each morning, it was an unusual daily occupation for adults.

Presently, as their little group gathered in the parlour, Dilwyn suggested that Betsy read from Psalm 46.

"God is in the midst of her;" Betsy's voice trembled as she spoke, "she shall not be moved; God shall help her, and that right early ... " Then, overcome by emotion, she broke down in tears and passed her Bible to Joseph.

"G. Dilwyn said for our encouragement this morning," she noted with surprised satisfaction some days later, "that he had seen since he had been with us the efficacy of reading in the Bible the first thing, he thought it a good beginning to the day!"

Despite their good beginnings, however, the days did not always continue well. Betsy found managing her household a struggle, and still painfully shy of giving orders, she was conscious of an embarrassing tendency towards familiarity with her servants. "How much more I act the part of a friend towards them," she said, "than in keeping it to myself."

She was conscious too of the frustrations caused by living over a business where she and Joseph were constantly on call for a stream of suppliers and customers, and where William, who was particularly short-tempered, was inclined to blame Joseph if anyone complained. "My brother William came in, in rather an angry tone," she wrote after one fractious incident, "saying something about *our* not wishing to treat the customers well." Mother and Father Fry, too, often made little effort to conceal a preference for William and a lack of confidence in their younger son. Yet while Betsy resented their castigation of her husband, and was often moved to pity by his crestfallen face, she sensed her own feelings to be ambivalent. Even as she loyally soothed Joseph's wounds, she knew there was substance to the allegations, and that what she had hoped was a honeymoon indulgence was in fact something more deep-seated and permanent.

On a morning in January 1801, when Joseph's resentment at once more being urged out of bed finally erupted into furious words, Betsy responded in a similar vein. It was one of many such confrontations, and although Joseph often came upstairs later from the counting-house to make amends, the difference in their attitude towards hard work and business lay as a rift between them.

So too did what Betsy regarded as Joseph's casual attitude towards money. Unlike her own inclination for tasteful furnishings, which she regarded as displaying an aptitude for wise investment, she regarded as spendthrift her husband's tendency to make spur-of-the-moment purchases. When he returned home one day, exceedingly proud, with a picture purchased at a sale for two shillings, she was so angry, and Joseph so hurt by her reaction, that he threw his prize onto the fire. Neither the argument, nor the memory of the flames engulfing his bargain, however, succeeded in stifling Joseph's passion, and months later, Betsy complained again to her journal. "Joseph vexed me today," she said, "by going to a sale and spending much money."

His attachment to reading vexed Betsy too, for she felt shut out from that part of his life. It also upset her that apart from her own morning readings, which were now a regular part of the Mildred's Court day, nowhere in her husband's life did the Bible feature. Convinced that she had found a recipe for future harmony, she suggested one day that they might read it together after supper. Joseph's response devastated her. She was *"going on* the wrong way," he retorted, and followed it with an accusation of religious enthusiasm.

Joseph was tired, he found business hard and not very rewarding, and as married life gradually became a routine he increasingly wanted a wife to relax with, who would soothe him and amuse him, not one who insisted he read the Bible. He was also becoming intensely irritated by Betsy's growing tendency to attend Meeting twice every day.

Betsy, however, was becoming desperate, for despite regular prayer and daily Bible readings, there was still no sign of the religious feelings she longed for. It was a lack made more poignant by a number of previously worldly Friends who were testifying publicly at Gracechurch Street to a renewed turning to the light, and also by others who spoke of enterprises to which God had called them. "Sarah Lines mentioned to the Meeting the manner in which she had accomplished her late journey," Betsy wrote after hearing Sarah speak, "and the feeling of reward she experienced."

Would she ever experience such a feeling of reward, she wondered, or had God forgotten her? Perhaps Deborah Darby's prophecy was all an illusion, whispered her old sceptical self.

Saddened by her absence of spiritual life, Betsy concentrated on good works.

Soon after settling in London, she had begun visiting the local poor, especially women, and almost always, Joseph went with her. It was that, together with the knowledge that his fortune now paid for her charity, that often reminded Betsy that Joseph was being as true as he could to the promise he had made before their marriage, that he would always support her, and never stand in the way of whatever religious path she chose to follow. Sometimes it almost compensated for their differences. "I call him a truly kind husband and that is a great blessing," she said.

She also encouraged poor women to call at Mildred's Court for gifts of food and clothing, and when they arrived clutching hungry-looking children she longed to do more to help them. But it was rapidly becoming clear that the visits and interruptions that had frustrated her at Earlham were to be repeated for ever in London. She liked having her own family to stay, especially her father and Uncle Joseph, but as well as the Gurneys, and the inevitable Frys, her enormous network of relatives, Barclays, Bells, Bevans, Hanburys and Hoares,[3] were constantly demanding her attention. Even when their visits were unannounced, it seemed they expected a welcome. "It was my intention to have done a little something this morning," she wrote after one unscheduled visit, "but being as usual interrupted, I could not go on in doing much, having many visitors."

"To spend one's life in visiting and receiving visits, is almost sad," she said, but so ingrained were their habits, and so leisured the lives of her wealthy social circle, it was impossible to break free. And although she tried hard, so lavish was the spread on every table and so rigorous the etiquette that insisted it be consumed, that she found it almost impossible to limit her intake of alcoholic beverages and rich foods.

Mother Fry also made constant presents of food, and the

relentlessness of it eventually made Betsy ungracious. When her in-laws arrived unexpectedly on Christmas Eve 1800, bearing a turkey, to their dismay, and Betsy's shame, she compared it disparagingly to the Norfolk bird sent by John Gurney that sat smugly in her pantry. A tense Christmas Day followed. "I do not think such family parties often answer," she confided miserably to her journal.

By the end of January 1801, Betsy was certain she was pregnant. Joseph, the Gurneys and the Frys were all ecstatic, and Mother Fry, in particular, was relieved to blame Betsy's Christmas bad humour on the then undiagnosed condition. But at a time when there were no anesthetics, and few remedies for complications arising from pregnancy or labour, many women were ambivalent about forthcoming motherhood: Betsy, who had lived in terror of death since her childhood, not surprisingly saw little cause for celebration, only a heightening of her fear. "I call it an anxious time," she said.

When the Gurneys' London physician, Dr Sims,[4] called to examine her, it roused unwelcome memories of the dark days of her collapse in 1796, and when he confirmed the pregnancy, she wondered morbidly if it would bring on similar symptoms. Almost as if the very thought itself had provoked them, surges of intense agitation almost immediately began laying hold of her mind. So powerful was the fear, and so graphic the possibilities that gripped her imagination, that by February she had almost convinced herself that she would never survive the forthcoming ordeal.

Feeling the new life quicken within her made her more conscious than ever of what lay in store. It also made her more conscious of her need for Joseph, who was always tender and loving towards her whenever she was tired or unwell. As her pregnancy advanced, and as a family became a reality, however, Betsy was forced to admit that her marriage was not a success. "I rather feared my beloved husband and myself had not been on those sympathising and happy terms I feel so desirable, almost necessary, to the comfort of married life," she confessed. Sadly, Joseph agreed, and during long walks together through the London streets, where they reflected on the past, and on their unkind treatment of each other, they vowed that the future would be better. "May I give up every other earthly consideration to please my husband and to render ours an increasingly happy union," she said.

At Earlham, in April, she missed Joseph desperately. "I felt want of him in the night," she said, "as I was but poorly, with a pain I suppose to be the cramp and my cough, and nobody minds me like him."

She was back in London in May in time for Yearly Meeting. The national assembly of the Society of Friends was held each year at Devonshire House,[5] its national headquarters in Bishopsgate, that was also so close to Mildred's Court that the Frys traditionally provided hospitality to the delegates. Many of them lodged throughout the two-week period in the house itself, while others, sometimes 60 at a time, ate breakfast, dinner or supper at the Fry table.

Despite her pregnancy, as well as attending two sessions of Yearly Meeting each day, Betsy was also determined to prove herself as good a hostess as Eliza Fry before her. In her eagerness, and to Jane King's frustration, she was forever in the kitchen worrying over the roasted meats, boiled fowls and poached fish making their way to the dining room, and fussing over the puddings, jellies and syllabubs that waited to follow. She also insisted on overseeing pitchers of hot water going upstairs and chamber-pots coming down for Friends who liked to take a wash or a nap after eating, and she fretted endlessly over her footmen, who despite all her urging, never seemed to be in the right place at the right time.

At Devonshire House itself, she sat uncomfortably on the wooden benches and tried to focus her mind on Quaker business and worship. To her dismay, she found herself thinking more often of the child within her, or about whether the dinner would be ready on time. And although she was gratified by the numbers of Friends anxious to wish her and Joseph well, and to reassure them that if they did their duty, blessings both spiritual and temporal would follow, when one female Friend suggested quite bluntly that such blessings flowed only to those who were obedient, Betsy was profoundly distressed. For, she sensed the speaker looking into her heart, and that rather than finding there an obedient wife, she had seen instead a restless and discontented young woman who secretly longed to be more than the helpmate of Joseph Fry and mistress of Mildred's Court.

She imagined her secret becoming clear to everyone after she went with a group from Yearly Meeting to meet Joseph Lancaster, a Friend who kept a school for poor children in the dingy streets of Southwark.[6] For so intrigued had she been by his radical new method, where older children called monitors taught lessons learned from the teacher to groups of their younger classmates, that at first she could hardly stop asking questions. Aware, eventually, that her fellow visitors had fallen silent, she had retreated in embarrassment to the shadowy walls where her thoughts drifted back nostalgically to her Earlham laundry. Later, when the time came to leave, she found it hard to tear herself away from the powerful sense of purpose filling the bare room, and clutching her husband's arm, she cast a long lingering look behind.

As summer settled on London, the rank vapours of the Thames drifted along Bishopsgate, along Cornhill, Cheapside and Poultry, before creeping finally into Mildred's Court, where Betsy saw unmistakable signs that her labour drew near. "I can hardly say how odd it struck me," she said in June 1801, "that milk should be in my breasts for a little child of my own within me." But despite the anticipation provoked by the creamy crusts that formed around her nipples, and by the growing strength of the child within, her dread was daily increasing. In the face of it, her faith wavered, and her old scepticism returned to deny the existence of a loving God ready to aid her ordeal. As she wondered if the pain of labour could be worse than the toothache that had plagued her throughout pregnancy, she became obsessed by an image of herself and the child going down together into the darkness. When her close friend, Mary Newman, died in childbirth, her anxiety became a torment, and in July, during Meeting at Gracechurch Street, she collapsed.

After that, as social engagements with relatives came abruptly to an end, so too did her twice-daily attendance at Meeting. Instead, she rested at home on her bed, listening to Joseph as he read to her from his beloved books. But inwardly she sensed it was a calm before a storm, and when Rachel and Hannah arrived in August to be with her during her confinement, even their familiar presence was unable to dispel her dread. "We had a pleasant evening at work for the little baby, who I much love in prospect but I do not like to build castles about," she wrote apprehensively.

Obsessively, she began to put her house in order. "For in such a time of trial," she said, "whether I live or die it will tend to my satisfaction of mind to know how my things are situated."

The pain was indescribable, Betsy remembered, and it went on for hours. When finally it came to an end, the agony and the effort had exhausted her so much that even the sight of baby Katherine, cradled in her proud father's arms, failed to move her. "I did not experience that joy some women describe," she admitted guiltily. All she could do, she said later, was to stare wearily at the child, and at Rachel and Hannah leaning anxiously over her bed, before closing her eyes in the face of the shadows that loomed behind them and bore down upon her.

Sunk in depression after the birth, Betsy became fearful, agitated, and over-anxious. Katherine's wails set her nerves on edge and reduced her to tears, while Katherine's splutters during feeding, or any rejection of the breast, caused her to panic. Eventually, Joseph became so resentful at being woken in the night that it provoked another round of arguments. Later, convinced that her milk no longer agreed with her baby, Betsy took to studying Katherine's tiny bowel movements, morbidly searching for signs of something amiss. As her anxious imagination conjured fearful maladies, in her dreams the sea returned once more to claim her. But now, as she fought to maintain herself in the face of the wind, she walked the wild shore with little Katherine clutched in her arms.

"My time is now principally occupied with little baby," Betsy wrote during an autumn visit to Plashet. "I have not here much else to attend to, but I do not feel satisfied as if my time were usefully employed."

Guilty that motherhood failed to fulfil her, and beset by anxiety over her baby's health, she sometimes looked sourly at the world.

"The noise of the mob nearly makes my head ache," she said crossly, early in October, as the prospect of an end to the long war with France brought all London out on the streets.[7] And when Joseph, Rachel and Hannah celebrated among the joyful crowds, and admired the illuminations decorating the city's West End, Betsy stayed pointedly at home. "It does not seem to me the right manner of showing our gratitude," she said, "as it appears to lead to drunkenness and vice."

Two weeks later, back in the familiarity of Earlham, she felt she had stepped back into a kinder and more comfortable world. John Gurney was ecstatic over his first grandchild, the entire household devoted itself to the new mother's comfort, and Betsy's sisters carried the baby away to nurse her and introduce her to every inhabitant of the family estate. At Goats Betsy was surrounded by well-wishers, and in the streets of Norwich, her poor and her laundry boys greeted her with shy enthusiasm. "How much more I am made of here than in London," she said wistfully, "indeed I believe I am estimated beyond my worth."

Eventually, however, came the inevitable return to London. To Betsy's surprise it was far less distressing than she had feared. Almost unnoticed, her life there had acquired a familiarity and a rhythm of its own, and what had formerly seemed unbearable now appeared possible, and what she had once regarded as strange now seemed almost commonplace.

For all Betsy's anxious dread, Katherine survived her inoculation against smallpox[8] and went on to survive the whooping cough. Despite the misgivings of Betsy's Plain Quaker conscience, the baby beamed whenever her young mother sang to her, and looked her best in the gay bonnets and baby gowns her aunts insisted on sending from Earlham. Her existence also enhanced the more positive relations with the Frys that had begun the previous year after Betsy summoned the courage to defend the Gurneys against Father Fry's criticisms, and to refuse her in-laws unlimited access to Mildred's Court. Now, with babies as the focus of conversation, Eliza became more companionable, while with a new grandchild to nurse, Mother Fry could be safely half-ignored and left to prattle cheerfully about her children, her husband and her home. Only when childhood ailments or Joseph's sick headaches roused the contentious subject of animal magnetism, did these mostly pleasant relationships falter.

Familiarity, Betsy felt, was also bringing her closer to her husband. Early in 1802, after admitting to her journal that it really had been a sense of duty that finally persuaded her to marry him, she was also relieved to confess how much she was now beginning to love him. If only they were less plagued by the company that had prevented them since their marriage from eating more than a quarter of their meals alone, she felt their relationship would blossom more profusely. For it was still only in their rare snug quiet times together, away from the cares of family and business, that they were able to relax, to attempt to understand each other's personalities, and to really enjoy each other's company. "The evening," she said, of 10 March 1802, "we rather dawdled away, reading our love letters." By July, she was certain she was pregnant again. In the same month, she began putting aside a little time each morning, before her Bible reading, for a period of silent meditation. "That I might find the will of the guide who I wish to follow," she said.

In September, at Joseph's request, Betsy went with him on a business trip to the Midlands that they extended into a holiday in the Lakes.[9] It was a bitter disappointment, and a brutal reminder that when they left their quiet intimacy for the bustle of life, then division, rather than unity, dominated their marriage. Betsy's depression, brought on by pregnancy, and her constant anxiety over baby Katherine's fretfulness, infuriated Joseph. His boyish enthusiasm irritated Betsy. "My Joseph was so exhilarated to be at the Lakes," she said in exasperation, "as to try my patience." While climbing Skiddaw struck her as pointless, attending Meeting each day sent Joseph to sleep.

This time, it was a relief to return to the familiarity of Mildred's Court, where among those waiting to greet her was her brother Sam. He had been apprenticed to the Fry counting-house earlier that year by John Gurney, who also paid Betsy for his keep, and although at first she had feared for her privacy, the whole family eventually agreed it was proving a successful arrangement. "I think I never knew Sam in so sweet a mind as he is in now," said Betsy's sister, Priscilla, "his present situation seems completely to suit his taste, and he shines in it more than he has ever done before. His partiality for Mildred's Court, and Joseph and Betsy, seems likely to increase, and he seems more attached to them than ever." It was partly the sight of Sam's familiar face that helped reassure the fraught couple that they were back on safe territory.

In March 1803, Betsy once more "entered the time of trial". To her relief, apart from one spasm so severe that she passed out, she experienced far less pain than she had during her first labour. She was also relieved that this time, the sight of a perfect little girl brought on the joyful flood of emotion that had been so lacking before. Very soon afterwards, rather than feeling depressed or weary, she was so full of boundless and sparkling energy that within weeks of Rachel's birth, she was back twice daily at Meeting and throwing herself into the hectic social life of Mildred's Court.

By the end of May, she had barely recovered from a complete physical and mental breakdown.

"I have gone though much since," she said, "in different ways, from real weakness, and also the trials of a nervous imagination, which no one knows but those who have felt them." Enmeshed in the depression whose onset had been so unexpected and so severe, once again she saw spectres of future horrors so terrible that she felt herself crumbling beneath them. "How hard they are to bear," she said, "for they lead the mind to look for trouble, and it requires much exertion not to be led away by them." The only thing that could prevail against them, she believed, was "the quieting influence of religion".

Yet despite her Bible readings, twice-daily Quaker Meetings, and now her morning meditations, religion continued to elude her, and when she looked back at the days of prophecy, it was as if they had never been. "I appear to have taken my flight from spiritual things," she said sadly.

Though yearning for living water, she felt trapped and weighed down by the world she inhabited. "Indeed my body affects my mind," she observed, "for the first part of the morning I feel active and clear, but by the time I have exerted myself, eaten and drank, I am so heavy, languid and stupid that I feel almost incapacitated the rest of the day." Eventually, even her journal, "the little friend of my heart", was laid by. "I do so little but nurse and take my pleasure, I hardly remember doing anything worth relating," she said.

Early in October 1803, despite tearful protestations from Betsy, who always sensed illness approaching whenever he left her, Joseph abandoned London for a two-week shooting party in Norfolk. On the evening following his departure, as she contemplated her empty fireside, and nursed a headache alongside a dull resentment against her husband, she also fretted over possible repercussions from criticisms she had made of animal magnetism during an illness recently suffered by Mother Fry. However, as she thought back on the days she had spent at Plashet nursing her mother-in-law, she reflected that in the sickroom there she had discovered satisfactions which more than compensated for the fatigue of travelling from London each day with two small children. The experience had stretched her, Betsy thought, not only demanding qualities of patience and compassion she was unaware she possessed, but also requiring her to be observant over medicines and the patient's condition. It had made her feel truly alive.

That night, Mother Fry's sickroom, together with the London poor and the Norfolk laundry boys crowded Betsy's dreams. In the morning, as she nursed baby Rachel, oversaw Katherine's breakfast, and read her Bible aloud to her children's uncomprehending faces, she felt a half-forgotten restlessness drawing her back to the window.

Outside in Mildred's Court she saw a hazy autumn mist that

promised later warmth, and peering through the pearly air towards the lantern on the church wall, to her surprise she saw in her mind's eye a wasted female figure. Recognising it as a once-regular caller, she suddenly realised how long it had been since that particular poor woman had made an appearance.

Presently, after leaving her babies with their nursemaid, Betsy left the house, and stepping out into the morning she glanced upwards to see the mist evaporating into a sky of azure brilliance. Feeling the sun warm on her head, she committed herself to God's care. Then she walked out of Mildred's Court into the teeming heart of London.

CHAPTER SEVEN

Now there is an opening made

When BETSY STEPPED OUT OF Mildred's Court in October 1803, she stood at the opulent centre of the richest city on earth.

Opposite her was the magnificence of the Lord Mayor's Mansion House; to her left, in Threadneedle Street, builders laboured on a new and bigger Bank of England; while across the street, at the Royal Exchange in Cornhill, merchants, shoppers and sightseers crowded over 150 shops that displayed, in lavish and spectacular splendour, the bounty of Britain's trade.

Yet within walking distance of the prosperity and pride lay slums full of poverty, filth and disease; mazes of tenements, narrow courts, and labyrinthine back alleys that had been thrown up, and then left behind, as London expanded away from its centre. In Smithfield, St Giles, Farringdon Without, and other regions encircling the city's rich heart, lived those least able to find work or stability; men and women whose poverty, frustration and despair too often found an outlet in domestic violence, drunkenness, vice and crime. Out of such slums, and from the dreary developments of north and east London, came urban highwaymen, burglars, cutpurses, gangs of muggers, fences, forgers and the passers of forged notes, prostitutes and pimps, as well as bands of small children who begged on the streets, picked pockets and stole from shops and market stalls. Unchecked, for there was no police force, the criminals terrorised London.

Spurning the comfort and safety of a silk-lined leather sedan chair, Betsy went on foot in search of the woman whose absence troubled her. Eventually, after making her way along Cheapside, and passing close to Newgate Gaol, she found herself in a warren of dingy alleys and courts where rubbish littered the streets and the air stank, and where dogs, pigs and dirty half-naked children clustered around puddles and squabbled over scraps, while sallow men and women watched them indifferently from doorways.

Conscious that she too was watched, that heads turned to follow her progress, she felt the atmosphere heavy with menace. Fear knotted her stomach, and she found that she was fighting to remind herself that she had asked God for his protection, and that she should therefore walk forward in faith.

The eyes that followed her, however, were curious rather than hostile, for in her plain gown and Quaker cap, rather than jar on her surroundings as another rich woman might have done, Betsy blended into them, and she passed through the stinking courts like a noiseless grey shadow. When she described the woman she sought, there was also something about the youthful Quaker, with her low voice, her polite manners and her air of faint anxiety that prompted people to answer frankly. As they did so, Betsy's heart eventually stopped hammering and she began more closely to observe the people around her. In them she saw men scarred by brutality, women and children pinched by want and young people numbed by vice: all of them tragic human beings in the grip of weakness and sin. Suddenly it seemed to her that in the squalid alleys of London, she heard the echo of a voice. No lives are so unlovely, nor so lost, said William Savery, that they are beyond the reach of the light which is Christ Jesus. And even you, it continued, can bring them to that same saving light.

For all her questions and the uncertain replies that led her deeper into the press of alleys and courts, the woman Betsy sought was nowhere to be found. But as she walked all morning she fell into conversation with other women, and most of them, she realised, were as anxious to tell her their stories of sorrow and misfortune, as they were to confess to desperate needs.

"I felt quite in my element serving the poor," she told her journal that night, "although I was much tired with looking about, it gave me much pleasure, it is an occupation my nature is so fond of. I wish not to take merit to myself beyond my desert, but it brings satisfaction with it more than most things."

Her sisters, however, found it disturbing. They had rather imagined that Betsy's passion for the poor would disappear after her marriage, or at least, follow a more conventional pattern of occasional good works. That she chose to walk London's filthiest streets and hold conversations with ragged women, seemed to them almost perverse. As perverse, indeed, as poor Betsy had always been, and as dreary as Mildred's Court itself. "We have had a regular Mildred's Court day," Louisa wrote home to Hannah, during a visit, "poor people coming one after the other till twelve o'clock, and then no quiet." Priscilla felt much the same. "Thee knows how dull Mildred Court can be," she told Hannah, "so I need not describe it to thee."

To Betsy, however, as 1803 drew to a close, life was at last seeming far from dull: rather, it was beginning to seem fulfilling. Just days after she returned from her search of London's slums, Gracechurch Street Meeting appointed her trustee of a will that bequeathed regular small sums to the Meeting's poor widows. Shortly afterwards, it made her personally responsible for the welfare of another.

Setting out to meet her new charge, Betsy made her way through streets that, although rapidly becoming familiar, still had the power to shock, and lying in an alley, where thin dogs sniffed hungrily, she saw a terrible sight. "I was grieved to see the sufferings of a poor babe in the streets," she said, "my heart almost prayed for it, dear lamb, it appeared almost forsaken."

The memory of the baby's pinched face haunted her. During visits to poor women with Joseph, she had encountered baby farmers, unscrupulous women who took in illegitimate infants left to a local parish, and who later abandoned them when funds were cut off. As she studied her own well fed and warmly clothed children, the fate of the innocent children of the poor lay heavy on her heart.

Towards the end of the year Betsy suspected she was pregnant again, but as the January snows of 1804 settled on London, she was so busy with others she barely had time to consider herself. At Mildred's Court, baby Rachel was unwell, while at Plashet, Mother Fry's illness had returned with symptoms that defeated doctors and animal magnetism alike. Eager to help, and once again taking her children with her, Betsy travelled regularly to East Ham. But in her sickness, Mother Fry forgot how her relationship with her daughter-in-law had mellowed, and while Betsy nursed her and fed her, the old woman grew querulous and spiteful. "In conformity with the fashions of the world," she grumbled about Betsy's hairstyle.

William and Eliza's unkindness was harder to bear. One evening during supper, with Betsy and Sam as their guests, they laughingly told the embarrassed young man just what they thought of Betsy's coldness. Hearing them, Betsy sensed something shrivel within her. Yet, stubbornly, she refused to be cowed. "I cannot say I thought anything altogether of their observations," she said, "they entertain me more than anything else."

For all the more cordial relations that had followed baby Katherine's birth, Betsy knew the Frys still resented her reserved manner and Earlham ways, and that in retaliation, sometimes they secretly mocked her. "What I believe they want of me is freedom and vivacity," she observed, "and being really free with people is not my nature. I think their taste and habits differ from mine exceedingly, and from my taste, grave characters suit me best, and I am more comfortable the more grave I feel."

Though she felt grave enough when Mother Fry died in March, as she brooded for hours by the corpse she also felt guilty and worried. "Although I have every reason to believe she died happy," she said, "I did not experience those awful sweet feelings I should have looked for at so serious a time."

John Gurney, who stayed on in London after the funeral, was troubled too, but not by any absence of feeling for Betsy's dead mother-in-law.

During the previous year, the treaty which provoked such

festivities in 1801 had been overturned, and as the French war resumed, Napoleon Bonaparte planned the conquest of England. As he did so, an invasion force mustered near Boulogne, transports gathered in the Channel, and throughout England wood for warning beacons was piled high on hilltops. At Earlham, John Gurney had four carriages and fresh horses kept ready to evacuate the entire household to Ely. But by the spring of 1804, the strain on him was beginning to tell. And if that were not enough, he told Betsy, a possible business action in Norwich could lose him £60,000, as well as bring disgrace to the family banking business where he had very recently been made a partner. That he confided in her so intimately made Betsy enormously happy. "I never remember taking so active a part in advice about my father," she said.

It also led her to consider some important issues. "I felt the difference of the understanding of men and women," she said, "men I think have clearer ideas than women." Even as she wrote the words, however, she wondered if they were really true. She had never heard any suggestion that Deborah Darby and her colleagues at Coalbrookdale suffered from cloudy thinking. She also reflected, with an uneasy combination of embarrassment for her husband and pride for herself, that ever since her discovery that Joseph muddled the figures, she had helped him with the business accounts. "Yet I think the judgement of women equal to that of men in most, if not all, cases," she concluded finally.

In the summer of 1804, as fears of invasion once again lay heavy on the land, Betsy gave birth to her third child. He was named John, after his delighted grandfather.

As before, the labour was surrounded by depressive illness, and later, while recovering, Betsy sought once again to understand its cause. In the end, in the absence of medical knowledge to the contrary, she could only continue to agree with the view expressed by William Savery, that ailments were sent and relieved by God, to benefit her in ways she could not entirely understand. Why else should it be, she reasoned, that "I have often found *help* and *release* from suffering when I have little expected it?"

Yet why should she find release, she puzzled, when others did not?

Earlier in the year one of the Earlham servants, "poor Becky", had committed suicide, and during a visit to Norfolk in May, as the death was discussed around the Gurney table, Betsy had experienced a growing sense of unease. When Dr Alderson described the recent death in Norwich of someone who had shot himself while his mind was unbalanced, it grew even more intense. For months afterwards, both deaths weighed heavy on her mind.

"To think that I had a complaint that could ever *bewilder* anyone so far as to lead them to take so dreadful a step," she said. It was a terrifying thought, for surely the ocean of darkness and death waited for suicides?

In her journals, Betsy never states explicitly that during her depressive episodes she actually felt drawn to suicide. It would in any case have been a hard admission for anyone to make at a time when the Christian church maintained that God would deny its victims heaven, and itself refused them burial in consecrated ground. However, she hints at it so broadly, and so consistently, that it does seem likely that during her blackest moments she sometimes felt herself tempted to take her own life.

Shortly after Becky's death, and brooding on the compulsions that led to suicide, Betsy nevertheless struggled to reassure herself that even when severely depressed, reason was not necessarily so disordered that all sense of right action was lost. Yet at the Friends' Retreat in York, during her visit there in 1799, she had most definitely seen for herself individuals whose thought patterns were chaotic and who had little or no ability to make rational or informed decisions. In such cases, she asked, did the terrible penalty still stand? She herself could not believe it to be so.

"When a knowledge of what is right and what is wrong is not granted, the individual is not answerable," she concluded finally.

Nevertheless, she remained troubled. "We know from all-wise motives, *madness* is permitted," she said, but just as with depression, God's purposes for it baffled her. "Perhaps," she speculated, it was "for the humiliation of those that are blessed." Without any medical or scientific knowledge on the subject, it was the only conclusion she could reach. As she wondered fearfully if her own depressions might carry her eventually towards madness, she strove to reassure herself. "Where there is much fever, or from any cause, extreme irritability, it may create temporary debility," she said, "but I do not think they have anything to do with *what is called insanity*."

Despite her conclusions that her symptoms were somehow part of God's purpose, Betsy was becoming increasingly accustomed to anaesthetizing the worst of them with the wine and brandy she already took for her health. Such remedies drove back the shadows, soothed her agitated thoughts, and together with laudanum they helped ease her physical pains, but her use of them made her feel guilty.

In the eighteenth century, strong drink and drunkenness had been widely tolerated, especially among the well-to-do, but by the opening years of the nineteenth, they were increasingly frowned on. "As an excuse for two of them," Betsy wrote in June 1805, after Gracechurch Street Meeting debated its members' drinking habits, "their infirmities were mentioned." In the end, however, it was agreed that even illness was no excuse. "It struck me it was better to suffer a little with patience than to take so dangerous a medicine," she said. But though she agreed with her colleagues, she remained painfully aware of her own susceptibilities. "I might face into the error myself in my weak nervous states," she admitted.

She also felt obliged to face up to other weaknesses. To her dismay, Joseph was becoming embarrassingly worldly; at Earlham, encouraged by Betsy's sisters, he played chess, sang, and played the piano, while in London, he missed Meeting so regularly that Cousin Joseph Gurney Bevan had finally been sent to admonish him. Convinced that the fault must be hers, that she did not strive hard enough to ensure her husband's spiritual welfare, Betsy vowed to be a better wife and to stand closer beside him in business and to encourage him in his Quaker path.

She was also miserably aware of her failings with her children, that had also been a cause of bringing Cousin Joseph to her door. She really would have to be firmer, he had told her, for if she continued to ignore Katherine's disobedience, and to allow her to do just as she pleased, then one day Betsy would bitterly regret it. But it was hard to admit that her daughter was totally out of control. "I believe he sees the worst side of her," she said consolingly, "as she is almost sure to be naughty if either he or cousin Mary are here."

It was something of a relief to believe that the shortcomings at Mildred's Court were mild in comparison with the enormous domestic deficiencies she observed in some other families, and when her Meeting decided to take them to task, Betsy applauded wholeheartedly. "Friends of our Monthly Meeting," she wrote approvingly in May 1806, "have lately made an appointment to visit its members, or I fancy, its delinquent ones."

To find herself included was a shock. "I suppose I was *rather* hurt to find friends *suspected me of delinquency*," the daughter of Earlham admitted painfully, but in the end she accepted what was sent with as much grace as she could muster. "On further consideration," she said, "my view quite altered. *A poor child like me, ought I* not rather to rejoice in being cared for and thought of, and do I not want stimulus and help in the important duty of governing a family?"

Two days later she took up an appointment as Visitor to the Friends' School and Workhouse in Islington. She had been nominated months earlier, but at that time was reluctant to take on too much outside her own home. But, although acknowledging the justification of the religious visit, perhaps something about it also roused her stubbornness, and despite being eight months into her fourth pregnancy, prompted her to make a start.

With her she took a batch of pretty finger cakes, just like the ones Grandmother Kett once brought to Earlham, as well as a new pamphlet on the Christian faith written expressly for children.

The sight of the workhouse children licking crumbs from their fingers and looking towards her expectantly, reminded Betsy very poignantly of her laundry. It was ironic, she reflected later, as she encouraged their stumbling reading, that she found working with such children so rewarding and easy, while similar tasks with her own little ones were so hard. Sighing, she shifted awkwardly as another soon to be born child stirred within her.

When finally the last child fell silent, Betsy took up the pamphlet and began reading aloud. Within minutes, she heard Ann Withers, her companion from Gracechurch Street, choking back sobs, and glancing up she saw that the teacher and several of the children also had tears in their eyes. Presently she began to elaborate on points raised in the pamphlet, and as she did so, she became aware of words flowing into her mind that were as unexpected as they were profound and uniquely appropriate. Speaking them aloud, she watched in amazement as those who had previously been on the verge of tears began openly to weep.

Where did the words come from, she asked herself later, that had prompted such tears? Had they been divinely inspired? No, she concluded eventually, they had originated in her own heart and understanding. But as she reflected on them, she also wondered if she was being carried closer to something that terrified her.

Ever since the day when she first raised her voice in public, Betsy had only ever spoken in administrative meetings of the Society of Friends. Yet by the summer of 1806 she had been uncomfortably conscious for almost a year of a small insistent voice prompting her to speak in the meetings for worship. "Very trying," she had said, on first becoming aware of it, "… so much so that I longed to run out of meeting." Rather than run, however, she had suffered, tormented over whether an urge to express a text of scripture that had very often occurred to her that day came from God, or from her own vivid imagination.

Ever since the dawn of Quaker quietism,[1] and its uncertainties regarding the origin of impulses to speak aloud, even experienced ministers often suffered agonies. Fearful that their response might be to what was creaturely and base, rather than the divine will, many often chose to remain silent. For Betsy, young, eager to please, and yet always fearing rebuff, the thought that during the long hours of silence she might rise to her feet and address the hushed rows of her fellows was an anguish almost too painful to contemplate.

Yet however much she tried to ignore it, in Meeting after Meeting, as Bible texts and the names of people needing her public prayers came unbidden into her mind, the inner voice constantly pressed her to speak.

During Yearly Meeting, late in May, she noted in her journal how a guest at the crowded Mildred's Court dinner table prophesied to her; "that I should also so prove among others to be as a city that is set on a hill that cannot be hid." Privately, she hoped it might be as a workhouse visitor that she should shine, not as someone who stood up in public waiting for God to put words into her mouth.

Less than two weeks later she gave birth to her fourth child, another boy, who was named William after his grandfather Fry. Afterwards, as she struggled with depression, she also resorted guiltily to laudanum to relieve an irritation of the bowels that was accompanied by agonising cramps in her stomach.

In September 1806, her Monthly Meeting appointed her representative to her Quarterly Meeting.

Three months later, with Joseph beside her, she was at Tasburgh Meeting House near Norwich, to see her sister Louisa marry Sam Hoare of Hampstead. Although she sometimes found Sam a little high-handed, and regretted that the Hoare bankers were Gay Quakers rather than Plain, together with both families Betsy applauded the match. Rachel Gurney described the wedding in her journal. "It was a most pleasant sight," she said, "to have so long a train of brothers and sisters in wedding garments, … the whole day was without a cloud."[2]

No one, however, said anything similar about the wedding of the younger John Gurney, and neither family applauded the match. For the good-looking, charming John, already a huge success at Gurney's Bank in King's Lynn, had become engaged to Uncle Richard's daughter Elizabeth, his first cousin. It was a union strictly prohibited among Friends, and many in the family felt it foreshadowed disaster. Few of them attended the ceremony in January 1807, and for Betsy, especially, the gloom cast by the unnatural marriage was darkened further by news from Goat Lane. To her horror, she learned that William Crotch had taken his own life, and as suicide returned once more to haunt her, she prayed that having so faithfully performed his duty to God, her old friend was now granted peace. At the same time, she also prayed for herself, "that whatever afflictions are vouchsafed, I may, if consistent with His will, be saved from such an end."

In the spring of 1807 Betsy left her four children with her sister Rachel and went with Joseph on a business trip to the north of England. Since their unsuccessful adventure in 1802, it was still only the second time in their married life that they had been alone together for anything more than hours, and reflecting on the constant demands of children, family and business, she looked back nostalgically to the rare snug evenings of their courtship and early married life. Journeying northwards through Sheffield, Leeds, and Newcastle and then returning south through Manchester, she tried to recapture the romance and intimacy that lived in her imagination. "How I have loved him the last few days," she wrote in mid-April, "what an increasing treasure would he become to me, if he could keep more constantly after good."

In May, they were both at Earlham to see Hannah marry Thomas Fowell Buxton. The bridegroom, a nephew of Uncle Gurney's wife, had been close to the Earlham family for years, and they had always sensed he was destined for great things. Since 1803, when he gained the first of many student honours at Trinity College, Dublin, they had become even more convinced. "He was indeed a noble youth," Kitty wrote years later, "full of well-directed ambition, and gifted with uncommon energy and perseverance in the right use of his talents."

It was a memorable wedding. "The house was overrun by bridesmaids in muslin cloaks and chip hats," Rachel recorded,

"... dressed alike in white with small nosegays, except the bride, who looked lovely, who was still more white, and was distinguished by one beautiful rose."

Watching her sister, who radiated happiness as she stood beside the very tall, studious-looking young man who so obviously adored her, Betsy's thoughts travelled back to the time when she herself hadn't felt much like a bride all day.

Betsy's fifth child, Richenda, was born in February 1808. *"In labour,"* she wrote ominously on the day her pains began. Three weeks earlier she had been at Hampstead, nursing Louisa's new baby, then at East Ham, nursing Eliza Fry's. It had all helped take her mind off the agony to come.

Another long depression followed the birth, while at the same time, Betsy's sense of domestic inadequacy was fuelled by Miss Mary Ann Davies, recently employed as governess to the older girls. "She has expressed great discouragement about the situation," Betsy said dispiritedly. To Miss Davies's concern, and Betsy's embarrassment, not only did Katherine remain a disobedient and disruptive child, but her sister Rachel seemed set to outdo her.

An inability to keep to her stern decision about alcohol added to Betsy's anxieties. Though constantly vowing to bear her pain until divine relief eventually arrived, when the stomach cramps grew severe, or the dark thoughts in her mind too insistent, she often reached out guiltily for the remedies that numbed them. Miserably she prayed for help. "Be with me if thou seest meet O Lord, guard me when I cannot take care of myself," she begged at the beginning of April, 1808, after being confined to bed for several weeks. "May nothing ever separate me from thy love, ... enable me not improperly to seek for consolation in any way inconsistent with thy will."

To her astonishment, the very next day she felt better. That she did so is perhaps another indication that Betsy's physical ailments were largely provoked by emotional distress. A week later, after getting up for breakfast, she went with Joseph to Barking to see her brother Sam marry Elizabeth Sheppard, a daughter of John Gurney's cousins, James and Sarah Sheppard of Ham House, West Ham. Though Sam had left Mildred's Court the previous year, when John Gurney launched him in business on his own account, the thought of not seeing her protégé married had completely restored Betsy to health.

In May, Betsy and Joseph gathered with the Gurneys once more, but this time, rather than wedding clothes, they wore black, for John's wife, Elizabeth, had died giving birth to her first child. To many of those present it seemed as if their ominous premonitions had come true. Betsy herself so nearly collapsed with emotion that later she was ashamed. But as the hearse and its black-plumed horses had moved slowly towards her along Earlham's avenue of limes, a cloud had passed over the sun, and in its shadow, she felt death's bony fingers gripping her heart.

Deborah Darby and a friend from Coalbrookdale stayed on at Earlham after the funeral, and when Betsy visited them again in the summer they expressed their belief that many among the Gurneys had been touched by the Holy Spirit. If they were faithful to its leading, Deborah said, they would become bright and shining lights to their generation.

Gloomily, Betsy wondered if that could still include her. Despite all prophecy, she still felt no quickening of spiritual life, and her work with the poor and the workhouse children showed little sign of leading to anything of greater magnitude. "Instead of being, as I had hoped, a useful instrument in the church militant," she said sorrowfully, "here I am a careworn wife and mother, outwardly nearly devoted to the things of this life."

Perhaps instead of herself, the shining lights would be Joseph John and Priscilla, who to Betsy's surprise were both drawing closer to Friends. Though she felt relief on their behalf, she also sensed apprehension for other members of her family who appeared to be abandoning their Quaker inheritance – not, as Uncle Joseph had once feared, for the world, but for Anglicanism with its liturgies and hireling priests. In Betsy's view, Kitty, Rachel and Richenda were far too influenced by members of the Church of England: by cousin Peggy Lindoc, who had abandoned Unitarianism when she married

William Jones, the Rector of Clare in Suffolk, and by the Reverend Edward Edwards, an Anglican clergyman at Lynn who had become the friend and comforter of their bereaved brother John.

Increasingly troubled, and anxious to plead the Quaker path of inner reflection, she sought out Kitty. It was the opinion of herself and her husband, she told her older sister, "that she has rather too much studied religious subjects for her good and whether more simply consulting her feelings in some things might not prove a safer guide."

Kitty was furious. That Betsy, the religious enthusiast, should dare to criticise her own search for faith was too much to endure, and in a rage she turned on her sister. Betsy was surprised and bewildered, for she had truly meant well. "I shew her a letter from Joseph," she said, "expressing his sentiments upon this inward seeking – which appeared to give her very great pain and made her express what I felt exceedingly that nobody gave her *such pain as I did.*"

Like many individuals who are passionate about their beliefs, Betsy sometimes appeared remarkably insensitive to the feelings of other family members. All too often it was Kitty, so obviously capable and intelligent, but who had been denied a husband as well as the opportunity for individual self-fulfilment, who appears to have suffered most. Betsy, meanwhile, reflected on how often her own family misunderstood her, so that sometimes there seemed a great gulf between them.

Between Betsy and Father Fry, however, after his wife's death the gulf between them had narrowed. For both had discovered, finally, that in each other's company they could enjoy simple pleasures; carriage drives in country parks, cosy teatimes with the children, or admiring together the gardens at Plashet. When he fell sick, in the autumn of 1808, Betsy was his chief nurse.

He died at Mildred's Court with Betsy beside him, a little before two in the morning on 15 October. Later, Betsy reflected on his journey towards death. During the first part of his illness he was afraid, she said, although reassured by the innocence of his life. But, after taking to his bed for the last time, "he appeared more powerfully to feel the necessity of feeling an interest in that power that can *alone* do all things for us." She had found it comforting to see Father Fry's fear change gradually to acceptance, and eventually to hope, and towards the end she was conscious of "a sweetness attending him". After he was gone, instead of feeling the anxiety that had accompanied mother Fry's passing, she felt her spirits rise.

Scarcely was she home from the funeral than she was sent for to nurse Hannah and Fowell through scarlet fever. She went despite having her new baby, Richenda, at the breast, having four susceptible little ones at home, and being extraordinarily busy with the relocation to Plashet where she and Joseph were to succeed the deceased Fry parents. She regarded it as "a great privilege", she said, to throw herself once more into nursing and the management of a sickroom. That she thought so perhaps indicates a growing fascination with the subject, as well as her constant need to "really be able to lessen the sorrows of the afflicted". Over Christmas, still supervising the relocation, she went to London to nurse a dying aunt.

"I do not think I have ever expressed the pleasures and enjoyments I find in a country life both for myself and the dear children," she said, as in March 1809, and once again pregnant, she completed the move to her new home.

As mistress of her own great house, Betsy's thoughts turned back to Earlham. Together with her Irish gardener, Dennis Regan, she filled her Essex gardens with the pale yellow primroses that adorned her native county, and as she explained to her children the wonders of the natural world – the life cycle of the frogs that hopped around the Plashet fish ponds, the structure of insects, or the development of flowers – she often recalled Catherine Gurney and the quiet efficiency with which she had managed her household and family.

Sadly, Betsy knew she had inherited none of it. Her servants still had the power to intimidate her, and she was frequently involved in misunderstandings with them, while between themselves they squabbled discontentedly. As her children continued in their embarrassingly unruly course, she was also miserably aware that her sisters had named them "Betsy's brats".

In September 1809, after the birth of her sixth child, another boy who was named Joseph after his father, Joseph Fry took a house at Tunbridge Wells where Betsy could recuperate in peace.

Early in October, sad news arrived there. Sarah Williman, the old Earlham nurse, had died at Lynn while nursing Dan through scarlet fever. "This awfully brings death home," Betsy noted in her journal. Weeks later there was more news, that although reassuring, still gave cause for concern. Priscilla had also taken the fever but was recovering, and John Gurney, who had undergone the second of two major operations, was also ultimately expected to mend. The thought of the pain he had suffered caused Betsy intense distress, and she knew that before submitting to the procedure he had feared for his life. She herself had prayed desperately that just like his fears in 1804 over the French invasion and his potential business losses, her father's dread would also ultimately prove groundless.

On 26 October, Betsy's sister Richenda arrived unexpectedly at the Tunbridge Wells house in an express coach. John Gurney was dying. As she heard it, Betsy suddenly remembered the dark cloud at Earlham, and the hand that had clutched at her heart. Almost immediately, with Joseph and the new baby beside her, she set out for Norfolk, desperate for the news that waited at each stage on the road. She reached Earlham at midnight on 27 October. Leaving the baby with Joseph, she ran to her father's room.

By the light of the steadily glowing candles, as her heart pounded and her breath came in gasps, she stared at the figure lying motionless on the bed. "And once more," she said, "*saw him* who has been so *inexpressibly* dear to me through life, since I knew what love was."

She was too familiar now with death not to see his presence strongly marked on John Gurney's face, "his sweet, and to me, beautiful face", but just as with Father Fry, she sensed that around the dying man "*all was sweetness.*"

As his last moments approached, despite being over-whelmed by waves of great pain, John Gurney spoke longingly of his dear Catherine who was gone before him. Then, reaching out to his children, he bade them hold on their way, and reassured them that their love of what was good, in the way each of them displayed it, had been a source of great encouragement to him.

Finally, almost inaudibly, he whispered that he feared no evil at last, but believed that through the mercy of God he should be received into glory.

He died very early on Saturday 28 October. Too distressed to be there at the end, later as dawn broke Betsy went alone into his shrouded room. There, in the pearly half-light, she was gripped by emotions so intense that she fell to her knees. "My soul was bowed within me," she said, "not only in love for the deceased, but also the living, and in humble thankfulness, so that I could hardly help uttering (which I did) my thanksgiving and praise."

Kneeling by her father's corpse, staring at the man who had been so central to her life, something in her depths began to stir. Fluttering and tremulous at first, it grew steadily more powerful, until, to her astonishment, the beautiful voice that John Gurney had loved, and Betsy had suppressed, burst from her mouth in a song of praise to Almighty God. "I cannot understand it," she said, "but the power given was wonderful to myself and the *cross none*. My heart was so full that I could, I believe, hardly hinder utterances."

"I have desired to leave this event," she said later, "but it was a glorious time, such a one as I never passed through, all love, all joy, all peace, or the nearest I think, to that state, that I ever experienced."

The night before the funeral, Betsy prayed: if such words, with such power, came to her again, and if it was God's will for her, then let her utter them.

Next day, the Gildencroft was full; with Gurneys, their relatives, the Earlham household and old family friends, as well as the people of Norwich come to pay their respects. Letting the solemn silence wash over her, Betsy was aware that the words she had uttered at her father's bedside, and that had been with her ever since, were still powerfully present. She also felt the insistent inner voice, that had been with her since 1805, prompting her to speak them aloud.

Following her father's coffin to the burying ground, Betsy sensed the impulse growing stronger. As it did so, she saw that the grass around the graves was intensely green, while the half-naked autumn trees seemed etched with almost unbearable clarity against the sky. Sunshine glanced fitfully through the branches, and a gusting wind tossed them, dislodging dry leaves.

When Uncle Joseph praised and lamented his dead brother, Betsy began to tremble.

Eventually, the new John Gurney of Earlham turned to lead the assembly away from the grave, and as he did so, a rush of wind tore through the trees, rattled the branches, and sent leaves whirling and scattering. As they flew past her, Betsy fell to her knees, and with the sun in her eyes and the wind in her ears she raised her hands to heaven. For a moment there was a startled silence. Then her voice, clear, sweet and melodious, rang out over the burying ground and into the clustering streets of Norwich. "Great and marvellous are thy works Lord God Almighty," she cried, "just and true are all thy ways, thou king of saints, be pleased to receive our thanksgiving."

Whatever the complex emotions were that bound Betsy to her father, which had continued to lie between them, and which for almost 30 years had evidently caused her to repress huge swathes of her personality and creative impulses, his death had at last set them free.

"I may be mistaken," she observed, "but my own view of myself is this. I am a little like a bottle that has long been corked up and pressed down, and now there is an opening made there appears much to run out."

CHAPTER EIGHT

The theatre of action

"**W**E WANT NO WINE**," murmured an elderly clergyman, "for there is that amongst us that does instead."

The Great Parlour of Earlham Hall was hushed, and as the silence lengthened and grew deeper, the guests bowed their heads in awe. Before them on the massive dining table, silverware and glassware gleamed and sparkled, while an abundance of warmly-toned autumn flowers contrasted vividly with a radiant white cloth. Through the high windows, with their views of green trees, came golden beams of September sunlight, slanting over the bowed heads and laden table, and resting finally on the simple white cap of a fair-faced young woman who knelt on a richly patterned carpet. Moments earlier, she had called down God's blessing on the newly formed Norwich auxiliary of the British and Foreign Bible Society.

After its foundation in 1804, local branches of the interdenominational Bible Society had sprung up all over the country. In Norwich, the foundation meeting in September 1811 had attracted a crowd of over 600, that included the mayor in his gold chain and the bishop, Bishop Bathurst, in lawn sleeves. Later the same day, Joseph John Gurney, the new branch's principal sponsor, hosted a dinner at Earlham for 34 guests, including the Reverend Joseph Hughes, the Baptist secretary of the Society.

"After dinner," Hughes recalled later, "... the pause encouraged by the Society of Friends was succeeded by a devout address from a female minister, Elizabeth Fry, whose manner was so impressive, and whose words were so appropriate, that none present can ever forget them."[1]

Many of the guests who were not Friends were startled – some even shocked – to see a woman take the initiative in prayer, but when they recalled how their hearts had burned within them, they were forced to reconsider. When God chose to visit his people, claimed one of their number, "neither *sex* nor *anything* else stood in the way of his grace."

Betsy recorded her own memories. "It was like having our high priest amongst us," she said, and she recalled how one dinner guest, clasping her hand, had said, "Through you, madam, we were brought to Jesus' feet."

Ever since John Gurney's funeral, when Betsy gave tongue to a voice and passions long suppressed, the power that released her had continued its work of transformation. "I feel and see things as I never did before," she said, "and, I think, what would be called, *opening*, spiritually."

She had described herself as a bottle, long corked up, with much to run out; now, with the opening made, she felt an ardent desire to share with the world the overpowering sense of love and thanksgiving that had come upon her at her dead father's bedside. But insecure and still apprehensive of the inner voice that urged her to speak, she sought reassurance. How could she be certain, she asked Uncle Joseph, whether the prompting was of the Holy Spirit, rather than her own fertile imagination, or even Satan tempting her with the promise of worldly glory?

The extraordinary events at the Gildencroft had convinced Joseph Gurney that his early sense of Betsy's gifts had been right, and he was eager to help her. "Walk by faith and not by sight," he said, and reflecting on his own long experience, he assured her that simple obedience to inner prompting almost invariably led to peace and an increase of faith, whilst refusal generally caused confusion. In time, he continued, she would learn discernment, and if now she stumbled occasionally or sometimes felt foolish, the knowledge that God's hand was upon her would carry her through.

"I have dared to open my mouth in public," Betsy wrote

boldly in December 1809, "I am ready to say what is come to me."

At Gracechurch Street, and at Plaistow Meeting House near Plashet, extempore prayers and praise flowed from Betsy's lips. Bible verses that impressed themselves on her mind were spoken aloud and followed eventually by personal testimony and preaching; the words and phrases a combination of her own carefully considered thoughts and others that appeared to enter her mind at need. In time, she learned to trust the inner voice, so that sometimes, with nothing at all in her mind, she rose at its insistence, opened her mouth, and allowed words full of "power and life" to flow out.

Despite the certainty that she spoke at God's command, however, and despite Uncle Joseph's support and an outward self-assurance, inwardly she remained insecure. "Can such a one as I have concerns," she often asked. She also worried about what Friends really thought of her, especially if she felt she had spoken too long or too often. Regularly at night she lay wakeful, replaying words and scenes in her mind as she attempted to recall expressions or reactions that indicated all was not well. Frequently she went in secret to ask "a feeling friend" for reassurance.

Yet Friends encouraged her and her reputation grew. Her low, melodious voice became familiar at Quaker Meetings throughout London, and many who heard it found profound truths and deep insights revealed to them, while in the deep silences that followed, they often sensed that heaven's peace itself enfolded them.

Sometimes, after such meetings, women approached Betsy privately to relieve anxieties long kept secret. Often they also asked her for advice, or to pray for them. Surprisingly, she also discovered that it was often the words she found hardest of all to speak when prompted, that touched such women most and brought them to her. At other times, she learned by hearsay that her words had relieved someone's long-stored troubles, or provided answers to questions and confusions.

"My dearest Joseph was kind enough to stay at home to nurse," Betsy wrote early in 1810, "to let me go to afternoon Meeting." But although she was grateful for that instance and for many others, Joseph's acquiescence fuelled a growing sense of guilt. For while there were many female Quaker ministers, few, if any, pursued their religious work while leaving young children in the care of their fathers. Increasingly troubled, she continually asked herself whether God could really be calling her to leave her family. But no matter how often she asked the question, which way she looked at it, or what answers she provided, there could be no denying that a powerful inner voice constantly bade her go out into the life of the world.

Once again, however, just like the conflict caused by her reliance on alcohol to ease physical and mental suffering, the discrepancy between the social conventions surrounding motherhood, and the reality of a mother who found fulfilment away from her family, provoked a huge inner discord. As one part of her struggled to focus on the family life she fully intended to devote herself to on her return, and another part felt exhilarated whenever she walked away, she began more regularly to confess her anguished thoughts on the subject to the haven of her journal.

As Joseph took on more of the burden of family and household, he was also forced to recognise that the eager promise once made by a young man in love – to always support Betsy in her religious work – was now becoming a central part of their marriage. Although it was not what he would have chosen, and as Betsy remarked to her journal, he was equally lost when it came to disciplining their offspring, there was something in Joseph that seems to have preferred life with the family at Plashet to the rigours of his desk in the City. He felt far more at ease in the country, and during Betsy's increasingly frequent absences he liked to share with his children the outdoor sports and games that he loved, while with a disturbingly exhilarating sense of guilt he often led them in gleeful singsongs, jolly country dances, and wild games of hide-and-seek. They liked being with him too, and they relished his easygoing nature, so unlike their mother, who was always so earnest, so insistent about prayer, so rigorous over Meeting, over Quaker dress and behaviour, and who so soon became flustered.

In June 1810, Betsy ministered alongside Uncle Joseph and Coalbrookdale's Cousin Priscilla, and despite the sorrow of the occasion – the funeral of a friend dead in childbirth – she found their family unity extraordinarily satisfying. "I might truly say my cup ran over, such sweetness covered my mind," she said.

In the second half of the year, despite another pregnancy, she began leaving Joseph and the children for much longer periods as she travelled to Quaker Meetings beyond London. In September she was in Essex, and in November, in Surrey. Early in December she travelled with Joseph to Earlham, where she also spoke at Norwich, while shortly after Christmas, she was once again in Essex.

Between journeys she found time to nurse relatives: Louisa's children in April, with whom she sat up all night as they burned with fever, and Louisa herself in May, during another labour and lying-in.

She also ministered regularly alongside Richard Phillips, an older colleague at Gracechurch Street, who, rather like William Savery earlier, attracted her with his confidence and experience. "I have desired, if it be right, that my union with my beloved friend RP may continue to grow, and may we prove true help mates to each other," she said, " … for I believe the babe may help those further advanced as well as they may help the babes."

In February 1811 Betsy gave birth to her seventh child. The labour came on more than a month early, in the middle of weeks of activity, but with Doctor Sims in attendance, the small and delicate being arrived safely, and was named Elizabeth after her mother. Like her mother, the family also called her Betsy. Unusually, there was little post-natal depression.

In March Betsy was formally recorded as a minister of the Society of Friends. "It brings me prostrate before the great I Am," she said, as she saw Deborah Darby's prophecy at last coming to pass. Three months later she was ministering again in Essex, this time in the company of another male Friend, the

American Henry Hull, and becoming uncomfortably aware that the almost inevitable closeness of a successful joint ministry could lead to more dangerous emotions. "I have felt so nearly united to our dear friend H. Hull in particular," she confessed, "that I feared natural affection being too much excited." Later in life she would often lament that her own husband was unwilling to be a partner in her religious activities, and recalling how she had once dreamed of travelling beside William Savery, it is possible to conclude that such a relationship, perhaps with an older and more experienced man, always remained her ideal. In a more vigilant frame of mind, however, having instructed herself not to be led into temptation, she went with Henry to Uxbridge and to Brentford, and then made plans to attend Suffolk Quarterly Meeting after a visit to Norfolk in September.

It was discouraging for Betsy to discover while at Earlham, that her sisters disapproved of her ministry. "Dear Chenda thought the children ought to be under more subjection," she wrote sadly, before adding that Louisa thought "I devoted that time to Friends, that I should devote to them." Although her brothers, John and Daniel, had always made it clear that they were opposed to any public role for Christian women, and John in particular made no secret of having found the events surrounding John Gurney's funeral particularly distasteful, Betsy had perhaps expected more of her sisters. Especially so perhaps, since the one who levelled accusations of incompetence and neglect was herself childless, while the other had not objected when Betsy left her own family to care for hers. That Priscilla, who now shared so much with Betsy in terms of faith, agreed with them, made it even worse. "Dear Priscilla cast me very low," Betsy said, "by saying her faith was at times try'd by my so often leaving my family."

Although Betsy was saddened, she was also uncomfortably aware that the accusations had substance. Sometimes, when her children's shrill voices and the relentless drumming of their boots on wooden benches forced her to leave Meeting early, she was both embarrassed and bitterly ashamed. It was some consolation that the older girls at least did seem to enjoy sharing her charitable work at Plashet.

She often took Katherine and Rachel with her to the girls' school she had founded with Mr Anglezark, the vicar of East Ham. It was housed in an ancient building just opposite Plashet's gates, and Harriet Howell, its young teacher, ran it on the Lancastrian system, Joseph Lancaster's monitorial method which had now become popular all over the country.

They also often helped in the room within Plashet House itself that held the supplies for Betsy's work with the local poor: rolls of calico and flannel, and racks of warm outer clothing. There was also a drugstore there, for during her years of family nursing Betsy had taken careful note of remedies prescribed, so that by 1810, whenever a servant, an estate worker, or a local villager fell sick, Mrs Fry was ready with medicines as well as nursing skills, blankets and prayers. She had also persuaded another of her family physicians, Dr Willan,[2] to instruct her in the technique of vaccination, and through her skill, the region around Plashet was kept almost free of smallpox.

The girls themselves especially liked visiting Irish Row, two strings of dingy cottages on the highroad between Stratford and Ilford. "At that time they were squalid and dirty," Katherine and Rachel recalled in their *Memoir*, "The windows generally stuffed with old rags, or pasted over with brown paper, ... puddles of thick black water before the doors; children without shoe or stocking; mothers, whose matted locks escaped from the remnants of caps, which looked as though they never could have been white; pigs, on terms of evident familiarity with the family; poultry, sharing the children's potatoes – all bespoke an Irish colony."[3] There they acted as their mother's almoners, as Madam Fry, as the Irish inhabitants always called her, distributed food and clothing, encouraged children to attend school, and with the agreement of the Roman Catholic priest, made presents of Bibles.

The girls also loved their visits to the gypsy camp that appeared in a green lane near Plashet each year when Fairlop

Fair drew close, where there were more clothes and Bibles to hand out to the swarthy, exotic inhabitants.

But there were also times when Katherine and Rachel felt uneasy. When they saw their mother sitting comfortably on an upturned bucket, or on the steps of a gypsy caravan, surrounded by a clambering host of dirty children, her two clean and comfortably clad daughters often fell silent. If they observed her lifting a particularly grubby infant onto her knee, and smiling into its eyes and talking to it in such a tender and familiar way that it wound its little arms around her neck, they wondered why she was never so easy with them.[4]

They were uneasy too, as was their father, when Betsy introduced extempore prayer and testimony into their household's domestic routine. Despite their objections, however, she remained resolute, for when the inner voice prompted, either during the morning Bible reading, or even before meals, she believed she was bound to obey. And she did know how they felt, she assured her family, and exactly how uncomfortable it could be, for among the personal shortcomings she often felt obliged to mention, she frequently included her own.

If the shortcomings concerned her still-intimidating servants, who now joined the family regularly for prayers, then Betsy generally experienced an almost paralysing sense of self-consciousness. Yet, stubbornly, she was determined to include them and consider their welfare, both in time and in eternity. "I do not think they have generally justice done to them," she said of servants in general, "they are too much considered as another race of beings, and we are apt to forget that the holy injunction holds good with them, 'Do as thou would'st be done unto.'"

She felt the same about her husband, her children, and her wider family. Even if Joseph insisted on reading novels and occasionally slipped off to a concert, if Katherine and Rachel appeared resentful of their mother's insistence that present piety would lead to later fulfilment, and if Kitty took offence over remarks about her spiritual path, Betsy resolved that she would continue to speak to them about her concerns, and pray for their right direction, just as she would wish them all to do for her. If they chose to regard her as an enthusiast, to ignore her, or even to mock her, she would nevertheless continue to do what she believed was God's work, and if necessary, suffer the consequences.

As the first decade of the nineteenth century passed away, however, and attitudes were changing rather than remaining an object of contempt, or a cause for concern among Christian parents, religious enthusiasm was rapidly becoming respectable. At the same time the philosophies based on Deism, that had questioned Christianity and scorned ardent faith, were themselves becoming less influential. Passionate prayer, preaching and public testimony to God's grace were now heard even within the established church, whose earlier rejection of the enthusiasts Wesley and Whitefield had led them to preach their message elsewhere, where it began the revival that was now flooding vigorously into the church that had once rejected it.

Among the most potent expressions of the Evangelical movement was the group later known as the Clapham Sect.

In the 1790s, while the young Betsy Gurney hungered for Virtue and was transformed by her encounter with William Savery, a group of British Christians were planning the transformation of their nation. Originally based at Clapham, close to the Gurneys' Barclay relatives, their leader was William Wilberforce, Member of Parliament, leader of the campaign against the slave-trade, and a man who believed God had called him to convert Britain to a nation based on Biblical principles.

It was the lack of such principles, Wilberforce believed, that had led to the infidelity and corruption he saw at the heart of Britain's national life, that spoke of contempt for God and his laws, and was reflected in the slave-trade, the exploitation of the poor, the brutality of the prison system, the drunkenness and reckless gambling of the rich, and the enormous sex industry that preyed on the young and the vulnerable. Equally he deplored the lack of example set by Britain's elite – its royal family, its aristocracy, its religious leaders, its businessmen and its politicians – and it was among them, in a disciplined and highly organised manner, that he and his group began their campaign.

"Real Christianity"[5] was the standard to which Wilberforce and his colleagues called the leaders of Britain. It was characterised by conversion and a conscious turning to Christ, together with a zeal for the improvement of self and society. The response was often startling. For in a country undergoing rapid industrial change, where there was corruption and little moral certainty, and which had been at war for over fifteen years, there was a desperate hunger for meaning. To many people, Wilberforce's call seemed like an invigorating wind gusting through stale and torpid air, blowing away the fog of dissolute and empty lives and replacing them with energy and purpose.

The testimonies that Betsy had heard at Gracechurch Street in 1801, from Friends turning once more to the light, were part of the wider movement. So too were her own household prayers, and her morning Bible readings that had been so innovative in 1800, but which by 1810 were becoming commonplace in a land where increasing numbers of individuals spoke of infidelity rejected, lives renewed, and of pledges made to Jesus, the Bible, and revelation.

Among those individuals were some of Betsy's relatives. In September 1809, shortly before her father's death, and with his full agreement, Kitty was baptised into the Church of England. The man who finally effected her conversion was her friend the Reverend Edward Edwards, who was himself the friend of Charles Simeon, vicar of Holy Trinity Church, Cambridge, where he mentored the university's Evangelical ordinands, Henry Venn, Charles' own mentor, and Henry's son John Venn, Rector of Clapham and the close friend of William Wilberforce. Later, Kitty was followed into the church by her sisters Richenda and Hannah, and by Hannah's husband, Thomas Fowell Buxton.

Early in life, Fowell had expected to inherit a large property in Ireland, but when his hopes came to nothing, and after his graduation and marriage to Hannah Gurney, he took a junior post in the London offices of the brewers, Truman & Hanbury, with prospects of a partnership after three years probation. Close to his first married home in Brick Lane, lay the Wheler Street Chapel, where, eventually, the Evangelical preaching of the minister, Josiah Pratt, brought Fowell to faith. Shortly after his conversion, during the scarlet fever where Betsy was his nurse, he had confronted the possibility of death. "No one action of my life presented itself then as any sort of consolation," he wrote to a friend, "'I know that my Redeemer liveth' was the sentiment uppermost in my mind."[6]

Earlier, Joseph John Gurney had undergone a similar experience. "I must bear steady testimony to the truth in this world," he wrote in 1808, "I must bow with resignation to the will of my God in all temporal and spiritual trials. In short, I must draw near unto Christ, and, if need be, take up my cross to follow Him."[7]

By then, Joseph John had travelled a long way from his timid childhood. A friendship with the Buxton boys, Fowell and his brother Charles, who liked to swim, climb trees and ride powerful horses, had helped overcome his early fears, while rapid promotions at the Norwich branch of Gurney's Bank had given him confidence. Two years with a private tutor at Oxford had also made him a scholar, particularly of the Bible and its ancient languages.

In 1811, under the guidance of Uncle Joseph, Joseph John and his sister Priscilla both became Plain Friends. They also brought something new to their Quaker tradition: the fruit of Joseph John's biblical scholarship and their friendship with Edward Edwards and his companions, which was also, in their view, very much in the spirit of George Fox and the first Friends. Quakers firmly wedded to quietism and exclusivity saw such a development as a threat, but others, eager to embrace its vibrant spirituality, rallied to it. Very quickly Joseph John Gurney found himself the leader of an Evangelical movement within British Quakerism that emphasised the Bible, social action, and working in partnership with other Christian groups.[8]

His sponsorship in 1811 of the Norwich Bible Society appeared to him to embody perfectly the Christian co-operation he sought to further, and his dinner guests were, he said, "a perfectly harmonious mixture of High Church, Low Church, Lutheran, Baptist, Quaker!"[9] For his sister Betsy, too, the meeting and subsequent dinner were "a sign of the times". Despite her earlier objections, by 1811 she too had become a friend of Edward Edwards, and a decided supporter of Joseph John.

A sign of the times, too, were the many other Christian organisations springing from the Evangelical movement, that sought to transform life and conditions both in Britain and overseas. And as newly converted men and women throughout Britain began seeing with new eyes, they also saw that thousands of their fellow human beings were not only strangers to the Gospel, but were also the victims of poverty, vice and enslavement. At the same time, many of those who emerged to lead the new movements were intensely practical individuals, who welcomed progressive developments in science and social issues. While they rejected its criticisms of Christianity, they accepted much else that had come from the Enlightenment, especially the theory that people were the product of their environment and could be changed and improved by the reform of public institutions.[10] When they combined this with an Evangelical passion to win lost souls for God, they represented a powerful force.

As they and their followers set to work, separation from the world no longer seemed a virtuous path for Christians. "Action is the life of virtue," wrote Hannah More, Evangelical author and the leading female member of Wilberforce's Abolition Society, "and the world is the theatre of action."[11]

In January 1812 Betsy set out on a long and demanding religious journey through southern England. With her went her sister Priscilla, who had reconsidered her earlier harsh opinions of Betsy's ministry, and Henry Hull. Together they travelled over 200 miles and visited 18 separate Meetings and many Quaker families. Later, in March, after nursing her younger children through feverish winter colds, when she sometimes stayed up with them for nights on end, she made a similar visit to Norfolk. But in April, to Betsy's anguish, the driving energy that had carried her through the miles was suddenly terminated by another black depression. Her only consolation was Joseph's tender care. "How sweet the endearing attention," she said.

Barely was the depression beginning to lift, and the children recover from a bout of whooping cough, than there was Yearly Meeting, that was itself followed by tragedy when Henry Hull's wife, son, mother and mother-in-law all died of a contagious disease. Though the shock, and the emotional strain of ministering to her friend wore Betsy out, there was to be no rest, for while Henry stayed with her at Plashet, so too did William and Eliza Fry, their three children and two servants, together with Joseph's unmarried sister Elizabeth, and his Cousin Sarah.

Betsy almost collapsed under the strain. "I am sorry to say," she said, "I have at times felt so *weighed down* and almost *panting for rest* that I have been almost irritable." Guilty that she had not been more accommodating and more cheerful, she put her bad temper down to the effects of her eighth pregnancy in twelve years, fear of labour and a constant toothache. Then, anxious to be positive, she counted her blessings: good friends, her attentive, if un-Quakerly husband, and her healthy children, some of whom were now reaching an age where she hoped religion, rather than self-will, would become their guide. She was grateful too for the Frys' wealth, that enabled them to welcome relatives and friends, entertain lavishly and be generous friends to the poor. For, she said, "*I fear really to pinch* would be *very difficult* to me."

Later in the year, however, shortly after the birth of Hannah, Bety's eighth child and fifth daughter, and another lying-in almost free of depression, the Frys were not only pinching, but facing bankruptcy.

Much of the blame was laid on Napoleon Bonaparte, since although his attempts to block European ports to British merchant shipping had largely failed, ongoing commercial conflict in Europe had dragged Britain into a war with the American Republic, her largest single market.[12] Industry was badly hit, for a while the national economy seemed threatened and there was a disastrous run on the banks. Fry's Bank, set up shortly after Joseph's marriage to Betsy to augment the tea business, was among those unable to meet its payments. Blame was also laid on William Fry, who over several years had unwisely lent money to Eliza's family. By implication, Joseph was also at fault, for not being more watchful of his brother.

No matter who was to blame, financial disaster on any level was an almost inconceivable thought. And almost overriding everything else was the reputation of the Society of Friends. For over a hundred years its leading families, all interconnected by marriage, had devoted themselves to business either as bankers or as merchants, and they had staked their collective reputation on their competence and honesty. Should one of their number fall from the high standards expected, it was seen as reflecting on the Society at large. Quakers who fell so far as to become bankrupts were publicly shamed and formally disowned.

At the same time, not only was personal poverty alien to a daughter of Earlham and a wife to the Frys, but ever since childhood Betsy had been reassured by family and friends alike that blessings were divinely ordained, and that Christians who did their duty would certainly continue to receive them. Though she could not resist the nagging thought that not all her family "walked in the fear and law of the Lord", the fact that she herself had struggled so hard to be dutiful, and must surely have made up for the deficiencies of others, reassured her that God would not abandon her.

"I do not think faith has ever led me really to believe we should not yet have prosperity granted us," she said optimistically, "though for a time we may not have the same abundance." Nevertheless she knew that even if Joseph were not personally responsible, any hint of financial irregularity would certainly affect her Quaker ministry. The Gurneys also knew that if the Fry enterprises were to collapse, then by implication they would share some of the disgrace, not only as businessmen, but as Quakers. To forestall disaster on any count their leading bankers took the matter in hand. Early in November,

John, now head of the Earlham family; Sam, whose Lombard Street bill-broking partnership, Overend, Gurney & Co., had prospered enormously since 1807; and Hudson, who since Uncle Gurney's death in 1811 was now elder statesmen of the whole family, all settled themselves at Mildred's Court to study the books.

Finally, after days of anxiety, the three men declared that although the bank was in jeopardy, the tea business remained relatively sound, and taken together they merited support. "There appears to be no doubt Gurney's would do what was needful for us," a relieved Betsy wrote in her journal. But, as they prepared to shore up the Frys, the Gurneys also demanded economies. To alleviate expenses they arranged for Betsy's four oldest children to spend a year with their Uncle Joseph John and their aunts at Earlham. There they would be kept and cared for, and although it is nowhere explicitly stated, the possibility remains that the Gurneys also intended to take the unruly young Frys in hand. At the same time, it was insisted that Betsy, Joseph and their four younger children abandon Plashet, that was so extravagantly wasteful of servants, candles and coals, and return to London and a frugal winter at Mildred's Court.

The shock to Betsy was enormous, and robbed of children and home she struggled to resist the mocking whispers of her old sceptical self. There was no God involved in human destiny, it said.

On the day she returned to Mildred's Court, the clutter left by the counting-house clerks who had used it as a lodging house reminded her so painfully of her first depressing entry there that she sat down and wept. Eventually, her face damp with miserable tears, she gazed from the familiar window out into the court below. Once again, she saw it filled with late-November gloom, while a black drizzle, full of London's soot and grime, fell upon the cobbles. How much she hated it, she thought, the dingy air and frowning walls that made her feel as if she were imprisoned within a gaol. "I have been of late like one with a cloud resting over me or in prison or in bonds," she said. Shuddering at the thought, she turned away and wondered what lay in store during the dark months ahead.

In February 1813, on a bitterly cold afternoon, Stephen Grellet, French aristocrat turned citizen of the United States and Quaker minister, together with William Forster, a British Quaker, hurried to Mildred's Court. They had just left Newgate Gaol and Betsy Fry was the closest Quaker woman they knew to that terrible place, and they desperately needed to unburden themselves to someone whose sympathy they could count on.

Earlier in the winter, after preaching to London's poor, Stephen had advertised a religious meeting for the denizens of the city's underworld, its thieves, pickpockets and prostitutes, and to his amazement, they had turned out in their thousands. His subsequent conversations with them had then led him to visit London's gaols,[13] and it was from the most notorious of them that he and his companion had come to Mildred's Court to be restored with hot tea and warm brandy, while his hostess, listening to them in silence, was conscious only of their words and the regular beating of her heart.

Inside the prison, Stephen Grellet told Betsy, after first visiting convicts sentenced to be hung, he and William had gone into the men's regular yards where young boys were imprisoned among experienced convicts who taught them all the corruption of their wicked trade. But, and Stephen's voice trembled as he spoke, it was when they visited the women's yards with their 300 inmates, whose gaolers had desperately tried to prevent their access, that they saw the most violence, depravity and despair. They had also visited the women prisoners who were sick, in their separate upper chamber, and on entering it, they had been utterly dismayed by the misery that greeted them. Speaking in a hoarse voice, Stephen described sick women laying on a bare stone floor, frozen in the bitter winter weather, on scanty straw rank with urine. He also described the coughs, the sores, the menstrual blood, and the blood that remained unwashed after childbirth. The babies, said Stephen, were virtually naked and cried pitiably.

Betsy set out for Newgate next day. With her was Fowell

Buxton's sister, Anna,[14] and they took large bundles of flannel baby clothes that had been stitched the day before at Mildred's Court by a group of Quaker women.

It was impossible for the gifts to be delivered personally, insisted Mr Newman, Newgate's governor. Not only were the sights and smells of the gaol too much for tender sensibilities, he claimed, but even if the ladies reached the womens' yards, the inmates would attack them. But, Betsy and Anna persisted, and with their allusions to wealthy families and influential connections finally wore him down.

Making her way along the prison's vaulted corridors, whose melancholy gloom was relieved only at long intervals by the baleful glow surrounding evilly hissing gas lamps[15], Betsy became aware of a distant noise and a gagging stink. As she drew closer to what was obviously their source, they grew respectively louder and more loathsome, and as she felt her stomach heave, she glanced at Anna and saw that her friend experienced the same lurching sickness. Presently, they approached a barred door where the smell of unwashed bodies, urine and excrement, alcohol and rancid food, sweat, blood and vomit, became all-pervading, while the noise, of hundreds of voices screaming, bellowing, wailing and sobbing, clamoured in the air and beat frantically upon the ears.

Facing the door, Betsy felt her flesh crawl, and a cold sweat break out on her forehead, while from somewhere deep in her mind came the conviction that she was walking into a half-remembered nightmare. The turnkey dragged open the heavy door, and the nightmare became real. As she stared through the iron grill, an awful recognition dawned on Betsy. Before her in a half-darkness lit by guttering rushlights and a distant fire writhed a seething mass of creatures, half spirit, half human, phantoms with substance, with contorted faces and twisted hearts. Unpredictable and malevolent, they meant everyone harm. Gasping, she stepped back as she saw, reaching towards her with greedy fingers, the spectres that had haunted her childhood, the loathsome creatures that lurked in the shadows and sought to drag her into a darkness from which there was no hope of return.

Presently, forcing the foul air into her lungs, she compelled herself to look again. When she did so, she saw that the creatures before her, who stretched their hands through the bars that confined them, were no nightmare, but human women in need of help. Few were properly clothed, all were dirty, some were obviously drunk, and while those in front whined for money to buy spirits at the prison's tap, those behind punched, clawed and scratched as they fought to take their place.

In her low voice, Betsy asked the turnkey to open the gate. For a moment he stared at her, then he refused. The women in his charge were animals, he said, evil and vicious, who could not be trusted. He himself only went in with another man, and the governor, on the rare occasions he entered, went in guarded. In response Betsy told him that she and Anna intended to clothe the Newgate babies and would not leave until they had done so. Eventually, after a long pause, the gate was opened and the two women walked alone into the women's yard. Behind them, the gate closed with a thud of certainty and the scraping of bolts.

For a moment, there was a silence like that that follows a sharp intake of breath. Then the prisoners surged forward, and surrounding the newcomers they peered at them, patted them, and prodded them, as if anxious to discover whether they were composed of the same human flesh as themselves. But they did no harm, and forcing herself with an enormous effort to stand still, Betsy saw to her horror that lice crawled in the eyebrows and hair of the stinking women that pressed against her. In the women's eyes as she returned their gaze, though she saw insolence, wantonness, confusion and despair, she also saw a terrible and Godless hopelessness.

In the infirmary upstairs, Betsy and Anna clothed every prison baby in new flannel clothes. As she worked, Betsy cuddled them to warm them, and almost without thinking, she reached out to their mothers with a friendly touch, a warm glance or the simple words that mothers share. In the end, clothing every Newgate baby and then delivering bundles of fresh straw for the sick, took three days, and on the final day, before they left, Betsy and Anna prayed. On the dirty floor, where insects crawled and the rats ran at night, surrounded by women who had barely heard of God and knew nothing of his love, the two women knelt down and commended Newgate and its sad inhabitants to his care. To their surprise, some of the women knelt down too, clumsily and uncertainly, and the sight brought tears to Betsy's eyes. Presently, she and Anna wept aloud, and then, as their final prayers pierced the dismal air, and drifted through the loathsome yard, the women around them wept too, for self-pity, for their children, for years of abuse and neglect and for their lives that were forlorn. Back home, Betsy stripped off her clothes that stank of Newgate, and had hot water carried upstairs for a bath. Afterwards, with clean hair and clean clothes, she went to the window that looked out into the Mildred's Court and stared for a long time into the darkness.

CHAPTER NINE

Newgate

*I*N THE SPRING OF 1813, the Frys returned to Plashet. The move, however, was an artifice, a keeping-up of appearances designed by the Gurney bankers to maintain confidence and prevent a further run on Fry's Bank. And although additional savings were also demanded, after 33 years of affluence Betsy found it hard to be frugal. As she struggled to achieve economies, her servants accused her of meanness, while the expectations of her visitors and guests, and those of the local poor, all of them oblivious to the real situation, remained as exorbitant as before. "We are *pressed* upon, at home and abroad," she said.

Early the following year, during more than three months of almost continuously icy weather, for Betsy there could be no question of economy. As the needs of the poor grew desperate, she became frantic to feed them. Dishearteningly, not all them appreciated her efforts, and when the dumplings in meat broth specially prepared in her own kitchen were thrown by one woman to her pigs, Betsy was mortified. Nevertheless, struggling to overcome the urge to regard her neighbours as merely ungrateful, she resolved to persist. "I truly desire to act in this work with a Christian spirit," she said, "still persevering to do my utmost for them and patiently bear their reproach."

It was during the freezing weather that Betsy delivered her first baby. Earlier in the day she had struggled through heavy snow to nearby Ham House, the country manor that Sam Gurney had inherited from his in-laws, ready to reassure her nervous brother and to comfort Elizabeth, his wife. When

Elizabeth's pains began, however, and it became clear that the blocked roads and worsening weather would prevent any doctor from reaching them, Betsy summoned up her courage and took charge of the delivery. Later, after easing the child from Elizabeth's body, she reflected on how her own experiences of labour and her presence at many others had enabled her to do what was necessary. She was also able to empathise with Elizabeth's fear, for once again, Betsy was pregnant.

As death seemed to harry her with a new ferocity, the conviction that this time she would not escape became a torment. So too, did the prospect of even more pregnancies. Struggling with her fear, and with the depressive illness that was so often accompanied by an irritation of the stomach and bowels, she discussed her symptoms with Dr Sims. He had thought about them deeply, he told her, and had finally reached the conclusion that the physical condition was largely the product of nervous anxiety. At first, Betsy was stung by his words. "I feel it rather humbling now after all the fuss that has been made, to have it made out only nervous," she said. However, she had struggled for years to understand the symptoms that plagued her, and with the doctor who was now so familiar to her reaching a new conclusion himself, it seems that his words prompted her to catch a glimpse of something deep. "It is better," she said, "to have our eyes opened to see the sores we may have, than for them to appear to us externally healed, and perhaps the wound deepening underneath." When the sores were seen and felt, she said, adding a reference to the woman described in Luke's gospel who touched the hem of Jesus' garment,[1] what an incentive that was to seek help from the great physician himself.

She also confided her fears to Joseph John. His response, however, was uncompromisingly down-to-earth. "Cheer up," he told her, "and endeavour to believe thyself in tolerable trim, as I am much disposed to think thou art in reality, however sinking thy feelings may be." As a firm believer in the medicinal powers of alcohol, he was also dismissive of her own reservations. "Have no scruples about the third or *fourth* glass being a little inconsistent with the *expected* proceedings of public friends!" he advised.[2]

Despite Dr Sims' observations, and Joseph John's recommendations, as labour approached, Betsy's dread and her physical suffering once more grew intense. Anxiously fearing the worst, she gathered her female friends around her to pray. Chief among them, and now her greatest comforter, was her sister Rachel. The years, and the shared love for Betsy's children that had blossomed within Rachel during their months with her at Earlham, had mellowed both women; as the differences of their adolescence faded into history, their old intimacy, born in their bright airy closet among their tea-sets and dolls, had returned to them once more. Together, as they prayed for Betsy's safe confinement, they also prayed for little Betsy, the premature child who lately had suffered miserably from illness, and also for their brother John, who had never recovered from his young wife's death.

In June 1814, Betsy's ninth child, Louisa, arrived safely, and although her pains were savage, Betsy survived. But in September John died, aged just 33. The final deterioration was rapid, and the sight of her once so promising brother overcome by attacks of physical paralysis and a mental condition that seemed to drag him back to infancy reminded Betsy very powerfully of the inmates of the York asylum that she had visited with her father in 1799. She would rather see John dead, she decided, than he should become like some of them. As death approached, however, John rallied, and in his last days he became lucid once more and turned to his Christian faith. Betsy ministered at his deathbed, alongside Joseph John, the Reverend Edward Edwards, and her sister Priscilla, who had herself been acknowledged a Quaker minister in 1813.

Though comforted by John's restored faith, Betsy arrived home after the funeral physically exhausted and emotionally drained. She was greeted there by news of the death of her cousin, Joseph Gurney Bevan.

The two deaths, so close together, fuelled her own fear and in the face of it, her faith quailed. "I cannot say that at present," she said, "death appears to have no sting for me, or the grave no victory." Nor could she help reflecting sadly on her cousin's warnings of so many years before. Despite her hopes, her constant prayers and her efforts to raise her children as good Quakers, the behaviour of the older Fry children had grown steadily worse. Katherine and Rachel were both selfish and had violent tempers, and they were often rude to their relatives and to their governess, Miss Davies, with whom they argued constantly. Betsy herself often wept at the harshness of their words to her. Rachel was especially rebellious, and took a particularly perverse delight in mocking Friends with sarcastic comments about Plain dress and Plain speech.

"I am sorry to say," Betsy wrote at the beginning of 1815, "that I feel that pressure upon me that I hardly know how to lift up my head." Children, servants, the local poor, the sick, the constant social round of family and friends, and the relentless struggle to save money while still keeping up appearances was a burden that was sometimes too much to be borne. The sense of release, when she left it behind, was immense. And though saying goodbye to her family continued to rack her with guilt, and she continued to question God's purposes, the call to go out into the life of the world was still too powerful to deny.

Too powerful to deny too were her constant worries about the opinions of Friends, that caused her to be for ever on the watch for the least sign of disaffection. But despite her guilt, the worry, and the weariness, it was in her life beyond home, in the theatre of action, that Betsy felt most truly herself. As she listened to pent-up anxieties, ministered to the sick, prayed with the dying and the bereaved, and allowed God's power to flow through her as she preached, she felt that she walked with balance and saw with clarity.

As the year advanced, in between the demands of her local ministry, her religious travels, and entertaining many guests, she spent increasingly long hours nursing little Betsy. Even Dr Sims confessed himself helpless before the distressing symptoms that made the little girl weep so fretfully, and Betsy was often up all night with her feverish child. In July, though desperately weary and growing ever more anxious, she nevertheless felt bound to leave her sick daughter and to travel with Joseph to Liverpool and Manchester. In the previous month, the long war with France had finally ended at Waterloo, and as the British economy, overheated by war, slid into recession, neither Fry's Bank nor the tea business appeared able to withstand the strain. While the country celebrated, Joseph Fry, with Betsy to support him, struggled through a series of fraught business meetings as he fought to stave off impending disaster.

Barely were they home again than little Betsy began sinking. In dark November, after a week of restless feverishness, she was carried one night into her mother's room, where early next day, with her parents beside her she died. "It has pleased Almighty and Infinite Wisdom to take from us our most dear and tenderly beloved child, little Betsy, between four and five years old," Betsy wrote in her journal. The pain was unbearable, faith failed to comfort, and later, she tore from her book many pages of her daughter's dying.

Looking at the lifeless body, Betsy saw there the curious emptiness she had first observed so long ago at Earlham when confronted with the corpse of poor Bob. Even though it helped to reassure her that little Betsy really had reached an "everlasting resting place in Jesus," when the time came she could not bear to part with her child. "The last relicks of my much *loved, kind* and to me beautiful lamb," were too precious to lose, she said, and when her brothers finally bore the little coffin away, Betsy fought desperately and hysterically to stop them. Only Joseph, so stolid and so reassuringly familiar, was able to comfort her. "My dearest husband very tender of a night," she said. Nevertheless, two weeks after the funeral, despite being more than four months pregnant, she set off for Dorset Quarterly Meeting. Being on the move eased the pain.

So too, to her surprise, did the thought of another child, and though little Betsy's body lying cold and alone in Barking burying ground was never absent from her mind, almost feverishly, she looked forward to the coming baby. With Rachel beside her, he arrived safely in April 1816, and was named Samuel Gurney Fry, though always called Gurney to distinguish him from his Uncle Sam. But, by August, his Uncle Sam, Sam's brothers, and their cousin Hudson, were once again coming to the aid of his family. Despite Joseph's efforts, little had been salvaged from the financial collapse, and the losses were enormous.

For a second time, the Gurneys agreed to rescue the Fry business, but so huge was the necessary injection of capital that Joseph and Betsy became almost entirely dependent upon them. It was deeply humiliating, but to Betsy, always so sensitive to the judgements of others, the shame of being a poor relation was particularly galling. She had seen it happen to other people, whose relatives had later treated them shabbily, and though she could not believe her own brothers would behave so cruelly, she sensed that none felt poverty so keenly as those who had once been rich and remained surrounded by rich relations.

She discovered she was right when her own rich relations, unconsciously rubbing salt in her wounds, this time took away six of her children to feed, clothe and educate at their own expense. The reason, she was told, was once again the keeping up of appearances, for before their creditors the Frys could not be seen to spend money on governesses and tutors, while before the world and for their own sakes, the children must be educated. And keeping it in the family ensured it was all done with discretion and the proprieties maintained.

Accordingly, arrangements were made for Richenda and Joseph to share the schoolroom at Ham House with Sam's children, for John and William to go first to Earlham, and then after Christmas, to boarding school, and for Katherine and Rachel to live with their Aunt Rachel and Uncle Dan, who would shortly move together to Runcton Hall, Dan's fine new home near King's Lynn. Secretly, Betsy was rather relieved to be rid of Rachel. "In dear Rachel's very contradictory state," she admitted, "it may even be well to have her under rather a different influence."

That some of that influence would come from non-Quakers, however, was an uncomfortable thought. Dan himself had become deeply antagonistic to Friends, while among his and Rachel's favourite visitors were their sister Richenda and Francis Cunningham, her Evangelical clergyman husband.

Disturbingly, the affable Francis had also very rapidly become young Rachel's favourite uncle, and she made it no secret that not only was she anxious to throw off her Quaker constraints, but that she found Francis' views much more to her taste. Though a respite from Rachel was welcome, it was with a heavy heart that Betsy left her daughters behind.

Despite their battles, she missed them dreadfully. "I found it even pleasant to go and stand by poor old Isaac the horse," she wrote to them, "and the cows and sheep in the field, that I might see some living thing to enliven poor Plashet." In November she moved back to London with Joseph, her three youngest children, Hannah, Louisa and Gurney, plus a few servants. Even under strict instructions to save money, it was a relief to close the empty, echoing country house for the winter and return once more to Mildred's Court.

At Christmas 1816 she went back to Newgate.

Gazing at the prison's frowning walls, and at the images of Justice and Fortitude, Liberty and Prudence, who looked enigmatically down from their gloomy alcoves, Betsy was not entirely certain why she had come. Perhaps it was the sharpness of the weather, reminding her of the days when she and Anna Buxton had clothed the Newgate babies, or it might have been the aching emptiness caused by her children being taken away.

Nor had Newgate ever been entirely absent from her mind. Both Fowell Buxton and Sam Hoare had become involved in movements for prison reform, and together with Sam, Betsy had visited Norwich Gaol and the women's wards at Cold Bath Fields House of Correction in London. There she had seen women raging and neglected, just like those at Newgate, and again it had shocked her. Later, she listened carefully whenever Fowell and Sam discussed the organisation they founded early in 1816, the Society for the Reformation of Prison Discipline, whose aim was to reform prison conditions and encourage rehabilitation programmes for young offenders.

Making her way through Newgate's mournful passages, where the gas lamps still hissed, Betsy felt alone and vulnerable. Yet as she drew closer to the women's yard, it seemed to

her that the inner voice spoke. She sensed it urging her forward, assuring her of God's covering, and that, as on so many
occasions before, words would come at her need.

On reaching the women's quarters, she found that conditions had changed a little since her last visit. Then 300 women,
tried and untried alike, had been crammed into two wards and
two cells, where they lived, cooked, washed when they could,
and slept packed together. By 1815, under pressure from
reformers, the Gaol Committee of the Corporation of London
had ensured that the entire space originally designated for
female prisoners – a whole quadrangle surrounded by six
wards and two cells – was reinstated. At the same time a dou-
ble grating, two rows of bars about three feet apart, had been
installed to prevent too close contact with visitors, who might
pass across anything from a bottle of spirits to a rope or a
kitchen knife. Now the women begged with wooden spoons
fastened to long sticks. Nevertheless, the racket and the stench
were unchanged, and as Betsy gazed on the melée, she felt the
same cold sweat standing out on her skin.

No, said the turnkey, he would not open the gate. But Betsy
was resolute, and with the authority of the governor's pass in
her hand, she insisted that he drag it back, and then lock it
again behind her. After he did so, and she stood alone before
the convicts, she heard a hush falling back throughout their
pressing throng.

In the silence, and in the eerie half-light, the Quaker minister and the mob of thieves, coiners and prostitutes stared at
each other. They saw a tall woman grown matronly with childbearing, who wore rich but plainly-styled clothes, no orna-
ment but a wedding ring, and whose fair, flushed face, framed
in a white lawn cap, wore an oddly poignant expression of
eagerness mingled with anxiety. Betsy saw only details,
grotesque tableaus lit by the wavering light. One group, frozen
in the act as they looked up in surprise, played with a filthy
deck of cards. Another appeared halted in the parody of a sexual act, at its centre a woman on the ground with another
astride her who wore a man's breeches, a cocked hat and a cra-
vat. Yet another group picked lice from the hair of two chil-

dren. Most of the women were half-naked, and the smell of alcohol, a sharply sour tone in the foul air, told Betsy that many were drunk.

Suddenly, like an expulsion of breath, the silence broke, expression animated features, and from somewhere deep in the crowd, came a rising tide of sound, foul words and laughter, as well as a tangible sense of threat. As panic began to seize her, Betsy silently pleaded for help.

Almost immediately she became conscious of a young woman who stood a little way off holding a fair-haired little girl. Not letting her eyes leave them, she moved towards them, and as she did so, the prisoners fell back in surprise. Then, taking the child in her own arms, and laying a hand on the young mother's shoulder, Betsy faced the crowd. "Is there not something we can do for these innocent little children," she asked, "are they to learn to become thieves and worse?"

The words had an extraordinary effect. Hardly any woman in that surging mass had ever been asked for her opinion before, or heard that the future might be different. But with four small words, "what can *we* do?" the light of hope immediately pierced the darkness. Someone brought Betsy a seat, and women with tears in their eyes, the reluctant encouraged by the more eager, gathered around the Quaker minister. Pressed upon by their foul-smelling and sweating bodies, and touched by their rags crawling with lice, Betsy told the women that she too was a mother, whose pain when her little daughter died had finally been eased by faith. Presently she spoke of God's passion for sinners and recounted the parable of the vineyard. Even as those hired at the eleventh hour were paid full wages by the lord of the place, she said, so even sinners coming late to repentance were welcomed into the fullness of salvation. "Jesus," Betsy said, "came especially to save sinners like us." A young woman looked up curiously. "Who is he, madam?" she asked.

Mr Newman, Newgate's governor, Dr Cotton, its chaplain, and two sheriffs of London listened politely to Betsy's plan. Then they dismissed it. Though it was laudable, sadly, it was also unworkable. Respectfully, they doubted that Mrs Fry knew much about schooling the poor, which was hard enough work in itself, but any attempt to educate the children of prisoners, they assured her, who were mostly degenerates like their parents, would certainly lead to disorder, and probably to violence. London's gaols, they said, overflowed with the scum of the slums, places no lady could possibly imagine, and whose inhabitants were filthy, debased and ignorant – ignorant of all the common habits of civilised life, not only of religious truth, added Dr Cotton. Idleness, gambling, drinking and swearing were the favoured occupations of prisoners, Mr Newman concluded flatly, not education.

Could she, Betsy asked politely, at least try her experiment. The request made the assembled gentlemen uncomfortable, for they had no wish to upset the Prison Discipline Society, with its influential members and whose patron was Prince William Frederick, Duke of Gloucester.[3] Uneasily they suggested another interview. It convened at the governor's house, and when all were gathered, Mr Newman announced with relief in his voice that a thorough review of Newgate had revealed that no space was available. Stubbornly, Mrs Fry pressed him. Was that the only reason? Reluctantly, he admitted finally that it was.

Leaving the four men behind, Betsy went into the prison. When she returned, she announced that the prisoners themselves had agreed to make a cell available, and that they had chosen Mary Connor, a previously respectable young woman convicted for stealing a watch, to be their teacher. At that, the authorities gave in. They were not, however, very optimistic. For, although, said Fowell later, "they approved her idea with cordial approbation, ... at the same time, [they] unreservedly confessed their apprehension that her labours would be fruitless."[4]

Next day Betsy returned to the prison, and after installing Mary Connor formally as teacher, she founded the first school in British prison history.

It seemed almost a small thing to her, just 30 children, mostly born in prison, but with a few young criminals among them, all crammed into one small cell where the heat and the

smell were intense. To others however, it was almost indescribably strange. Mary Sanderson, who went with Betsy on
the first day, and who told Fowell later that she felt she was
going into a den of wild beasts when Newgate's doors closed
behind her, wondered how her friend could be so composed.
Betsy, however, surrounded by the rough-featured children
who reminded her so poignantly of her laundry, felt quite in
her element. "I have lately been much occupied with forming
a school at Newgate," she wrote on 24 February 1817, "...
which has brought much peace and satisfaction with it."

There was little peace or satisfaction, however, to be found
in the condemned cells that lay deep in the prison's bowels;
only death in his most ugly and brutal guise. When she first
entered the prison she had barely thought how her services as
a Christian minister might be called for, but when the other
prisoners begged her to visit a young woman condemned for
killing her own baby, faith told Betsy not to shrink. Later, sitting alone with the distraught and grief-stricken mother, she
wondered what festering sores had given rise to her terrible
crime. The thought of the forthcoming death struggle at the
end of a rope also haunted her imagination.

That she had visited the young woman at all, quite shocked
Joseph John. "When I heard of thy visiting that poor woman at
Newgate," he wrote from Earlham, "I felt anxious about thee,
knowing how racking such things are to the spirit and how
exhausting to the frame." Perhaps, he suggested, Betsy should
think carefully before proceeding. "I think it right to suggest
the consideration whether that wisdom which dwells with prudence, justifies thy entering, at Newgate, *into that most trying
line of service.*"[5]

Betsy was already making plans, however, and as she did
so, she felt her spirits lift and any weariness fall away.

Almost as soon as her 30 scholars took their places, other
mothers began begging admittance for their children too. At
the same time, adult female prisoners began pleading to be
taught to read and sew. If only they had such skills, they said,
they need never steal or beg, walk the streets, or be dependent
on the whims of men again. To Betsy, the virtue of their request

was obvious. In the short time she had been at Newgate she had seen very clearly what went on inside its walls. During the day there was nothing to do except drink, play games or tell fortunes with cards, chew tobacco, sing lewd songs and fight. At night, male prisoners and turnkeys entered the women's yards and used them as brothels. Apart from begging with their wooden spoons, there was no means of acquiring money. If these abused and raging women were to be redeemed, then their request for education must surely be answered.

"Newgate is a principal object," Betsy wrote to her sister Rachel in March, "and I think until I make some attempt at amendment in the plans for the women, I shall not feel easy." For surely, she reasoned, God would not have taken her to the gaol unless there was work for her to do? "I have felt in thy taking care of my dearest girls," she told Rachel, "that thou art helping me to get on with some of these important objects."

Though she felt enthusiastic, Betsy was also nervous of making a start. She had already found it painful to ask for help with the school, she said, especially when some people had been less than forthcoming, and in some cases, quite critical. Her brief negotiations with Newgate's authorities had also told her that if she continued such work, there would be many similar encounters with men in authority. Did she really want to be involved in such a world? Was it right that even more than before, she would be led away from her family? And was it the sin of pride urging her forward, or was God really calling her to something that was new? She was also acutely aware that no woman had ever done anything so bold.

From the brief entries she made in her journal at this busy time, and from others that followed later, it is clear that Betsy recognised the events at Newgate as critical, and that in some sense, there would be no turning back. It is also evident that as she faced a future that was unknown on many levels, a mass of conflicting feelings surged within her. She was about to take on such a task at a time when women had no public role; she would inevitably be leaving her family for longer periods; and as a Quaker minister, she might be succumbing to what was creaturely: all these considerations caused intense anxiety, as did the thought of the reactions likely to result from family, Quaker colleagues and the world at large. At the same time, for a woman as driven as Betsy so obviously was, the prospect of working among a group of people who were so desperately in need, and the knowledge that she had the skills and experience to undertake the task of relieving them, the prospect must have been exhilarating indeed. And, also humbling, for by now, her Christian faith was well-established, and although it wavered at times of stress, she appears convinced that she moved at God's command and that the inner voice that prompted her, was indeed that of her Master. And although she expressed apprehension at working alongside public men, for a woman brought up among the sophisticated company of Earlham, whose adult life had been spent among London's wealthy, cultivated and well-informed Quaker community, the prospect of spending time among people who had the control of human destiny in their hands would not have been entirely daunting. In fact, for all the misgivings on the subject that she continually expressed, Betsy's later history was to prove that she moved among the rich and powerful with as much ease as she moved among the prisoners of Newgate.

When Betsy finally spoke to Fowell and Sam Hoare about her plan for a workshop where female prisoners could learn a trade and then be usefully employed, it was a blow to hear them reject it. Repeating almost the same phrases that Mr Newman had used for the school, the two reformers insisted that Newgate's women were unteachable. Though they listened patiently to her accounts of poor girls at Earlham learning to make gowns, they assured her that the thieves of London were different, that they had no desire for steady employment, and any initial enthusiasm would evaporate when other amusements presented themselves. The materials would be stolen or destroyed, scissors and needles would become weapons and the workshop would be overtaken by riot.

Their rejection roused Betsy's stubbornness, while a growing conviction that it was right for her to go ahead was bolstered by a voice that lived in her memory. "There are no lives so unlovely, none so unworthy or so lost," said William Savery, "that they are beyond the reach of God's transforming light." At the same time, Betsy's own reason told her that if lives were to be transformed, then someone must be the catalyst. "Even you," said William Savery again. "A light to the blind, speech to the dumb and feet to the lame," said Deborah Darby like an echo. Together they persuaded her that despite her own anxieties, and the doubts of others, she must nevertheless walk forward in faith.

In April 1817 a new society was born. It was exclusively female, and it consisted of eleven Quakers plus Mrs Anglezark, the wife of the clergyman at East Ham. It was called the Association for the Improvement of the Female Prisoners in Newgate, and its object was "to provide for the clothing, the instruction, and the employment of the women; to introduce them to a knowledge of the Holy Scriptures, and to form in them, as much as possible, those habits of order, sobriety and industry, which may render them docile and peaceable whilst in prison, and respectable when they leave it."[6] The twelve women pledged themselves to take turns in visiting Newgate daily, to pay the salary of a resident matron and to provide funds for necessary materials and arrange for sales of work. They also hoped to prove Fowell and Sam Hoare wrong.

Joseph Fry, however, became their ally. Doing so helped restore the confidence that had been badly shaken by the disaster that had overtaken him, and also reassured him that although the woman he continued to love and admire was moving far beyond him, he could still play a crucial role on her stage. It was with a warm glow of satisfaction, therefore, that he welcomed Mr Newman, Dr Cotton, and Sheriff George Bridges to Mildred's Court, and told them that as a leading London businessman it was his privilege to endorse his wife's cause. Betsy was delighted by his support, but also grateful for the secrecy that shrouded his finances; as she smiled at her guests she wondered how they would react if they knew that the comfort that surrounded them, seemingly so integral a part of the Fry business empire, was actually provided and maintained by Joseph John and Sam Gurney.

Mr Newman was not entirely convinced by the arguments

of Mrs Fry, but he did finally agree to attend a meeting at Newgate on the following Sunday with the convicted prisoners only, who, it was agreed, should begin the experiment. When the day came, however, as he looked upon the 70 women, all unkempt hair and rags, who filled the space before him with an unstable provocative energy, he doubted even more whether they were worth Mrs Fry's concern.

He was still wondering whether he had been foolhardy to give his agreement when he saw her stand up to outline her scheme. Would they, she asked the prisoners, be willing to abide by a set of rules, which must be established if the workshop was to go ahead? Unanimously they assured her they would. One of the sheriffs then spoke to them, promising the City's support if the rules were kept and the prisoners worked hard. Clearly thinking it unlikely, he leaned towards Betsy and her committee. "Well, ladies," he said, with a disparaging nod in the convicts' direction, "you see your materials."[7]

Days later, the same assembly met again, this time on the new wooden benches installed in a freshly whitewashed laundry. Might it be a portent, Betsy wondered, as once again she addressed the prisoners.

This time she spoke to them of the benefits gained from hard work and sobriety, from virtue and religion, and she contrasted them with the idleness and dissipation of the lives that had led the prisoners finally into ruin and Newgate. She spoke too of their guilt in the sight of God, and appealed to them to choose the paths of righteousness.

Motioning towards her committee, she told the convicts that they had come to Newgate eager to rescue their fellow-creatures from evil, and to impart to them the knowledge which they, from the benefit of their own education and circumstances, had been privileged to receive. However, she continued, the ladies did not intend to be authoritarian. Rather, they wished for all to work in harmony, so that the convicts could learn skills for later use beyond Newgate, where they could also take with them money saved from the sale of their prison work, that would enable them to live new redeemed lives. In fact, she said, the Ladies' Committee had already agreed to add one shilling of their own to every five a prisoner earned. But such things could only be achieved with the full agreement and co-operation of the prisoners. Would they consent, she asked, looking at them directly, to hear and vote on a list of rules, and to freely comment on anything that puzzled them or with which they disagreed? The convicts listened open-mouthed. None of them had heard anything like it before, where poor, ignorant, imprisoned women were asked to share in shaping their own destiny. Cautiously at first, and then enthusiastically, they all agreed.

Rules

1. That a matron be appointed for the general superintendence of the women;
2. That the women be engaged in needlework, knitting, or any other suitable employment;
3. That there be no begging, swearing, gaming, card-playing, quarrelling, or immoral conversation. That all novels, plays, and other improper books, be excluded; and that all bad words be avoided; and any default in these particulars be reported to the matron;
4. That there be a yard-keeper, chosen from among the women: to inform them when their friends came; to see that they leave their work with a monitor, when they go to the grating, and that they do not spend any time there, except with their friends. If any woman be found disobedient, in these respects, the yard-keeper is to report the case to the Matron;
5. That the women be divided into classes, of not more than twelve; and that a monitor be appointed to each class;
6. That monitors be chosen from among the most orderly of the women that can read, to superintend the work and conduct of the others;
7. That the monitors not only overlook the women in their own classes, but if they observe any others disobeying the rules, that they inform the monitor of the class to which such persons may belong, who is immediately to report to the matron, and the deviations to be set down on a slate;
8. That any monitor breaking the rules shall be dismissed from her office, and the most suitable in the class selected to take her place;

9. That the monitors be particularly careful to see that the women come with clean hands and face to their work, and that they are quiet during their employment;

10. That at the ringing of the bell, at nine o'clock in the morning, the women collect in the work-room to hear a portion of Scripture read by one of the visitors, or the matron; and that the monitors afterwards conduct the classes from thence to their respective wards in an orderly manner;

11. That the women be again collected for reading, at six o'clock in the evening, when the work shall be given in charge to the matron by the monitors;

12. That the matron keep an exact account of the work done by the women, and of their conduct.[8]

As she read the list, and then the names of the proposed monitors, Betsy saw every convict hand raised in favour. In the silence that followed, she announced that her committee had obtained from Mssrs Richard Dixon & Co, of Fenchurch Street, London, an agreement that a percentage of the rough stockings and other apparel, supplied by them to the British convict settlements in Australia, could be replaced by similar items produced at Newgate. Finally, after reminding the prisoners once more of their own responsibility for the success of the enterprise, she implored God's blessing and read the thirteenth chapter of Luke, the parable of the barren fig-tree. In the solemn silence that followed, Governor Newman gazed at his prisoners. To his surprise he had been deeply moved; by the scheme, by Betsy's faith, and by the expressions of earnest attention and hope that sat so poignantly on the ravaged faces before her.

Barely two weeks after Betsy's workshop began, the Reverend C.B. Tayler recorded his impressions of the women's wards once known as "Hell above ground". He found the transformation hardly believable. Rather than the clamour and wild women he remembered from previous visits, he was met by a newly appointed yards-woman, who, after bobbing him a curtsy, led him through a well-swept quiet yard to a long chamber. There a woman in Quaker dress sat reading to a group of 16 other women who were all busily sewing. Each one wore a clean blue apron and bib, while around each neck hung a red ribbon bearing an individually numbered ticket. The room was clean and smelled freshly of whitewash, the women rose respectfully at his entrance to curtsy and then merely glanced at him curiously before resuming their work. "Instead of a scowl or ill-suppressed laugh," he said, "their countenances wore an air of self-respect and gravity, a sort of consciousness of their improved character, and the altered position in which they were placed."[9]

"Already, from being like wild beasts, they appear harmless and kind," Betsy said of her convicts. "I am ready to say, in the fullness of my heart, surely 'it is the Lord's doing, and marvellous in our eyes.'" Looking back through the years, she also marvelled at how resourcefully God had prepared the ground, using even her disasters to achieve some purpose. But, as she looked forward, she knew that already the world was clamouring to know more about Newgate and Mrs Fry. Would she have the courage, she wondered, to walk out and face it?

CHAPTER TEN

Too much divided

*T*HE QUAKER HEROINE, the notorious gaol, and the ongoing miracle: although Betsy had tried her best to work quietly, it was a story of too much drama and romance to remain hidden for long. Within months, all over the country, people were talking about the woman who walked alone through Newgate and tamed its savage inhabitants. News spread too about the prison workshop, that within weeks of its foundation had become part of the overall prison system of the City of London; of how the Lord Mayor, aldermen and sheriffs had attended a special meeting to celebrate the incorporation; and how the City Corporation agreed to share the costs of the Matron with the Ladies' Committee. Newgate itself, it was said, was become quite a show, as reformers, clergymen and civic officials rubbed shoulders with royal dukes and foreign ambassadors, all eager to see and learn from the extraordinary transformation, and to hear from Mrs Fry herself, how each day she and the Ladies investigated convict histories, allocated the workgroups accordingly and oversaw the workshop. People also spoke of how many of those same visitors also attended Mrs Fry's public Bible readings that were held at the prison each Friday, and how they often left Newgate in tears.

Newgate's chapel had never seen anything like it. In that stone cold room at the heart of the gaol, where male and female prisoners sat segregated on rising tiers of wooden seats, few people had ever paid much attention to religion. It had been far more common to see convicts talking, laughing or shouting at each other, their babies wailing or sucking noisily at their mother's breasts, while visitors, who generally came to indulge a macabre fascination with crime, commented loudly and unkindly about the convicts.

However, when people spoke of Mrs Fry's readings, it was with awe.

Late in 1817, the Reverend C. B. Tayler attended one of them and left an account in his journal.

Tier above tier rose the seats at the end of the room, a gallery of wooden steps many feet high, ... and on that gallery the female prisoners, many of them the very refuse of society, were seated; ... It was indeed a shocking and most distressing spectacle, that range of about a hundred women's faces, with the various types of vice and crime written on the lines of almost every one. But there they sat in respectful silence, every eye fixed upon the grave sweet countenance of the gentle lady who was about to address them. A table was before her, on which lay the Holy Bible, ... and after a pause for silent prayer of some minutes, she quietly opened the inspired volume. She turned to the Prophet Isaiah, and read aloud the fifty-third chapter, ... Never till then, and never since then, have I heard anyone read as Elizabeth Fry read that chapter – the solemn reverence of her manner, the articulation, so exquisitely modulated, so distinct, that not a word of that sweet and touching voice could fail to be heard. While she read, her mind seemed to be intensely absorbed in the passage of Scripture, and in nothing else. She seemed to take in to her own soul the words which she read, and to apply them to herself; and then she raised her head, and, after another pause of silence, she spoke to the wretched women before her.

Her address was short, and so simple that it must have been intelligible to the capacities of her hearers; and it was soon evident that it had come home to the hearts of many there by the subdued expression of their countenances, and by the tears that flowed freely from eyes which perhaps had never shed such tears till then. She set forth clearly, forcibly, though with a mild persuasiveness, the wonderful love of God in sending His own Son to die in the place of sinners, and in accepting the sacrifice of Himself as an atonement for their sins. She told them that it was He who was led as a sheep to the slaughter; He who was despised and rejected of men; He who has borne *our* griefs and carried *our* sorrows, and then most impressively she added, "And the Lord hath laid on Him the iniquity *of us all*." What struck me as most remarkable in her speaking, and no doubt that which won its way so powerfully to the hearts of those abandoned women, was, that she always seemed to class herself with them; she never said "you", but "us", when speaking of those who were lost, giving them to understand, though not in distinct words, that in the sight of God they were all alike sinners, all alike lost, if not washed in the precious blood of Christ, which alone cleanseth from all sin ... I have heard many eloquent preachers, but I have never, before or since, listened to one who had so thoroughly imbibed the Master's spirit, or been taught by Him the persuasive power of pleading with sinners for the life of their own souls.[1]

As women all over Britain discussed Mrs Fry and the Ladies' Association, many of them also discovered that something inside them was aroused. For in doing what no woman had done before, by taking her bold and public initiative, Betsy had opened the door to possibilities hitherto inconceivable. In their thousands, from all over Britain, and then from all over Europe, women inundated her with letters. Could they form a Ladies' Association in their town, they asked; could they too, visit female convicts in prison? Hundreds more letters came from men, many of them magistrates, asking what was the basis of her system, and could they introduce it in the prisons they oversaw? Other people wrote asking for advice on family matters, for financial assistance, and even for help in finding work.

Although she had known there would be public interest, Betsy was totally unprepared for the amount of it and for the huge deluge of letters, while the extraordinary fascination shown by complete strangers for her own person fuelled her anxieties and her fears. So too did the high regard of public men.

In May 1817, together with other members of the Ladies' Association, she was asked to discuss her work with the Lord Mayor at the Mansion House. Was it a temptation, she asked apprehensively, "being made so much of; so much respect paid me by the people in power, in the City?" Would it lead to worldly pride? But, while her past and the fear of spiritual transgression pulled her one way, the future and the theatre of action pulled in the other. If the work were to go forward, she knew that not only must she walk with the rich and powerful, but to some extent, conform to their expectations. "A degree of this sort of conduct appears almost necessary," she said.

Yet while many admired her, she also had to face detractors who maintained that public life was no place for a woman. At Yearly Meeting, a number of delegates expressed the view that her busy ministry and high-profile prison work was leading her to neglect her family. Meanwhile, in the world at large, she was also accused of vanity, of running after fame, of furthering the interests of the Gurneys and of deliberately sending away six children in order to spend time at Newgate. Such criticism reflected her own ambivalence. "Others appear to feel for me, that I am too much divided," she said. Yet despite it all she continued, convinced that she did God's work. "What can I do, but follow the openings?" she asked.

Her family, however, rallied to her support.

Hudson was particularly impressed, and together with Uncle Barclay, he agreed to support a fund set up by the Ladies' Association to provide additional clothing. Descriptions of women arriving at the gaol in rags, with the Ladies forced to stand between their near-nakedness and male officialdom, roused their compassion, and both men were exceedingly generous. Like many others touched by Betsy's work, they also began to see the prisoners in a new light, no longer an anonymous mass of creatures barely human, but tragic human beings, with real needs, who carried within them the potential for redemption.

Even Katherine and Rachel, returning from their Aunt Rachel at Runcton to Plashet for the summer, were pressed to assist with the huge mass of correspondence. As they set to work, it almost seemed to Betsy that her prayers for them were being answered. She not only yearned for her daughters to walk the Friends' path to salvation, she also wanted to see it reflected in useful lives on earth. "The poor and the schools will be glad to have you home, I think, for help is wanted in these things" she had written to them earlier. "Indeed if your hearts are but turned the right way, you may, I believe, be made instruments of much good; and I shall be glad to have the day come, that I may introduce you into prisons and hospitals."

Neither Fowell Buxton nor Sam Hoare needed any such inducements. After admitting that they had earlier been wrong, together with Sam and Joseph John Gurney, they endorsed and supported Betsy's work. Fowell was particularly passionate, for having achieved his goal of a partnership in the brewery, he now felt able to build on his work in the Prison Discipline Society by standing for parliament with prison reform high on his agenda.

Since medieval times, the treatment of Britain's convicts had been public and brutal, as the state sought to ensure that as many people as possible witnessed the floggings, mutilations, humiliations and executions suffered by wrongdoers. Thus they would learn, it was widely believed, that retribution was swift and terrible, while at the same time being deterred from committing similar crimes themselves. It was not until the Enlightenment, with its theories that maintained that human nature was not immutable, and that individuals and communities were shaped partly by environment and education, that there was any real insight into the nature of crime, or the suggestion that criminals could be transformed into honest and useful citizens.

One of the first individuals to make such a suggestion was John Howard, a Londoner born in 1726, whose Christian faith led him to investigate Britain's gaols and houses of correction. Throughout the eighteenth century, these were administered by local justices, their gaolers made their living by charging for board and lodging, and no distinction was made between prisoners awaiting trial, convicts awaiting transportation to the American colonies, and debtors. What Howard discovered as he pursued his investigations, both horrified him and caused him to conclude that the ways in which prisoners were kept and treated were not only inhuman, but led almost inevitably to an increase in crime. His book, *The State of the Prisons in England and Wales*, published in 1777, was an inspiration for the reformers that followed.

Despite Howard's conclusions, however, most Members of Parliament were uninterested in penal reform, and almost casually they increased the number of offences carrying the death penalty. By the beginning of the nineteenth century, it stood at over 160, from the theft of five shillings to the most abominable murder. It was only Britain's magistrates and judges, defying Parliament by commuting almost four-fifths of death sentences to transportation, who provided any amelioration to what was aptly titled The Bloody Code.

But the movement for reform could not be halted. In 1808, at the instigation of the Solicitor-General, Sir Samuel Romilly, and despite fierce opposition, Parliament was persuaded to abolish the death penalty for picking pockets. Also at Romilly's instigation, a House of Commons Report, produced in 1811, expressed the opinion "that many offenders may be reclaimed by a system of Penitentiary imprisonment by which [the Committee] mean a system of imprisonment not confined to the safe custody of the person, but extending to the reformation and improvement of the mind and operating by seclusion, employment and religious instruction."[2] The Millbank Penitentiary, a state-run prison under the direct control of the Home Office, with its first stage completed in 1816, was the result.[3] Within its walls, prisoners occupied separate cells, each with a small barred window, a toilet, a hand-basin, a hammock and a loom. Its staff also included a medical officer and chaplain, a matron in charge of the women and a master manufacturer overseeing instruction in about 20 different trades.[4]

Though reformers like Fowell Buxton sensed the quickening of change, they also knew they would have to contend not only with forces of reaction, but also with the results of a turmoil engulfing Britain. The end of the Napoleonic Wars brought back to Britain half a million men with few skills except war, while as the iron-works closed that had once manufactured armaments, thousands more men were thrown out of work. At the same time, in the British countryside, new machinery was making ever increasing numbers of people redundant. Many of those forced unwillingly from their work also went hungry, as the price of bread was kept artificially high by the Corn Law rushed through Parliament in 1815 to protect the profits of Britain's wealthy landowners.[5] As the unemployed, the dispossessed and the hungry were cast adrift, many of them turned to crime. Those who were caught and convicted added their numbers to a prison population that included thousands of debtors as well as murderers, highwaymen, forgers and thieves. In 1818, Britain's gaols contained 107,000 persons, and the number was rising rapidly.[6]

Newgate, with over a thousand prisoners, was Britain's largest and most notorious gaol, but although others were smaller, they were generally its equal in gloom, brutality, vice and disease, plus a stench that polluted the regions around them. Many were old gatehouses in city walls, whose cells looked out into the streets, while others were the dank dungeons of old castles. Most were overcrowded, with inmates crammed together indiscriminately: petty thieves with murderers, youthful beginners with old offenders, men among women, sexual predators among vulnerable young people and children. Sometimes the violently insane were locked in with ordinary convicts, while those suffering contagious diseases were shut up with the healthy. Gaol fever – a form of typhus – was rife, as were smallpox, syphilis and all sorts of skin complaints. Vermin crawled on everything, sometimes so densely that clothing seemed to be in actual movement from armies of lice. Female prisoners were often regarded as fair game by turnkeys, who also, for small bribes, looked away as prostitutes were brought in for the men. Alcohol also arrived in vast quantities, much of it bought with "garnish", money begged from visitors or extorted from fellow prisoners to provide riotous drunken parties. Supervision was minimal, escape being chiefly prevented by heavy irons attached to staples in walls and floors. Food too was sparse and water supplies were inadequate. Few gaols had proper systems of sewage disposal and what privies there were remained choked with excrement and vomit. The stink, as Fowell remarked after a visit to Bristol gaol, was "something more than can be expressed by the word 'disgusting'".[7]

Prisoners who survived the gaols generally left them penniless, often with their health broken, coarsened in their morals, but well-educated in crime. That many of them longed for something better, Betsy had often heard from Fowell, Sam Hoare and the men of the Prison Discipline Society. At Newgate, she heard it herself from women. Having heard it, she believed she saw God's purpose at work, and recognising that she could not turn away from what was set before her, almost inadvertently she joined the ranks of the prison reformers.

In February 1818, as the overflowing gaols and the increase in crime caused a desperate government to look for solutions in the work and theories of the reformers, Mrs Fry was invited to give evidence before a House of Commons Committee. Preparing for the interview, and travelling into London with Joseph John, she thought back to the day at Ackworth when she had trembled at making her first, hesitating observations before a body of intelligent and knowledgeable people. Would speaking to Members of Parliament be any harder, she wondered.

She began by recounting the birth of the Newgate workshop, and emphasising that although its rules were occasionally broken, this was exceedingly rare. "I think I may say we have full power amongst them," she said, "for one of them said, it was more terrible to be brought up before me, than before the judge, though we use nothing but kindness."[8] For all their worldliness, the politicians who made up the Committee were fascinated by Mrs Fry. With her candid blue eyes, her rich clothes and her Quaker cap, she was a striking figure, and for all her ladylike manners, her combination of religious conviction, earnestness and knowledge was compelling.

Mrs Fry was also anxious to emphasise that if her reforming programme was utilised, then the lives of female prisoners could be transformed. It was not merely intended to make them docile in gaol, she said, but honest and self-respecting in the world beyond its walls. She focused on three major points.

First, religious instruction was vital. Reassuring the

Committee that her teaching was not sectarian, she described its extraordinary effects on women who had little previous knowledge of Christianity, neither its basic truths, nor the morality contained within it. So eager were they to hear and learn, she said, that they flocked to the twice-daily Bible readings, and while almost all had been forced to consider their manner of living and their habits, some had actively changed them. Some had also learned to read, in order to study the Scriptures for themselves.

Secondly, she spoke of the benefits of categorising convicts according to crime and criminal history, and then of keeping the groups separate. By allowing them to mingle indiscriminately, she said, the wards became schools of crime as well as breeding places of disease. Both problems were exacerbated at night, when completely unsupervised, the convicts slept crammed together on mats on the floor, 30 to a room. Basins, soap and towels, she added, would have a powerful effect, not only on personal cleanliness, but on moral hygiene too.

Third was the value of income-producing employment, which not only utilised the hours efficiently, but provided a basis for self-respect and honesty. In the ten months of the workshop's existence, she said, 80 female prisoners had produced 20,000 articles, mostly knitted stockings and socks, of which only three items had been lost, and that by accident, rather than theft. The earnings, approximately 18 pence each week, supplemented by the Ladies, were used partly to buy additional food and clothing, while some was stored in a fund against the day of release.

When asked if reward was an important part of her system, Mrs Fry agreed that it was. She went on to describe how the class monitors reported regularly to Newgate's new matron, who herself kept a record of good marks, and how the promise of much sought-after prizes, small articles of clothing, Bibles and Testaments, encouraged both good behaviour and industry.

To stress how well the system worked, Mrs Fry described two recently released convicts with whom the Ladies maintained contact. One of them, she said, who had been taught to knit while in prison, now earned part of her living with her needles. The other, who was lent money by the Ladies to help establish her new life, called regularly, and proudly, each week at Mildred's Court to make her two-shilling repayments.

Finally, boldly, Mrs Fry made a radical suggestion. "It has been said," she began, "that there were three things that were requisite in forming a prison that would really tend to the reformation of the women; but there is a fourth."[9] The Committee eyed her expectantly. In order to achieve real and lasting reformation, she continued, women should be kept in prisons that were exclusively female; staffed by female warders and visited by lady inspectors, where the only men admitted were a doctor and a minister of religion.

She also suggested, again very radically, that training, employment, the payment of wages, and a savings fund, should be the complete responsibility of government. "In a prison under proper regulations," she concluded, "where they had very little communication with their friends, where they were sufficiently well-fed and clothed, constantly employed and instructed, and taken care of by women, I have not the least doubt that wonders would be performed, and that many of those, now the most profligate and the worst of characters, would turn out valuable members of society."[10]

The Report, *Prisons of the Metropolis*, was published by the House of Commons in 1818. In its postscript, it included the sentence: "the benevolent exertions of Mrs Fry and her friends, in the female department of the Prisons, have indeed, by the establishment of a school, by providing work and encouraging industrious habits, produced the most gratifying change. But much must be ascribed to unremitting personal attention and influence."

In the same month that Betsy gave evidence to the Parliamentary Committee, her unremitting personal attention was also devoted to two women at Newgate condemned to death. In her efforts, she was admired and supported by the leader of Britain's Evangelical Christian community, William Wilberforce, who through the Bible Society had become the firm friend, first of Joseph John Gurney, and then of his wider family. Early in 1818, Wilberforce wrote to Mrs Fry.

Kensington Gore, Tuesday 17th February, 1818

My dear Madam,

I think I need not assure you that I have not forgotten you this morning. In truth, having been awake very early, and lying in peace and comfort and safety, the different situation of the poor women impressed itself strongly on my mind.

I shall be glad, and Mrs Wilberforce also, I assure you, to hear that your bodily health has not suffered from your mental anxiety, and I will try to get a sight of you when I can, to hear your account and remarks on the effects of the events of the last few days, both on the poor objects themselves and their prison companions.

With real esteem and regard,
I am, my dear Madam
Yours, very sincerely
W. Wilberforce[11]

One of the women referred to was Charlotte Newman, convicted of forgery, and she too wrote to Betsy on the morning of 17 February. But, unlike Wilberforce, Charlotte did not lay in peace and comfort; she waited alone in the condemned cell for Newgate's chaplain to lead her to the scaffold.

Condemned cell

Honoured Madam,

As the only way of expressing my gratitude to you for your very great attention to the care of my poor soul; I feel I may have appeared more silent than perhaps some would have been on so melancholy an event; but believe me, my dear madam, I have felt most acutely the awful situation I have been in. The mercies of God are boundless, and I trust through His grace this affliction is sanctified to me, and through the Saviour's blood my sins will be washed away. I have much to be thankful for. I feel such serenity of mind and fortitude. God, of His infinite mercy, grant I may feel as I do now in the last moments ...

I once more return you my most grateful thanks. It is now past six o'clock, I have not one moment to spare; I must devote the remainder to the service of my offended God.

With respect, your humble servant.
(Signed) Charlotte Newman.[12]

Edward and Priscilla Wakefield, with Mrs Wakefield's sister Catherine Bell, Elizabeth Fry's mother *(Francis Wheatley: Norwich Castle Museum and Art Gallery)*

John Gurney Esq of Earlham, Elizabeth's father *(lithograph, after John Opie: Norwich Castle Museum and Art Gallery)*

The Court House,
Magdalen Street,
Norwich, Elizabeth's
birthplace *(Jean
Hatton)*

Earlham Hall, Norwich, now the law school of the University of East Anglia *(Jean Hatton)*

Elizabeth Gurney (later Fry), aged ca. 19 *(Amelia Opie: Religious Society of Friends, London)*

Amelia Opie, 1798 *(engraving, John Opie: Norwich Castle Museum and Art Gallery)*

Hudson Gurney Esq *(Mrs Dawson Turner, after John Opie 1979: Norwich Castle Museum and Art Gallery)*

Sunniside, built 1750–51 by Abraham Darby II. Demolished 1856.
(Ironbridge Gorge Museum Trust)

The upper part of Coalbrookdale (William Westwood 1835). The house to the left is
Dale House, built by Abraham Darby I, 1715–17, enlarged and improved by his
grandson Abraham III in 1776 *(Ironbridge Gorge Museum Trust)*

Elizabeth Fry *(oil painting, Charles Robert Leslie RA: Religious Society of Friends, London)*

Joseph Fry (1777–1861) *(oil painting, Charles Robert Leslie RA: Religious Society of Friends, London)*

Elizabeth Fry reading to the prisoners in Newgate, 1818 (*From an engraving by T. Oldham Barlow after an oil painting by Jerry Barrett: Religious Society of Friends, London*)

Joseph John Gurney
(1788–1847) *(watercolour by George Richmond, ca. 1830: Religious Society of Friends, London)*

Samuel Gurney (1786–1856) *(oil painting, artist unknown: Religious Society of Friends, London)*

The children of Joseph and Elizabeth Fry, with Rattle the dog. Those living at home in 1830 were: Katherine, centre, b. 1810; William Storrs, b. 1806; Joseph, b. 1809; Hannah, b. 1812; Louisa, b. 1814; Samuel Gurney, b. 1816; Daniel Henry, b. 1822 *(from a reproduction: original drawing by Charlotte Giberne, 1830: Religious Society of Friends, London)*

Plashet House: photograph taken a few days before demolition in late 19th century *(Religious Society of Friends, London)*

Gurney family photograph, ca. 1842. Photograph from a sepia albumen print, probably from a daguerreotype. Depicts Joseph John Gurney with his third wife Eliza in the back row; his sister Elizabeth Fry in the centre front row; one of Elizabeth's daughters (probably Katherine) to her right. To her left are JJ Gurney's daughter Anna and his son John Henry; Josiah Forster is to the left of Katherine *(Religious Society of Friends, London)*

The other woman was Mary Ann James, who was also convicted of forgery, and who wrote to her fellow prisoners. Both letters found their way into the newspapers, where their measured and contrite tones created huge sympathy for the victims and helped fuel a growing opposition to use of the death penalty for anything other than crimes of violence. It was an opposition enthusiastically supported by Joseph John and Sam Gurney, Sam Hoare and Fowell Buxton, as well as by William Wilberforce, while in the House of Lords, one of the few to support their cause was Prince William Frederick, Duke of Gloucester.

It was not only the frequent injustice, and the innate brutality of execution, that concerned the reformers, but also its brutalising effects. In their view, rather than deter crime, it served only to harden the hearts and blunt the sensibilities of all who came into contact with it.

In the face of their fate, before their fellow prisoners many condemned convicts became swaggering and fatalistic, mocking the law and denying God. Before the public, who thronged Newgate's chapel before hanging days to see them marshalled around a symbolic coffin and berated for their sins, they affected indifference. Later, in their cells, peered at by men who bribed the turnkeys for a sight of them, they frequently drank themselves to oblivion.

The huge crowds who flocked to see the hangings, rather than being made thoughtful and contrite, generally regarded the day as a macabre holiday. There was also something about the scaffold draped in black, the dignitaries who sat stony-faced upon the platform, and the gloomy tolling of the prison bell, that produced in them a hideous excitement that robbed them of compassion and transformed them into brutes, who jeered at the convulsions of men and women strangling at the end of the rope. During her years at Mildred's Court, Betsy had often heard the tolling of Newgate's bell, followed by the roar of the mob.

Betsy had considered the subject of public execution long before her introduction to Newgate. Joseph Gurney Bevan, her father's cousin, had been a member of the Society for Diffusing

Information on the Subject of Punishment by Death,[13] formed in the early 1800s to support the efforts of Samuel Romilly, and she had heard him discuss the topic at many Quaker dinner tables. It had become real to her, however, when she met the tragic young mother executed in February 1817, and then Elizabeth Fricker, another convict condemned to hang the following month.

"Is it for man thus to take the prerogative of the Almighty into his own hands?" she asked after Elizabeth Fricker's death. "Is it not his place rather to endeavour to reform such; or restrain them from the commission of further evil? At least to afford poor erring fellow-mortals, whatever may be their offences, an opportunity of proving their repentance by amendment of life?" Visiting more of the condemned, both women and men, praying with them, hearing their stories, comforting their relatives, and agonizing over their orphaned children, Betsy became increasingly convinced that capital punishment was both evil and wrong.

When Harriet Skelton, one of her favourite prisoners, was condemned in March 1818 for passing a forged banknote, Betsy threw herself into a campaign for reprieve. As she did so, she was caught up in an emotionally charged situation aggravated by the complexities of the law, the attention of the press, and the affronted dignity of public men.

Under pressure from reformers, and embarrassed by large numbers of small-time forgers sentenced to death, Parliament had earlier passed an Act empowering the Directors of the Bank of England to allow a certain number of them to escape the capital sentence. After pleading guilty to a minor count, they were sentenced instead to transportation. The selection, however, was random, with the possibility that among those selected, some might still be hanged as an example to others. Those believing themselves innocent often felt safer in pleading not guilty. Harriet, who always claimed she had acted unknowingly at the instigation of her husband, was one of them.

When Harriet's appeal was rejected, and believing she had turned down an opportunity offered by the Bank, Betsy approached the Home Secretary, Lord Sidmouth. But though he had been sympathetic to previous requests, this time he was deaf to entreaty. He still recalled very clearly, from the days when he was a young man in his thirties, the violence that surrounded the French Revolution. Now, in the face of a spate of machine-breaking by the unemployed, and an earlier attack on the Prince Regent's carriage by hungry citizens, he was beginning to believe that reform was the prelude to similar uprisings in Britain.

Sidmouth was also annoyed by the publicity drawn to the case, when, unwilling to abandon Harriet, Betsy involved some influential friends. One of them was William Frederick, who personally visited Harriet in her cell, but though he appealed again to Lord Sidmouth, and then, together with Betsy, visited the Directors of the Bank, their efforts were in vain and Harriet was hanged.

Even after Harriet's death, the affair dragged dismally on. In her desperation, Betsy had spoken critically to the Bank's directors, and also to Lord Sidmouth who chose to regard some of her remarks as untruthful. Anxious to justify herself she called on him in the company of the Countess Mary Harcourt, one of several aristocratic and influential ladies who were both inspired and fascinated by Mrs Fry. The Home Secretary, however, remained hostile, and still smarting from their interview, Betsy went on with Lady Harcourt to the Mansion House, where Queen Charlotte was presiding over the examination of hundreds of poor London school children.

Also in attendance were a profusion of royal princesses, the Lord Mayor and eight bishops, who together with the Queen, were the focus of attention. Yet as the heroine of Newgate made her entrance, the earlier hush and solemnity that had surrounded them entirely disappeared.

"A buzz of 'Mrs Fry, Mrs Fry,' ran through the room," Betsy's daughter Katherine wrote, in an account composed for her Aunt Kitty. "We heard people pointing her out, one to another," she continued, " 'That is she with her hair over her forehead.' 'That must be Mrs Fry with the Bishops,' 'Look now! you may see Mrs Fry; she rises to receive the Queen's salute.' "[14]

As Queen Charlotte stopped to speak to a commoner, so unusual was the event, and so enormous the public reputation of Mrs Fry, that throughout the Mansion House a clapping began that eventually became a cheering. When it spread to the crowds waiting outside, and then across the street to Mildred's Court, it lured Joseph Fry out into the spring sunshine. "Why," people told him, when he asked its cause, "the Queen is speaking to Mrs Fry!"

The event itself, and the day of such contrasts, echoed Betsy's continuing ambivalence at the show her life had become. "I believe that certainly it does much good to the cause, in spreading it amongst all ranks of society, a considerable interest in the subject, also a knowledge of Friends and their principles," she wrote on the following day, "but my own standing appears critical in many ways. In the first place, the extreme importance of my walking strictly, and circumspectly, amongst all men, in all things, and not bringing discredit upon the cause of truth and righteousness." She had hardly been circumspect in her dealings with the Bank and with Sidmouth, she reflected, while she was also embarrassed by sensational newspaper reports of her leaning on an Alderman's arm at the Mansion House. Desperate to calm her anxiety, she reassured herself that far more important than good or evil reports, was to live in the fear of God. Yet even as she instructed herself to keep that before her at all times, she recognised how hard it was, for a woman in the public eye, to walk a balanced path.

Months later, a potential riot at Newgate threatened enough adverse publicity to seriously undermine Mrs Fry's reputation. As the day approached for another shipment of women to be sent to Britain's convict settlements in Australia, Betsy had sensed a tension beginning to charge Newgate's air. When she learned what lay in store, she grew increasingly fearful.

Howling with rage, cursing, scratching, and punching anyone who tried to restrain them, on the night before they left the gaol, a turnkey told Betsy, drunken mobs of female transports hurled furniture at their gaolers and fellow prisoners, broke windows, and trampled broken pottery and ripped clothing into the puddles of spilled wine and gin flooding the floor. They might even, he suggested, break down the door of the workshop where the scissors and knitting needles were all stored, reduce it to chaos, and then attack themselves and others with the tools.

When Betsy spoke to the transports, she discovered they were terrified. Transportation as a means of ridding Britain of her unwanted convicts had been used since the reign of James 1. Although it had ended with the loss of the American colonies, it had begun again in 1787, 17 years after Australia was claimed for Britain by Captain James Cook. But New South Wales was a world away from Virginia, and convicts feared it. Few of them had travelled more than a few miles from home, and the distances involved were unimaginable, while for men and women barely able to read, the continent of Australia itself was inconceivable. At the same time, convict ships were reported as being similar to slave ships: overcrowded and stinking, with little food and bedding, where prisoners wearing nothing but rags were kept chained and lying in water, and where they either died or reached their destination ravaged by scurvy and dysentery. Female prisoners also learned that there was neither accommodation nor employment waiting for them, and that when new ships arrived, officers and troops from the settlement, together with established convicts, came on board to take women as unpaid servants and concubines. Newgate's women also dreaded leaving the gaol, for when the transports left, chained and shackled on open carts, they faced a jeering crowd who followed them, pelting them with rotting fruit and vegetables, all the way to the quayside at Deptford. Hearing of it, Betsy promised to see what she could do.

Mr Newman was sympathetic. In just over a year his attitude towards Mrs Fry had changed. He had seen her work hard, and her dogged persistence bear fruit, and at her suggestion he agreed to a plan which she then took back to the transports. They accepted it with relief, and in return they assured her that there would be no drinking and that all would be orderly.

On the morning the transports left, only the crowds were disappointed. For when the prison gates opened, and the mob surged forward, all that met them was a neat procession of closed Hackney coaches, followed at the very last by the private carriage of Mrs Fry, who with her Bible on her knee, smiled benignly as she passed by.

At Deptford, where the convict ship *Maria* waited to receive them, women arrived in small groups, at irregular intervals, from all over the country. They travelled on the outside of public stagecoaches, on carts, in fishing smacks, and on river boats. Almost all were heavily ironed, on their wrists and ankles, and often by hoops around their waists. They were also shackled to each other, so that if one wanted to relieve herself, no matter where they were, the others must follow. Some carried a pitifully small bundle of clothes, while others carried young children. Others, to the horror of Betsy and the Ladies, arrived grieving for infants torn from them and left behind. Elizabeth Pryor, one of Betsy's closest colleagues, agreed that she would in future lead representations to Whitehall, so that letters could be sent quickly to reunite children with their mothers before the ships set sail.

Faced with an enormous task, Betsy and the Ladies set to work. For the five weeks that the *Maria* lay in the Thames, they divided 128 convicts into groups of twelve, based wherever possible on age and their crime, and encouraged each group to choose a monitor from among their ranks. The Ladies also obtained brightly coloured scraps from London's haberdashers, so that on the voyage, the women could stitch the patchwork quilts that were popular in New South Wales. The proceeds from the quilts, and from knitting, Betsy pointed out, would provide a little store of money to lay the foundation of eventual new lives. Additional clothing was provided too, as well as a supply of Bibles, prayer books and religious tracts for each monitor. A teacher was chosen to teach adults to read, and another for the fourteen children on board who were to have a school in a little space in the ship's stern.

Finally, however, came the day of departure. It was a morning of uncertain weather, of blustery wind, glancing sunbeams and showers of quick, sharp rain. It was also a day of new beginnings, and to mark the solemnity of the occasion, the convicts were lined up neatly on the quarter-deck facing Mrs Fry and the captain. Meanwhile, above them, and also on ships all around, sailors swarmed high into the rigging for a better view of the curious scene. Others leaned precariously over their vessels' sides. Presently, as Mrs Fry began to read from her Bible, a hush fell over the whole assembly, until it seemed that the only sounds on the river were the silvery tones of Betsy's voice, the wind buffeting the ship's sides, and the melancholy cry of the gulls. At the last, Betsy knelt down on the deck and commended the *Maria* and her cargo to God.

Later, she saw the ship hauled out into the Thames, and then finally disappearing around the river's bend. As the day wore on, and as she followed the convicts in her imagination, she saw England pass finally away from them and she heard them mourning for their native land and all that was familiar and dear. Then, as the hours passed, she imagined the convicts feeling the ship quicken beneath them, as the tide and the wind took her, and her bow dipped into the troughs of the sea, and rose high on the wave. She imagined that she heard their cries of loss and fear. Finally, she heard the timbers groan as the *Maria* turned her face to the south, and with the salt wind thudding in the sails above them, and the night gathering around them, she finally lost sight of her convicts in the dark as they began their long, long voyage to the southern oceans and Botany Bay.

CHAPTER ELEVEN

A sweet united band

"WE ARE A SWEET UNITED BAND in spirit and in nature," Betsy noted contentedly in August 1818, as she relaxed in the parlour of a Quaker home in Belford, Northumberland.

Travelling with her, and underwriting their whole enterprise, was her brother, Joseph John Gurney, recorded earlier in the year as a Minister of the Society of Friends and already showing promise of great things. "Joseph appears to me the most highly gifted I ever remember a young minister, as to power, wisdom, tongue and utterance," Betsy wrote admiringly. "What an unspeakable cause of thankfulness to have him brought forth as a bright shining light."

Another bright light in their company was Joseph John's wife, Jane Birkbeck, whom he had married in September 1817. Like Betsy and Joseph John, she was a decided Friend, and she numbered both Gurneys and Sheppards in her Quaker ancestry; even though she had brought Kitty's 25-year reign to an end, she had been welcomed as a very appropriate mistress of Earlham.

The fourth member of the party, and in her mother's opinion at least, hardly a shining light, was Betsy's 15-year-old daughter Rachel. Apart from her general hostility towards Friends, Rachel had recently been the subject of unsettling rumours and as much as she hoped that her wilful and stubborn daughter would be influenced by Joseph John and Jane, Betsy also wanted to keep an eye on her.

Though Rachel resented being forced away from home, she

also couldn't help rather enjoying herself. For to travel with her mother and uncle was to be part of an extraordinary progress that combined grandeur and wealth with reforming zeal and religion.

To carry the party eventually as far north as Aberdeen, Joseph John had marshalled the vast resources of Earlham; a procession of gleaming carriages, an array of liveried footmen and grooms, troops of male and female servants, and an enormous quantity of trunks, boxes and hampers. It was an impressive sight, and at all the great houses and towns on their route, there was no doubt among observers that it was all done for the benefit of Earlham's most famous daughter, Mrs Elizabeth Fry. For although Joseph John had felt called to minister to Scotland's Quaker community, to promote his brand of Evangelical Quakerism, the claims of the Bible Society, and to visit Scottish gaols, it was Mrs Fry who attracted the crowds and who fired the enthusiasm of local newspaper editors.

A Scottish lady described Mrs Fry for a friend. "She is about 40, tall, sedate, with a physiognomy gentle, but very observant, at first not calling forth much sympathy," she said. But as she saw Mrs Fry's reserve gradually melt, she changed her mind. "Mrs Fry's voice and manners are delightful," she concluded, "and her communication free and unembarrassed." She then went on to describe Mrs Fry's appearance before the women of the Glasow gaol. "The reading was succeed by a solemn pause," she said, reaching the end of her account, "and then, resting her large Bible upon the ground, we suddenly saw Mrs Fry kneeling before the women. Her prayer was beyond words – soothing and elevating, and I felt her musical voice in the peculiar recitative of the Quakers to be like a mother's song to a suffering child."[1]

Despite the apparent outward freedom, however, inwardly, as ever, Betsy was troubled. That she was leaving Joseph and the other children for such a long time made her feel more guilty than usual, while she also feared a less than enthusiastic reception from her northern Quaker brethren. Since 1811, and the foundation of the Norwich Bible Society, she had grown increasingly close to Joseph John, so much so in fact, that in meeting they often appeared to speak with one voice. At the same time, her friendship with William Wilberforce, Charles Simeon and Edward Edwards was continuing to reinforce her support for the Evangelical message her brother preached. But, just as in England, to deeply traditional Scottish Quakers, and to those in isolated communities, the Gurneys' habit of kneeling in prayer, their passionate preaching, their devotion to the Bible, to interdenominational activities, and to the affairs of the world, were often profoundly unsettling.

The magistrates and prison authorities of Scotland were also frequently unsettled by their Gurney visitors too. Many of them were thoughtful and compassionate men, anxious to reform inhuman conditions, and eager for help and advice. Others, less welcoming, but conscious of the public eye and the power of the press, were unable to refuse the well-connected Mrs Fry and her imposing brother. Almost all of them, however, eager and reticent alike, were equally shocked when it was proposed that they enter their own gaols and talk to the turnkeys and prisoners. Rarely had such an idea occurred to them, but as they followed the well-informed and compassionate Quakers into the stinking cells, and observed and listened to their inhabitants, many of them began to see with new eyes and were converted to the cause of reform.

A record of the gaol visits was published in Edinburgh the following year by Joseph John as *Notes on a Visit made to some of the Prisons in Scotland and the North of England, in company with Elizabeth Fry*. In almost every case, it said, conditions in Scottish gaols were atrocious, and most prisoners, whether tried or untried, male or female, were kept in "a damp, dark and filthy cell; it may be with only straw for [his] bed; assailed by the most noisome smells." While the inmates in these unhealthy places were either crammed unpleasantly together, or else kept entirely solitary, in either case there was little opportunity for exercise, no useful labour, decent food or proper latrines, nor the services of a doctor or minister of religion. And without them, the report concluded, there was little prospect of rehabilitation and therefore a consequent decrease in crime. The report also highlighted a feature that was singular to Scottish gaols: that since gaolers traditionally lived away from their prisons, not only were the possibilities of inspection or proper care limited, but an almost free communication with the public meant that alcohol and the introduction of prostitutes were equally unlimited.

Among its examples, the report cited the gaols at Dunbar and Haddington, two small towns east of Edinburgh. At Dunbar, the gaol consisted of two filthy rooms, one for debtors and the other for criminals of all descriptions. At Haddington, the gaol, filled to overflowing with men and women arrested at a riot, contained them all in four small, dark rooms where one wooden tub served as the latrine for all. Haddington Gaol also held a prisoner who had tried to escape, and who was therefore subjected to a punishment common in Scottish prisons: to be attached by the feet to an iron bar in such a way that made it impossible to sit or lie down comfortably, to remove clothing, or to relieve oneself properly. In Joseph John's view, such treatment was a form of torture. An equally unpleasant, if not worse punishment for attempted escape, said the report, was to be "consigned to the yet more terrible dungeon, denominated the black hole".

As Betsy and Joseph John wrote up their notes each evening and planned their future publication, Betsy also confessed to her journal her own continuing unease. Despite the formation of Scottish Ladies' Associations, and her success in the gaols where prisoners were touched by her words, she remained painfully conscious of the worldly snares that waited to trap her. In Edinburgh, she said, where she and her brother had visited the prison with the Lord Provost and other dignitaries, she had talked rather too loudly, and far too proudly, about her meeting with Queen Charlotte at the Mansion House. She was also conscious that the vast crowds who thronged the meetings organised by Friends in the towns she passed through, often attracted there by features in the local newspapers, were drawn as much by a fascination with Mrs Fry herself, as by any more serious motives. "Quite a jubilee meeting," she commented about the fashionable hordes who followed her at

Edinburgh, while in Liverpool, on the way home, the abundance of feathers and ribbons adorning the public hall, "such a flock of the gay," made her wonder if it was not all designed to tempt her to worldly pride.

The same temptation seemed to lay waiting at Knowsley, the ancestral seat of the Earl of Derby, where the whole family and their many guests were all determined to honour Mrs Fry. "If a duchess in the land I think that more would not have been made of me," she said, and although she struggled to maintain a coolness, as the attention and the company warmed her, almost imperceptibly, "quite the old Betsy came once more upon the stage." Betsy herself was mortified. "My internal feeling was humiliation and self-abasement," she said later, "yet the surface of my mind was rather light, vain and foolish, and I rather enjoyed the novelty and cheerfulness of the scene." Yet as she regretted her failure to be more resolute, she also marvelled at God's purposes. Before the Gurney party left, Lady Derby marshalled her whole household, including every servant, over 70 people in all, into her vast dining room, for Betsy and Joseph John to lead them in prayer. Gazing around the great room, where glittering chandeliers hung from gilded ceilings, where the eyes of Derby ancestors stared down from paintings adorning the walls, and where the candlelight was transformed into an almost ethereal glow by many gleaming mirrors, Betsy saw the whole assembly kneel down before God. "Many of the party were in tears," she remembered, "some exceedingly affected."

Betsy herself had been exceedingly affected by something she had witnessed at Haddington Gaol, where she and Joseph John had found a lunatic confined in a dank and gloomy cell, a man whose origins no one knew, but who had been caught damaging the garden seats of the local gentry. "Being considered mischievous," said *Notes on a Visit*, "he was confined to this abominable dungeon, where he had been, at the date of our visit, in unvaried solitary confinement, for eighteen months."

She had already seen many like him in Britain's gaols, either kept like the Haddington lunatic, isolated and often chained to walls or heavy furniture, or else allowed to mingle freely among other prisoners who either feared their madness or taunted them for their feebleness and confusion. Joseph John, as he followed his sister into Britain's gaols, was often struck by her special concern for the lunatics they encountered; her manner was so tender and loving that he sometimes sensed she shared a special fellowship with them.

Betsy herself knew that she did. She had never forgotten Earlham's Becky and Goats' William Crotch, and since their deaths she had concluded that those like herself, who were afflicted mentally, should use their knowledge and insight to help their fellow sufferers. Yet fear of madness still haunted her, and in November 1818, when the reformer's friend, Sir Samuel Romilly, took his own life after the death of his wife, it returned with a vengeance. "It took rather painful hold of me," she said, "as such things are apt to do, as my fearful imagination is set off by them."

She was already depressed, for any elation at the success of the northern tour had been almost dispelled by what waited at home. She had been away almost two months, and on returning to Plashet she had found Joseph, Katherine and her younger daughter Louisa all unwell, anxious for her presence, and demanding to be nursed. Joseph had also neglected the accounts, and as Betsy worried over her family's continued financial predicament, and their expenditure which regularly exceeded their income, she spent weary evenings pouring over columns of spidery figures. She was also disturbed to discover that during her absence Joseph had attended many concerts, even the opera, and read as many novels as he could lay hands on. The poor had been neglected too, and required endless consoling visits, while Aunt Hanbury, at Brick Lane, was so sick that she must be brought to Plashet for Betsy to nurse. Most disturbing of all was Rachel, who returned from Scotland as deeply resentful as ever, and had become subject to bouts of hysterical tempers and weeping. Betsy blamed herself. She was guiltily certain that it was her failings as a wife and mother that caused her family's problems and transgressions. Desperately, she prayed for improvement, and for the power to bring her erring flock to the path of true religion.

Newgate, however, brought her some consolation. "My prison concerns truly flourishing," she said, "surely in that, a blessing in a remarkable manner appears to attend me more apparently than my home concerns."

Yet her worries continued. The accusation that she neglected her children, provoked now by the bad behaviour of the younger ones, especially by John who was constantly in trouble at school, still persisted. There were also claims that her Newgate Bible readings, while admirable in themselves, had become far too much of a show. Betsy, however, was unwilling to abandon them. While she recognised that many people attended for dubious reasons, either because it was the fashion, or from morbid curiosity, she also knew that sometimes lives were profoundly changed. For this reason alone, she said, she would not be hasty either in preventing public access, or in discontinuing the sessions entirely.

The book that described the Scottish prison visits was also a power for change, as it highlighted both the humanitarian aspects of prison reform and its potential to mitigate crime. Betsy's friend Lady Harcourt spoke for many. "Oh! My good friend," she wrote in a letter of February 1819, "what a blessed tour you have made, and may Heaven reward your wonderful exertions, by making them effectual to the purpose intended."[2] Mary Harcourt also promised to send a copy of the book to William Frederick, currently residing in Paris, and also, she said, to put a copy into the hands of the Prince Regent himself.[3] By then, however, Betsy was in no condition to appreciate her friend's good intentions.

At the age of 38 she was pregnant for the eleventh time, but her symptoms were disturbing and they led Dr Sims to suspect an imminent miscarriage. Early in February, shortly after she returned from taking her two older boys to a new school in Darlington, where she hoped their bad behaviour would improve, he had confined her to bed. There she sank into a depression and began thinking once more about death.

Staring weakly at the grey winter sky lowering over Plashet, as her physical symptoms grew steadily worse, and her stomach and bowel cramps reappeared, Betsy felt her faith tremble in the face of it. "I even *could not pray*. I felt I had not faith nor power," she wrote on one occasion. She also thought nostalgically of her work at Newgate, of the publicity that had so recently surrounded her, and of how much things could change in a year. "What was not said of me?" she asked, recalling the previous winter. "What was not thought of me? may I not say in public and in private, in innumerable publications, &c. &c." Despite her earlier reservations, she now missed it much more than she cared to admit.

Eventually Dr Sims concluded that the baby was dead. The thought of it, and the idea that death, which she had feared for so long, should have made its home within her, was so abhorrent and disgusting that it finally forced Betsy to her knees. Let me bear it, she pleaded to God, whatever it might be. She finally bore it in May; it had been dead for four months, and as she looked at the shivelled creature that emerged from within her, she felt she saw death glaring balefully from its tiny wizened face. She trembled at the sight.

In September she was called urgently to Priscilla, who had been spitting blood and was terrified that it heralded consumption,[4] that most dreaded of nineteenth-century diseases, whose end was a physical deterioration followed by an agonising death. So desperate was Priscilla, both for reassurance and for Betsy's nursing skills, that for weeks she refused to allow her sister to leave her side. Finally Priscilla's symptoms eased and she appeared to rally, and the whole family breathed a sigh of relief; their memories of John's death were still raw. However, as Betsy attempted to resume her public life and her ministry, symptoms of sickness and calls for her presence appeared on every side. In October, after her daughter Katherine suffered cramps in her bowels, Betsy and Joseph took her to Broadstairs for the sea air. In November Joseph's unmarried sister Elizabeth Fry spat blood too, and early in 1820, young Rachel suffered the same symptoms.

But the worst was yet to come, and even Betsy, whose gloomy imagination so easily conjured castles of dread from the air, could not possibly have imagined how terrible it would be. Meanwhile, once back in London, life went on; "almost like living in a market or a fair," she wrote to her boys away at school, "only that I have not merchandise to sell." In her letters, she also told them about her recent meeting with a missionary back from India, and of the awful story he told. "I think in one province," she said, "about 700 poor widows burn themselves every year, when their husbands die." She also discussed it with Fowell, who agreed to campaign in the House of Commons for a law to outlaw suttee in British India.[5]

After being elected Member of Parliament for Weymouth in 1818, Fowell had moved his family away from Brick Lane to Hampstead, close to Sam and Louisa Hoare. Both families were now members of the Church of England, and both were devout, devoted and happy. "More of heaven I never saw," Charles Simeon wrote of them to Joseph John in 1820, "than in the two families at Hampstead."[6] In the early months of that year, as freezing weather and the results of a failed harvest in 1819 combined to produce a humanitarian disaster, Fowell and Sam were the driving force behind London's first nightly shelter for the homeless. Assisting them were Mrs Elizabeth Fry and many City merchants.

Within six hours of an initial public meeting, Mr Hick, merchant of Cheapside, had thrown open a huge warehouse on London Wall, and as straw bedding was strewn on the floors, and hot soup began bubbling in enormous kettles, Betsy and Mrs Hick formed a Ladies' Committee. For almost two months it ran Bible classes morning and evening, clothed half-naked women, taught pauper children the rudiments of reading, found employment for men, especially in the Merchant Navy, and from the many donations that flooded in, provided grants to the public hospitals for the sick. By the end of February 1820, some 1,522 people had passed through the doors of Mr Hick's warehouse, and Betsy, Sam and Fowell had cause to thank God for a job well done.[7]

It was on Fowell and his placid wife, Hannah, however, that death wreaked a ferocious devastation. In March their adored eldest son, ten-year-old Thomas Fowell, arrived home from school with a fever. Fearful, but almost certain of her nephew's eventual recovery, Betsy hurried to Hampstead to take up her role as chief nurse. But despite tender care, medicines and prayers, within three weeks young Fowell was dead, followed over the next five weeks by three of his sisters. Betsy was devastated, especially as one of the little girls, five-year-old Rachel, had reminded her very painfully of her own little Betsy. As her faith faltered before the tragedy, it was Fowell and Hannah, the grieving parents, who helped to restore it. "Their resigned and patient state," she said, "has been a striking instance of the power of religion and also an example to us, their poor fellow mortals."

Despite the reassurance, the deaths were a grim reminder of mortality, though they also made Betsy nostalgic for the delights that new life brought with it. "Thankful as I feel to avoid lyings-in," she said, "yet I think my pleasures are certainly diminished in not always having babies to nurse." Even if her own young children were rowdy, their good health was a comfort to her, and she still delighted sometimes in wandering with them through the gardens at Plashet, or sharing their pleasure in the seashells her friends sent to them from all around the country. It brought back memories of Bramerton and her mother, and allowed her to be once again the child Betsy, innocently observing the bounty and beauty of nature. "I am often astonished," she said, "when my mind is so exceedingly occupied, and my heart so deeply interested, how I can turn with my little children to these objects, and enjoy them with as great a relish as any of them."

But, even as she enjoyed her younger children, their older siblings continued to grieve her. They had "peculiarly tempted minds", she said, and sometimes their insolence and the furious arguments they provoked seemed almost too much to bear. One day she vented her pain at Rachel in her journal, but on re-reading the entry, she tore out the page. "The dearest child has been much more sweet and good," she wrote more hopefully some days later, so it was distressing to see a more severe return of Rachel's hysterical tears, this time accompanied by fainting fits and convulsions. As she nursed her daughter through what were very familiar symptoms, Betsy hoped desperately that a little bout of illness would encourage Rachel to reflect on her treatment of her mother, and that a new and closer relationship would emerge.

For a time it seemed that all would be well, and she was delighted that Rachel and Katherine, as well as Joseph, were able to join her when she travelled north in September on prison concerns. "We have, generally speaking, been sweetly united and enjoyed our journey so far very much," she wrote gratefully at Nottingham. However, as they travelled through the Midlands and North-East England, apart from briefly encouraging her husband and daughters to help her collect seashells on the windy beaches of Northumberland, she was unable to give them much more of her time.

After her earlier visit north with Joseph John, there had been criticisms of their subsequent report by some Yorkshire magistrates, who had insisted that changes made since the Gurneys' visit had in fact been there all along. Knowing that this was not the case, and determined to prevent anything similar occurring in the future, Betsy had evolved a very precise and time-consuming procedure. Firstly, armed with letters of introduction either from officials or from private friends, she called on the local Visiting Magistrates responsible for the prisons she wished to see. Then, with their authority, and in the company of officers of the prison, interested magistrates, and often with local ladies, she went into the gaols. Once there, as she moved from yard to yard, and from one ward to another, she took detailed notes from gaolers and turnkeys, and also assessed the buildings for their potential for improvement. Afterwards, she wrote a report which she sent to each magistrate and prison governor visited.

Wherever possible, as she returned towards London from her northern trip, Betsy also founded Ladies' Associations from the throngs of women eager to follow her example. She also addressed many public meetings on the subject of prison reform and the death penalty. At Seaton, County Durham, early in October, she amazed herself when for the first time in her life she took sole responsibility for organising a meeting attended by people of all walks of life, which she then presided over almost alone, and successfully controlled despite its being large and sometimes rowdy.

Back at Plashet, and recalling their brief moments of family togetherness, once again Betsy vowed to be a better wife to Joseph and to spend more time at home. It was a vain hope. She was by now Britain's most high-profile prison reformer, and after the royal family, its most high-profile woman. As an expert in her field, each week she received hundreds of letters, and her presence was constantly in demand. Every Friday after her public Bible readings at Newgate, she went out on prison business, often to the Lord Mayor at the Mansion House, to the aldermen or sheriffs in their City homes, or to the homes of influential Londoners who might be persuaded to support her cause.

During the previous year, some of her misgivings about her dealings with the rich and powerful had been partially assuaged by Joseph John, who agreed with Wilberforce that in order to transform society it was essential to work among the arbiters of opinion and the makers of laws. "My deliberate opinion is," he had replied, after she finally revealed her fears to him, "that thy introduction to the great ones of the earth, is in the ordering of Divine Providence; and this decides the question at once – as to thy being endangered by it, I think nothing of it."[8] Together with other family members he also encouraged her to use her influence and speak more frequently on behalf of other causes, most notably the Bible Society, and the campaign against slavery that was rapidly becoming the great passion of Fowell Buxton.

Whenever she could, Betsy also spent time each week at Newgate, classifying new prisoners, taking her turn in the workroom, sometimes calming frayed convict tempers, and visiting the condemned cells. Often rising at four in the morning to ensure she fulfilled her busy programme, she visited London's other prisons regularly too, the Borough Compter, Tothill Fields, Coldbath Fields and the Millbank Penitentiary among them. Once there, as well spending time with the prisoners, conducting prayers, and visiting the condemned, she also met with governors and chaplains to advise on the appointments of the matrons and female officers that were the result of her ceaseless lobbying and influence. She also met regularly with her Ladies in committee, and with them she visited former prisoners in their homes, encouraging and assisting them to live decently and maintain their honesty. Together with Elizabeth Pryor and other ladies, she also visited every convict ship that left London for Australia, and as she did so, she began a campaign to change the dismal conditions endured by women convicts in New South Wales.

"Honoured Madam," said a letter from Parramatta, dated 23 February 1819,

> Having learned from the public papers, as well as from my friends in England, the lively interest you have taken in promoting the temporal and eternal welfare of those unhappy females who fall under the sentence of the law; I am induced to address a few lines to you respecting such as visit our distant shores ...

The writer was Samuel Marsden, a protegee of William Wilberforce who had eventually become the leading Anglican clergyman in New South Wales. He was also chaplain at Parramatta, near Sydney, home to the prison colony known as The Factory.

> For the last five-and-twenty years many of the convict women have been driven to vice, to obtain a loaf of bread, or a bed to lie upon. To this day, there has never been a place to put the female convicts in, when they land from the ships. Many of these women have told me with tears, their distress of mind on this account, some would have been glad to have returned to the paths of virtue, if they could have found a hut to live in, without forming improper connexions.

Yet despite Samuel's petitions to the Colonial Office, to Members of Parliament, and to the Archbishop of Canterbury, nothing had ever been done. What was particularly hard for him, he said, were his visits to the deathbeds of such women.

While I use the Scripture language my soul yearns after them, I should wish to impart to them the consolations of the gospel, and point out to them the Lamb of God, but my tongue often seems tied, I have got nothing to say to them. To tell them of their crimes, is to upbraid them with misfortunes: they will say, "Sir, you know how I was situated, I did not wish to lead the life I have done, I know and lament my sins, but necessity compelled me, to do what my conscience condemned; I could not help myself, and must have starved, if I had not done as I have."[9]

Though Betsy had known the details of Marsden's story ever since she met the first transports at Newgate, his letter made them so real that the thought of female convicts forced to live their lives degraded and ashamed, and then dying with no assurance of salvation, goaded her to action. Together with her Ladies she began raising Marsden's cause among her influential friends, while at the same time she also established contacts with similar women in Australia whom she encouraged to form Ladies' Associations of their own. But even as she dwelled on deathbed scenes faraway, she was called to a deathbed in Norfolk.

Priscilla's consumption had eventually returned with renewed virulence, and in March 1821 it finally reached its climax. Her brothers and sisters took her to Cromer Hall, the home Fowell had bought by the Norfolk coast for what remained of his family. Betsy nursed her sister there for almost six weeks, and as she did so, she struggled once again to maintain her faith in the face of death. "The present is with me a low time," she said, "spiritually and naturally, a time of fears and doubts which my unbelieving heart is naturally so subject to." Sometimes it even seemed that faith was all but extinguished. "Ah, dearest Lord, help my unbelief," she pleaded. But finally, on the morning of 25 March, when together with her five other sisters, Joseph John, Fowell and Francis Cunningham, she ministered at Priscilla's deathbed, she felt it all flood back. "Our dear sister Fry," wrote Joseph John, "wonderfully strengthened in faith and empowered by the Spirit, addressed the dying beloved one in a strain of confidence and ensured encouragement, as it were, helping her over the waters of Jordan."[10] Later that day, Betsy wrote to Joseph and Rachel. "About nine o'clock this morning," she said, "the scene closed, and our most tenderly beloved sister went to sleep in Jesus."

For Betsy, however, even after six long weeks in Norfolk with the dying Priscilla, there was little time to rest. Almost from her first successes at Newgate, her fame had spread overseas and she was regularly visited by foreign visitors and by ambassadors, while her huge post-bag almost always contained letters from the European capitals that had been so uniquely united by the travellers and philosophies of the Enlightenment. In some of them – in St Petersburg, led by the Princess Sophia Mestchersky; in Paris; in Turin, led by La Marquise de Barol; and in Amsterdam – ladies anxious to become prison visitors formed associations based on the Newgate model and wrote to Betsy for advice. To provide for them, and also for the growing number of Ladies' groups in Britain, and to properly oversee the convict ships, in mid-April 1821 Betsy founded The British Society for Promoting Reformation of Female Prisoners. The Duchess of Gloucester, William Frederick's wife, agreed to be its first Patron.

Less than a month later, on 23 May, Betsy's friend Sir James Mackintosh brought a motion in the House of Commons "for mitigating the severity of punishment in certain cases of forgery, and the crimes connected therewith."[11] The House was packed for the debate, and many Members, previously uncertain, or even hostile to reform, were finally swayed by the passion of Fowell Buxton, which he combined with an impressive array of statistics. Although the Bill fell by a small majority, the moment was historic. It was from that speech in May 1821 that Thomas Fowell Buxton, reformer and Evangelical Christian, became recognised as one of Britain's leading parliamentary advocates in the cause of humanity and also that the reformers sensed that victory was at last in sight.

Early in June, at a meeting of the Society for the Improvement of Prison Discipline held at Freemasons Hall, they gave expression to that belief. It was reported in *The Times* of 4 June: in the chair, it said, was the Society's Patron, William Frederick, Duke of Gloucester, and prominent in the audience, and greeted by cheers, were Thomas Fowell Buxton and Mrs Elizabeth Fry. The paper also reported the cheers from the distinguished audience that followed the speech by Lord John Russell, a supporter of reform since his entry to Parliament in 1812.[12] He expressed a belief that Britain was about "to become distinguished for triumphs, the effect of which should be to save, and not to destroy" and that "instead of laying waste the provinces of our enemies, we might begin now to reap a more solid glory in the reform of abuses at home, and in spreading happiness through millions of our own population."[13]

Later that same month, Betsy's own happiness, and her entire life, was shaken profoundly, when she discovered the cause of Rachel's erratic behaviour. His name was Captain Frank Cresswell, the relationship had begun long before the bout of service in India from which he had recently returned, and he was as handsome an officer as any that Betsy had once flirted with at Earlham. He was not however, a Quaker, and with painful memories revived of Rachel's namesake and Henry Enfield, the Gurney's gathered under the chairmanship of Hudson, to consider Rachel's future. But this time, the judgement was different, and as they concluded that times had changed, the family recommended that young Rachel be allowed to follow her heart. It was a blow for Betsy, who reflected bitterly on how her daughter was throwing away what her mother had struggled so hard to achieve. She also knew that she and Joseph would be censored for it by their Plain colleagues.

By July, however, she had allowed herself to compromise a little, and as she shopped for Rachel's trousseau, she was nostalgically recalling the days when her own fine wedding-clothes had been delivered to Earlham.

Rachel and Frank were married in Norfolk on 23 August 1821 by Francis Cunningham, and her Aunt Rachel watched with mixed emotions. Since the day that she and Harry Enfield had parted, two of her younger sisters, Hannah and Richenda, had married men not Friends and both had found great happiness. Now her niece was following in their footsteps. It had been her misfortune, she realised, to have been a young woman in love at a time when family and religious codes were harsher, and for years afterwards, as she struggled both with depression and with faith, she had questioned her Quaker inheritance. "I have lately felt," she wrote in 1807, "no good or sufficient reason for appearing, as a Quaker, so different from other people, and have doubted whether it is worthwhile to adopt any further singularity than true moderation and perfect modesty would lead to." Finally, in 1820, influenced by Josiah Pratt, the Evangelical preacher who had so profoundly brought about Fowell's conversion, she was privately baptised into the Church of England at Harrow Church by Francis Cunningham's brother John.

After Priscilla's death, Betsy was the only member of the Earlham sisterhood to remain a Quaker. Now one of her children had abandoned Friends too. "My dearest Rachel married at 9 o'clock," she recorded in her journal on 23 August. "I deeply felt about that time a sweet feeling was my portion, though certainly very low. Visited the widows, the fatherless, my poor Kate with me. Quietly at home the rest of the day." In order to show the necessary public disapproval, both she and Joseph, together with Kate, had stayed at home. Kate and Joseph had hated it, and after it, Betsy threw herself into her work at Newgate, and into religious visits with her sister-in-law, Elizabeth Fry, to Friends and to prisons throughout Kent, Sussex and Surrey. Rachel, however, was unforgiving, and for two months she corresponded with her mother only by letter. "How much that dear child can wound me!" Betsy said bitterly, after receiving one of Rachel's vitriolic missives.

The sight of Rachel and Frank together, and their new-married joy that was so evident, melted Joseph Fry's heart immediately, and when his daughter and her new husband arrived at Plashet early in November, he gathered her into his arms and could barely stop shaking Frank's hand. He also liked the young man who he thought was a steadying influence on his volatile daughter; he had been glad to give his permission for the marriage and desperately disappointed not to have given her away. Betsy was cooler. "We were all calm and got through it as well as we could expect," she noted severely after their first evening together. Three days later, as she got through entertaining a large party of Gurneys assembled to approve the young Cresswells, she began to hope that her whole large family, despite its failings and its differing opinions, might eventually become more harmoniously united. By December she had melted enough to stay at Rachel's new home at Blackheath, where she also called on Frank's parents. While there, she also discovered an unexpected advantage in her new role as mother-in-law to a family in the area. During her visit to Rachel she found herself close enough to Brixton to make a short inspection of the gaol.

It is not of
our own orderi...

"*T*HIS IS A BLESSING I...
announced to her journal on 16 November 182...
Providence has brought them together!" The b...
babies, Betsy's eleventh, and her daughter Ra...
their safe arrival, on the first day of the m...
quished the fears that in the summer of the...
again rocked Betsy's faith.

Early in June, just as she set out to escort
Princess of Denmark to Joseph Lancaster's sch...
Road, Betsy had learned that her sister-in-la...
lay dangerously ill. Though the royal visit itself —
cess, and had seemed to lay the foundation for...
cessful foreign connection, it had been har...
prevent her thoughts straying to Earlham. Thre...
heard that as she and the royal couple were fêt...
of flag-waving schoolchildren, her sister-in-law...
ing two motherless children. Once again she...
felt death's chilly breath on her brow.

Now 42 years old, pregnant for the twelfth
again fearing for her life, Betsy berated hersel...
faith. "Why need I dread so much?" she asked...
"Have I not often known naturally and spiritu...
where I could see no way, and hard things mad...
by now, she told herself, she should be able to...
Yet she was unable to trust, and apprehensive...

volatile daughter; he had been glad to give his permission for the marriage and desperately disappointed not to have given her away. Betsy was cooler. "We were all calm and got through it as well as we could expect," she noted severely after their first evening together. Three days later, as she got through entertaining a large party of Gurneys assembled to approve the young Cresswells, she began to hope that her whole large family, despite its failings and its differing opinions, might eventually become more harmoniously united. By December she had melted enough to stay at Rachel's new home at Blackheath, where she also called on Frank's parents. While there, she also discovered an unexpected advantage in her new role as mother-in-law to a family in the area. During her visit to Rachel she found herself close enough to Brixton to make a short inspection of the gaol.

It is not of
our own ordering

"**T**HIS IS A BLESSING INDEED," Betsy announced to her journal on 16 November 1822, "surely a kind Providence has brought them together!" The blessing was two babies, Betsy's eleventh, and her daughter Rachel's first, and their safe arrival, on the first day of the month, had vanquished the fears that in the summer of the year had once again rocked Betsy's faith.

Early in June, just as she set out to escort the Prince and Princess of Denmark to Joseph Lancaster's school in Borough Road, Betsy had learned that her sister-in-law, Jane Gurney, lay dangerously ill. Though the royal visit itself was a huge success, and had seemed to lay the foundation for an equally successful foreign connection, it had been hard for Betsy to prevent her thoughts straying to Earlham. Three days later she heard that as she and the royal couple were fêted by hundreds of flag-waving schoolchildren, her sister-in-law had died, leaving two motherless children. Once again she flinched as she felt death's chilly breath on her brow.

Now 42 years old, pregnant for the twelfth time, and once again fearing for her life, Betsy berated herself for her lack of faith. "Why need I dread so much?" she asked herself uneasily. "Have I not often known naturally and spiritually way made where I could see no way, and hard things made easy?" Surely, by now, she told herself, she should be able to trust her God. Yet she was unable to trust, and apprehensively she gathered her female relatives and friends, and her female servants, to pray for her safe delivery.

When their prayers for both Rachel and herself appeared answered, her previous lack of faith humbled and shamed her – especially when, four weeks after the birth and virtually free of depression, she resumed her public work. Early in December she ministered at Plashet Meeting, and two weeks later, with little Daniel Henry, whom the family called Harry, in her arms, she was back at Newgate. Later the memory of her baby's aggrieved cries during the chilly coach journey to London caused pangs of guilt, but she felt that the warmth of their reception at the gaol more than compensated. The fact that Mrs Fry brought them her baby to pet reinforced her message to the convict women, that when she said "us", she meant it. Later, kneeling among them in prayer, she was freshly overcome by the importance of the prison cause. "If those who espouse it are enabled to persevere," she said, "what good may be *done in preventing* much crime that has been both committed and perpetrated in prisons."

Late in January 1823, shortly after her brother Daniel married Lady Harriet Hay, a daughter of the Earl of Erroll, Betsy was called to Hampstead to nurse Louisa through labour. By now her attendance at such events and at family sickbeds was almost a foregone conclusion, for although she was reluctant to admit it to herself, experience, close observation and reflection on the causes and symptoms of disease had developed her nursing skills to a degree far beyond what was normally expected of women.

Yet, despite her skill, and despite her success as a reformer, a visit to Louisa in any capacity always made Betsy feel inadequate. As she observed her sister's polite, well-behaved children, her well-ordered household, and her happy marriage to a successful businessman committed to the cause of reform, she felt the contrast painfully. That Louisa's children also came so willingly to morning prayers was particularly galling,[1] and she often asked herself how her sister, who appeared so easygoing, could succeed where Betsy herself had failed. Her sense of failure was additionally reinforced whenever she caught sight of the books Louisa wrote on childcare, that were so widely acclaimed,[2] or remembered that it was Louisa who first coined the phrase "Betsy's brats".

Early in February, and anxious to encourage her own husband, Betsy took Joseph with her when she was invited to the Mansion House to dinner. In March, she took him again when she and Fowell Buxton met Robert Peel, who after replacing Lord Sidmouth at the Home Office in 1822, had almost immediately begun to investigate Britain's criminal law.

Unlike his predecessor, Britain's new Home Secretary was very much a man of the nineteenth century. Eager to be well informed, he ensured that he was regularly briefed by experts in their various fields, and although not by nature a reformer, he nevertheless recognised that if Britain were to succeed in her quest for economic progress at home and world dominance abroad, then she must become more centralised and efficient. As such, he also recognised that the nation's social policies could no longer be left to often inefficient local authorities or to benevolent individuals, but must be firmly anchored in the structure of the state.

With six years experience of prison work behind her, Betsy agreed entirely with the Home Secretary. In her evidence to the House of Commons Committee in 1818, she had recommended that training and employment in prisons be the responsibility of government. Later, in a letter respecting convict ships, she wrote, "I am anxious that a few things which would greatly tend to the order and reformation of these poor women, and protect their little remaining virtue, should become established practices, authorized by government, and not dependent on a few individuals, whose life, and health, and every thing else, are so uncertain."[3] Another who shared the same view was Admiral Sir Byam Martin, Comptroller of the Royal Navy between 1813 and 1832.[4]

Convict ships, like slave ships, were largely converted merchantmen, fitted and victualled by private contractors, whose human cargo was frequently abused by unscrupulous masters and crews. Since 1792, the presence of Royal Navy surgeon-superintendents, answerable to British government authorities, had reduced some of the worst abuses, but with an average of 20 ships sailing each year to Australia between 1815 and 1822,[5] conditions remained largely overcrowded and stinking. Although almost every woman transported (one in seven of the convict total) had been convicted of petty theft, society as a whole often chose to regard them as whores, and there was a reluctance to see their travelling conditions improved. However, after representations from Mrs Fry, and against the objection that female prisoners would therefore receive comforts unavailable on troop ships,[6] Sir Byam finally ensured that female ships carried a plentiful supply of soap and towels.

The Convict Ship Committee, a sub-committee of the British Society, using their own funds plus aid from generous supporters, also helped provide for the long-term welfare of the transported women. From 1818 onwards, each female convict who chose to take advantage of it, was provided with her own little store of goods, including a Bible, a Hessian apron, a black stuff apron, a black cotton cap, a large Hessian bag to keep her clothes in, and a small bag containing tape, one ounce of pins, and 100 needles; in all a total of almost 50 useful items for women who would otherwise often arrive in a new land with nothing. (Appendix 2.)

At Betsy's instigation, the Committee also provided libraries for each ship, including religious works, biographies and tales of travel and adventure. It was also the Committee's relentless lobbying that finally forced local authorities and central government to provide enough decent clothing to last out the long voyage. Sir Byam himself backed an initiative that allowed surgeon-superintendents to issue the certificates of orderly behaviour that could sometimes assist convict women to find employment in the households of free Australian settlers.

However neither Betsy, the Convict Ship Committee nor Sir Byam were under many illusions. Betsy herself remarked in October 1821, that not every prisoner was grateful, and many were resentful and mocking; while despite Mrs Fry's "miracle", outbreaks of rowdiness and violence still took place at Newgate. On board ship, where convict women and seamen were confined in cramped conditions for weeks on end, sexual encounters and frustrated bad behaviour often relieved the seemingly endless monotony. Anyone associated with them also knew that many convicts bore a deep and lasting hatred of the system that tore them from their home, and wanted nothing more to do with any part of it. Equally, many women had been driven to crime by the circumstances of their lives, and they yearned to make a fresh start. "Surely for the welfare of such," Betsy wrote to Sir Byam, "both here and hereafter; and the hope that even the worst may be preserved from further evil; ... it is worth the effort to make even a convict-ship a place for industry, instruction and reform."[7] It had also been worth the effort, she believed, to approach Lord Bathurst, Secretary of State for War and the Colonies, since it was after her representations to him that Samuel Marsden's barracks finally began to rise at Paramatta.

Almost immediately after receiving that news, she turned her attention to the conditions for women arriving at another convict settlement, to the south of Australia in Van Dieman's Land. "In the first place," she began, in a letter to a friendly Member of Parliament, "we deem it expedient that a building be erected in Hobart Town ... "[8] A Matron, a school for adults and girls, classification of prisoners and opportunities for employment were all carefully detailed in a series of points that Mrs Fry hoped would also eventually reach Lord Bathurst's desk. To Robert Peel's desk, in the same year, went a report concerning twelve women who arrived in handcuffs to board the convict ship, *Brothers*, eleven more who were iron-hooped around their waists, and one from Cardigan whose leg-iron had bitten so deeply into her flesh that she fainted in agony when it was finally removed.[9]

Many years later, one of the transported prisoners wrote to Betsy. Her memories of Mrs Fry were fond ones, she said, and as well as belatedly thanking her for her gift of sugar and tea, she wanted her to know that life in her exile home had been kind. Some 20 years after leaving Newgate, she was happily married, the proud owner of many chickens and pigs, and now bought her tea by the chest. She also retained a memory of her days on the convict ship, for the patchwork quilt that covered her marital bed was made of the pieces given to her by the Ladies on the day she embarked for Botany Bay.[10]

In the Newgate workshop itself an enormous quantity of goods were produced, far more than even the benevolent Mssrs Richard Dixon & Co, were prepared to dispose of, and as stocks mounted, the Ladies' Association occasionally invited their influential friends to public sales of work.

The idea was a novel one, and although it had originally been suggested by Betsy, both daughter and wife to merchant families, and although such public sales later became commonplace, in April 1823 she wondered if such blatant fundraising was consistent with her own religious principles. For there was no doubt that when Mrs Fry stood behind the trestle tables loaded with knitted and woven goods, the crowds grew thicker and the chink of coins much louder. There was also no doubt that when she took a turn serving tea and pretty cakes, there was a general bustle towards her, and that before very long she would be surrounded by colourful flocks of elegantly dressed women, all anxious to be seen with the heroine of Newgate, and to carry away a few words to repeat to their friends.

Was it another snare to trip her? Betsy asked herself. She was already convinced she was in danger, for at the end of March, Joseph had suddenly announced that he had commissioned Charles Robert Leslie, the history and portrait painter,[11] to make separate portraits of Mr and Mrs Fry. At first Betsy tried hard to dissuade him, but Joseph was so convincing in pointing out that with so many indifferent aquatints of Mrs Fry already in circulation, there was a need for one accurate likeness, that eventually, reluctantly, she had yielded.

Gradually, she also reconsidered her attitude to the sale of work. Reflecting on Joseph John's view, that Divine Providence lay behind her success, and recognising how much the prison cause benefited from her presence, she resolved to trust God and lay aside her reservations. "I have the comfort to feel at this time," she wrote, "for all my many fears on the subject, *particularly for myself,* a considerable portion of sweet peace and hope, and belief that for all the remarkable manner in which we have been brought forward in these services, it is not of our own ordering, but we may acknowledge in deep humility of heart, it is the Lord's doing and marvelous in our eyes."

A month later she needed all her reserves of faith after a virtual riot shattered the fragile peace of Newgate's workshop. Despite her earlier recognition that not all convicts appreciated her efforts, the event was nevertheless disheartening. "I met with ingratitude such as I never remember among the prisoners," she said bitterly. Struggling to overcome the sense of rejection that engulfed her, she reminded herself that in life there were times of encouragement and building up, and times of discouragement and treading down, and that in the end, all was in the hands of God. "If He who has hitherto in a remarkable manner appeared to bless the work may be pleased for a season to permit a cloud to pass over it, what is that to me?" she asked.

Even as she tried to lift her flagging spirits, in mid-May her young friend, Mary Hanbury, died in childbirth. Betsy felt the blow keenly. She had personally supervised the labour, and watching helplessly as Mary's life slipped away, her faith once again quailed before the inexorable power of death. Later she ministered to the bereaved family. At the same time she suckled Mary's motherless child alongside her own little Harry. "A low time," she said.

That she shoud give the substance of her own body to feed another woman's child, is yet another indication of the extraordinary complexity of Betsy's character. A driven woman who rarely allowed herself to rest, and whose spur to action and determination to achieve can be seen as resulting from a sense of unworthiness, nevertheless, she was also possessed of an extraordinary generosity of spirit. It was surely a feature that attracted many people who might otherwise have been repelled by her unremitting determination to do them good.

Depressed by the riot, even though the convicts had finally, shame-facedly apologised, grieving for Mary, and at 43 years old, physically drained by suckling two babies, it was a struggle for Betsy to get through Yearly Meeting. For it was there, among so many dutiful Quaker families, that she was always reminded so forcefully of the deficiencies of her own. As she stretched her resources to provide the usual hospitality, she knew that many among her guests continued to maintain that Fry shortcomings were the result of motherly and wifely neglect, and that the affairs of the world were neither the business of a Quaker, nor of a woman. For a while she felt herself adrift, a ship without a pilot. "Where am I?" she asked, "What am I about? Am I sick or in health? Going backwards or forwards?"

Her solution was more work, and she threw herself relentlessly into the prison cause, Newgate readings and speaking engagements with Joseph John and Fowell. In the evenings, she either entertained at Plashet or went out to dinner, where the talk was often of penal reform, the final abolition of slavery, or the Bible Society; if her companions were not already supporters, then Betsy was ready to convert them to the cause. Often she was so busy that she had little time to reflect on her actions, only to acknowledge what she believed was their source. "I believe they are not of my own seeking," she said, "quite the reverse, and in many of them a blessing has appeared to attend me in them. I desire not to repine in the least degree but be thankful that I am enabled thus to be employed."

Joseph Fry, however, had no desire to be similarly employed, and unlike his wife, he hoped to grow more leisurely as the years advanced. Late in the summer he bought two small cottages set in a green haven of lawns and willow trees close to Dagenham, deep in the Thames marshes, and reached only by a cart road or by boats on the placidly shining river. There he planned to spend lazy days fishing, with only his sons and daughters for company, and, he very much hoped, the wife he saw so rarely. In her honour he named his little rowing boat *The Betsy*.

Betsy herself was uncertain; she was uncomfortable about the expense, and uneasy at Joseph's devotion to a sport shunned by many Quakers and which her brother, Joseph John, never failed to oppose.[12] But, gradually, lulled by the gently lapping water and the wind sighing through the reed-beds, her overtaxed soul relaxed and she allowed her concerns to drift away. It was there too, in their reedy hideaway, that the patiently devoted Joseph managed to recapture a little spark of their youth, the snug quiet times where their relationship had almost blossomed before being overtaken by company, Betsy's Quaker ministry and by Newgate. So comfortable was it at times, that Betsy was almost ready to forgive her husband his shortcomings. "Very loving and sweet to me," she said of him in October, after she went through the painful business of weaning little Harry in the peace of Dagenham and Joseph's tender care.

Invigorated by the rest, and once more reassured that she was doing God's work, late in the month Betsy left Harry with Joseph and set off with Joseph John and her sister-in-law, Elizabeth Fry, for Bristol Quarterly Meeting. While in the West Country they also visited Bath Meeting, local magistrates and local Ladies' groups, toured a prison and publicised the reformers' agenda at two public meetings. Betsy also called on cousin Priscilla, now living in Bath, and on Hannah More, Wilberforce's faithful female supporter and author of many of the Evangelical tracts that Betsy now carried with her wherever she went.

From her meeting with Hannah More she returned to Plashet full of fervour. "I believe it right for me to make a stir in our parish about the Bible Society," she wrote enthusiastically. Then, with every expectation of success, she encouraged her neighbours to throw themselves into the work, and for rich and poor alike to overlook their differences, break down the barriers that divided them, and unite in the common cause. She found their response profoundly depressing, for not only were they largely indifferent to her project, but to her dismay she discovered that rather than rejoice at the prospect of Christian unity, many of the rich shuddered at the thought of uniting with the poor, while many of the poor loathed the rich. Seeing her shining vision inexorably laid waste, it was hard, even for Betsy, to retain a spirit of Christian love. "Ah, for a little help, dearest Lord," she prayed, "in this, as well as many other callings."

With the dawn of the new year, 1824, she began to feel that she needed that help more than ever. "My public concerns are at this time very pressing," she said, "for I have to remove prejudices in the minds of many, which prevent ladies visiting prisons."

This had first become evident to her during a visit to Dorking in mid-February, when the Ladies' Association there had complained of outright opposition. Very soon, similar reports began pouring in from all over the land. Sadly, they were prompted by what had originally appeared to be a culmination of something Betsy had worked for since the day she first entered Newgate.

The sense of the reformers in 1821, that change was within sight, had been correct. It was reinforced in the same year by legislation,[13] which although largely confined to a declaration of principles, was at least a firm indication that the cause of penal reform was gathering momentum. From 1822 onwards, with Robert Peel anxious to amend the criminal law, to bring all prisons gradually under central government control and to impose standards and uniformity, the momentum gathered speed, and his Prisons Act of 1823 was a milestone in British penal history.[14] It also included many of the principles that Mrs Fry and the reformers had fought for. Henceforward, gaolers became salaried employees of local authorities and were no longer able to charge fees; prisoners were to be classified; and rules were laid down that covered issues of health, clothing, education and labour. Where men and women inhabited the same prison, they were to be confined in segregated areas, and women were to be supervised entirely by female wardens. The general use of irons was prohibited, so too was solitary confinement, while local justices of the peace were authorised to investigate complaints of punishment deemed too severe. The justices were given other powers too, to organise the gaols according to a prescribed pattern, to ensure that the new regime was reformatory on behalf of every prisoner, and to furnish the Home Secretary with quarterly reports. In the same year, another piece of legislation ensured that henceforward all prisoners would be carried through the streets in covered vans.

While Peel's 1823 Act was intensely radical, however, it contained two substantial defects. It failed to create an Inspectorate to ensure its implementation, and it applied only to the prisons of London and Westminster, of 17 designated provincial towns, and to 130 of Britain's innumerable county gaols. In effect, it meant that where the policy prevailed, much of its fulfilment was left to local magistrates, some of whom were either hostile to the reforms or struggling to implement them with inadequate funds, and where it did not, the old order remained as before. In neither case, but especially where magistrates were hostile or struggling, did those in charge always relish the thought of self-appointed teams of local ladies examining their shortcomings, making suggestions and sending critical reports to Mr Peel. At its moment of triumph, the success of Betsy's cause seemed now to be a hindrance to its continuation.

"The burden and perplexity of the opposition to improvement in prisons," she said despairingly, "is almost too much for me."

Up to that point, although her public path had been hard, it had also appeared relatively straightforward. When she preached at Newgate, or worked among the prisoners, when she spoke from public platforms or shared her ideas with public men, although she believed she saw herself tempted by worldly pride, she had nevertheless always been able to reassure herself that her path was divinely ordained. Only once before, in her dealings with Lord Sidmouth, had she inadvertently stepped into the complex world of politics. And although Harriet Skelton had died, she herself had escaped relatively unscathed. Now, however, it appeared that her cause was endangered by a degree of political complexity which no woman of her background had ever dealt with before.

As Betsy struggled to see her way forward, the conflict between her fear of worldly contamination and her desire to play a role on the stage of the theatre of action grew increasingly sharp. It grew sharper still as into the conflict went her guilt at leaving her family, and her doubts over whether it really was God who prompted her or her own sinful vanity. Even her old scepticism once again returned to haunt her. In the face of such overwhelming odds, the idea of mounting a public defence, or of attempting to rally her influential acquaintances to her support seemed an impossible task. Yet at the same time she yearned to save her cause. The conflict, both outside and within, gradually began to overwhelm her.

"I have felt for some little time past very delicate," she wrote in the second week of March 1824, "and as if I was really over-done, bordering on a shaking state, and as if I could not go on much longer." She could barely stay awake, she said, and was sometimes sleeping all day. Shortly afterwards, after determinedly forcing herself out of bed for the morning Bible reading, she collapsed.

The speed with which the illness took hold terrified her. Suddenly, almost without warning, it seemed, she was confined to bed, sunk in a tearful depression, blaming herself, and thinking of death. Was the sickness her own fault, she asked guiltily, for being so immersed in the things of the world? Should she have spent more time developing a life of faith instead? Was she ready to die? She also fretted over a planned religious visit to Worcester and Birmingham.

Desperate not to abandon the cause in its time of need, but against all advice, she forced herself out of bed and into the luxurious olive-green coach lined with thick carpet and watered silk that was the pride of her brother Sam. Long years as close neighbours had deepened and strengthened the ties that had first begun at Mildred's Court, and while the by now enormously wealthy Sam was unwilling to relinquish the rewards and responsibilities of his City firm, he had become increasingly willing to finance the reformers' agenda. It was in his company, with his wife Elizabeth, and with all their expenses underwritten by Sam, that Betsy hoped not only to survive the journey and the heavy round of Quaker meetings and prison visits, but to minister successfully in all of them. That she did so, while feeling so ill, was to her a remarkable proof of God's providence. "Indeed a remarkable evidence," she insisted, "that there is in man something *beyond the natural*, that when at its lowest, weakest state, wonderfully helps and strengthens. None can tell what its power is, but those who submit to it."

It was the opinion of Dr Sims, however, that the illness had been provoked by a miscarriage, and he advised Betsy to take a much longer rest in bed. She ignored her symptoms, however, and drove herself on; early in April, with so much doubt about the future of ladies visiting prisons, she felt bound to preside over the third annual meeting of the British Society. Though at times she could barely keep her eyes open, while at others she felt she no longer inhabited the same reality as her colleagues, she was grateful to be there.

In the event, it was a historic occasion. The Duchess of Gloucester, the Society's Patron, presided in the Chair, and the hall itself was filled to overflowing with women from many Christian denominations, who as they sought to bring transformation to others, had discovered that their own lives were also transformed. As they discussed their earlier struggles, and, despite its limitations, the achievement of Robert Peel's Prison Act, there was a sense of purpose in the air that was almost tangible. "How many prisons are now visited by ladies," Betsy noted with satisfaction, "and how much is done for the inhabitants of the prison-house, and what a way is made for their return from evil."

Among those ways were three small beginnings that had been made in Westminster, Liverpool and Dublin. They had various names – Shelter, Asylum and Refuge – but the original concept had been Betsy's. They were the first residential establishments of their kind where discharged female prisoners were offered the employment and support necessary to begin the long and difficult return to productive, law-abiding lives. The meeting also discussed another of Betsy's suggestions, that a similar shelter be set up for some of the very young girls who stole, begged and prostituted themselves on Britain's city streets. After it was agreed that efforts would be made to establish such a refuge before the annual meeting of 1825, Betsy offered to write personally to Mr Peel, begging his support.

In the anti-climax that followed the meeting, Betsy returned to Blackheath where she was staying with Rachel and Frank, and with the applause still loud in her ears, she bent over her journal.

By now, as her illness grew more acute, and was combined with even more weeks of overwork and stress, she was also in a state of complete denial. "Deep as my interest has certainly been in the destitute and forlorn," she told her journal, "yet how much more, both in time and heart, have I been occupied with my own family. I fancy that my natural affections are very acute; and that if it had not pleased a kind Providence to lead me into some other services, and in His tender mercy to bless me in them, I think there would at times have been great danger of my being pressed down out of measure by home cares."

Having safely reassured herself, she felt she saw her words reflected in the care and attention she was currently receiving from her once-rebellious daughter, proving that the long years of maternal devotion had finally been rewarded. Rachel herself was certainly worried enough about her mother's health to take in the younger children while Joseph and Kate took Betsy away to Brighton.

Once there, Betsy's collapse became total. Clothed in a fog of depression, she did little except sleep fitfully during the day, lie wakeful at night, brood over the endlessly shifting sea, and drink more than she knew was good for her. "Obliged to be constantly taking some stimulous to keep circulation going on, so apt to be cold, sick, spasmodic and faint," she said. Though the remedies soothed her and drove away the worries caused by Peel's Act, as well as the nagging inner voice that accused her of neglecting husband and children, they also fuelled her guilt. Anxiously she tried to reassure herself that she had them under control. "I believe I may say as it respects spirits I am clear," she said, "and I think I may say it is also my true desire in other things, such as the wine and malt liquor that ... " When she looked over her confession she tore out the following page.

It was while gazing idly at the sea one day, mesmerised by the glints and sparkles that shimmered across its blue surface, and powerfully conscious somewhere in her being of its

231

immensity and depth, that Betsy became aware of the District Visiting Society taking shape in her mind.

On the rare days she had ventured outside the Brighton house, she had been painfully struck by the huge numbers of beggars who clamoured around local inhabitants and seaside visitors alike. Her house, too, had sometimes seemed almost under siege from people attracted by the charitable reputation of Mrs Fry. Thinking about them, she also found herself thinking of Earlham, the compact world where everyone knew each other so well that while need could not be hidden, neither could dishonest attempts to obtain relief be disguised. Might it be possible, she wondered, to establish something similar in Britain's growing towns where so many people remained strangers. Turning the problem over in her mind, she recalled a conversation in 1822, when Dr Thomas Chalmers, the Evangelical leader of the Church of Scotland,[15] had described to her his efforts to take Christianity to the Glasgow poor. Could an equally successful scheme be initiated at Brighton? Betsy asked herself.

As she did so, almost immediately she began to feel better.

"A good deal occupied with endeavouring to form a charity for the good of the poor," she wrote at the beginning of July. When crowds flocked to a public meeting she called, many of them women eager to be involved in the proposed society, she felt her recovery gaining pace. Her plan, she told her audience, was simple, and drew both on the ideas of Dr Chalmers, and her own experiences over many years. Its beneficiaries would be the poorest and most needy families, whose needs would be assessed by local female visitors, who, as the months and years passed, would build up an intimate store of knowledge, as well as a friendly acquaintance with their poorer neighbours. The poor, meanwhile, as well as receiving any necessary assistance in terms of food and clothing, were also to be encouraged, with the aid of an initial financial inducement, to save a regular small amount in a Savings Bank. Both parties would benefit, Betsy maintained: the poor through habits of order, industry and achievement, and the wealthy through an increase of kindness, interest and usefulness. When the Bishop of Chichester agreed to be its patron, and the Earl of Chichester its first

President, a satisfied and invigorated Mrs Fry declared the Brighton District Visiting Society founded.

Yet even as she brought the Visiting Society into being, another idea was germinating in her mind. During the nights of her sickness, claustrophobia had sometimes driven her to an upstairs open window, where she gazed for hours from her lofty vantage point towards the shingled beach. She had become increasingly intrigued by something odd she saw, and she began to watch out for him: a solitary figure who day and night, through fair weather and foul, paced the lonely shore in a perambulation as regular as the rise and fall of the tide. She eventually learned that the lonely walker was a blockade-man,[16] and that the singular task of his fellowship was to patrol England's coasts to prevent smuggling.

Out in her carriage on one of her better days, she passed the isolated and windswept outpost that was the Coast Blockade Station, where, after being informed politely by its inhabitant that he was forbidden to communicate with strangers, she handed him her card. Later she often thought about him, and about his silent wife, their troop of round-eyed solemn children, and the lonely life they shared together in their cliff-top home.

Some days later a young naval lieutenant held Betsy's card in his hand as her maid showed him into the parlour. He was the commander of the Blockade Stations near Brighton, he said with a smile, as Betsy invited him to sit down, and he had come in person to answer her enquiries. It was also a pleasure, he added, to meet Mrs Fry. Presently, as he sipped his tea, he explained how the blockade system worked. Guarding Britain's coasts was a dangerous and often unpleasant occupation, he said, for not only were the men obliged to be out in all weathers, but they were also unpopular with local people, partly because they were forbidden to communicate with them, and partly because their presence deterred the illegal trade. Often they were themselves attacked by smugglers. "They might almost be said," the lieutenant added, "to be in a state of blockade themselves."[17]

Betsy asked his opinion of her idea of providing each station with a small library of useful books, rather like those on the convict ships; religious titles, biographies, and accounts of travel and exploration. In response the Lieutenant assured her that such a gift would be very warmly received.

The books were indeed received warmly, and some months later the young officer forwarded to Betsy a letter from the blockade-men at the Salt Dean Naval Watch-House near Brighton.

> Sir
> We, the seamen of Salt Dean Station, having the pleasure to announce to those ladies, whose goodness has pleased them to provide the Bibles and Testaments for the use of us seamen that we have received them. We do therefore, return our sincere and most hearty thanks for the same, and we do assure the ladies, whose friendship has proved so much in behalf of seamen, that every care shall be taken of the said books; and at the same time great care shall be taken to instruct those who have not the gift of education, and we at any time shall feel a pleasure in doing the same.
> We are, Sir,
> Your most obedient and dutiful servants,
> William Bell
> D. Stringer
> in the name of the Salt Dean party.[18]

Returning to Plashet after almost twelve weeks away, Betsy pondered on her long illness. First there had been the sudden and unexpected plunge that had seemed designed to prevent her from continuing her public career. Then it had taken her to Brighton, where she had been enabled to achieve so much for the benefit of others, before finally being carried through. There was no other explanation that she could see but that it was all part of God's plan. "A humble trust often arises," she wrote, "that these illness are in a peculiar manner dispensations permitted for my *deep humiliation*, more so I believe, than almost any outward dispensation could be. They so remarkably prove to me my own *great frailty*, and all my powers, natural and spiritual, are *of the Lord*."

CHAPTER THIRTEEN

The storm

"*I*N BEGINNING ANOTHER BOOK, my heart feels tendered within me under the consideration of the many I have already filled, with a history of what appears to me an interesting life."

Early in January 1825, letting her gaze rest on the empty white pages before her, Betsy reflected on all that had passed since William Savery had bid her turn to the light. Could she ever have imagined, on that long-ago day at Goat Lane, the extraordinary journey ahead? Or could she have conceived, as she made her first faltering steps towards faith, how Earlham, its inhabitants, and herself, would eventually play a major role in Britain's wider Christian life?

Under Joseph John's mastership, the old house had increasingly opened its doors to influential Christians of many denominations who worked together in unity for the furtherance of many causes. Under the benevolent eye of Kitty, who after Jane Gurney's death had once more resumed her sway, William Wilberforce relaxed in the Great Parlour with Fowell Buxton and Francis Cunningham, as Charles Simeon described to them the latest stars in his long line of Evangelical ordinands. In the library, Dr Christopher Wordsworth, Master of Trinity College, Cambridge,[1] told stories of his famous brother William, to the Bishop of Norwich and his fascinated family. In the Little Parlour, rather more quietly, Rachel often listened pensively as the now-widowed Amelia Opie reflected on her life since becoming a Friend.[2]

Each year the Norwich Bible Society held its annual meeting at Earlham, while in the same week the Church Missionary Society and the Jews' Society,[3] also convened there. Many years later Joseph John's daughter, Anna, recorded her memories of the parties of 90 or more men and women who gathered around her father's great table.

> It was so different from a party called together for mere amusement, so fine a feeling pervaded the whole; while he, [Joseph John] as master, was wonderfully able to keep up the tone of the conversation, so that I should think it never sank to a mere chit-chat level. My impression is, that while he greatly felt the responsibility of these occasions, he most truly enjoyed them, having often round him those whose conversation was a feast to him, such as Wilberforce, Simeon, Legh Richmond,[4] John Cunningham, and many others.[5]

For Betsy, Earlham's interdenominational events meant that she maintained close contact with Wilberforce and his circle, and while they were always well aware of her latest work in Britain's prisons, she herself was also caught up in the current of ideas flowing from the Evangelical movement into the Society of Friends.

Later in January, during a visit to Brighton with her daughters Katherine and Richenda, she reflected on the success of the District Visiting Society, and also considered the changes that were taking place in the country at large. From the days of her youth, when so many in society had seemed intent only on pleasure, it was now becoming almost fashionable to be industrious, to be good, and to be involved in worthwhile causes. Much of it, she knew, was due to Wilberforce and his circle, and a little, she hoped, to herself.

She was also beginning to feel more confident that to play a role on the world's stage was no longer wrong, either for a Quaker or for a woman. In fact, she observed, it seemed to be a feature of the present day that an ordinary woman, "nothing extraordinary in point of power, simply seeking to follow a crucified Lord," could lay the foundation of organisations supported by people from all parts of society and all Christian denominations.

But, although society might be changing, there were no changes in the financial problems of the Frys, and before the end of the month she was reminded of them forcibly by her brother-in-law William Fry. Their discussion was acrimonious, and as William complained bitterly of earlier shabby treatment by the Gurney bankers, Betsy became increasingly uneasy. Following the financial disaster of 1812, she had truly believed that anything due to him had been paid, but now, in the face of so much stored-up resentment, she was less certain. For a while, on William's behalf, she was ready to blame Joseph. "If I had not to look to a very expensive husband and children," she wrote in exasperation, "but *only myself* ... I believe I could make any sacrifice to please him and his family."

Confronted once more by the spectre of financial uncertainty, Betsy reminded herself how often rescue had come at her need. On one recent and particularly hard-pressed occasion, she noted optimistically, an unexpected £500 had arrived from Joseph John just in time to shore up appearances that were in imminent danger of collapse. "Where there is an *upright desire* ... to do *strictly right*," she maintained, then she had no doubt at all that the Lord would continue to provide.

However, she was unable to convince herself that Joseph Fry had acted either uprightly or done what was strictly right, when he arrived home from a trip to France in February laden with valuable paintings and cases of elegant ornaments. Horrified that he had wasted the money, just as he had when they were first married, and as he often still did whenever he felt that Plashet needed renovation or decoration, Betsy worried that her extravagant husband courted disaster.

She was in a happier frame of mind at the fifth annual meeting of the British Society in April, when she was able once again to see herself as a sign of the times. "The British Society meeting got through to *real* satisfaction," she wrote, "and I may say to myself, the poor humble unworthy instrument amongst women in this country in this prison cause, it is really wonderful to myself what has been accomplished in the last few years." She also noted the success of the Brighton District

Visiting Society and the work among the blockade-men. "I there sowed in tears," she said, "and I now reap in joy."

Hannah More, her much-admired fellow female Christian pioneer, had presented her with a copy of her work, *Practical Piety*. On the flyleaf, the inscription read:

> As a token of veneration for her heroic zeal, Christian charity, and persevering kindness to the most forlorn of human beings. They were naked, and she clothed them; in prison, and she visited them; ignorant, and she taught them, for His sake, in His name, and by His word who went about doing good.

The words always reminded Betsy of Deborah Darby's prophecy, which had now so fruitfully come to pass, and as she thought of the minister of Coalbrookdale, she reflected that in Deborah Derby, in Hannah More, and in herself, she saw three women taking the stage in a world that was providing new opportunities for their sex.

It was the opportunities of the changing world, together with a growing concern for young people, that encouraged her, at Yearly Meeting, 1825, to call a grand rally of Quaker youth.

The Fry children were not the only young Friends dissatisfied with their Society; they were just a small part of a continuing drift away that had begun during the years of quietism, and which Betsy had seen grow increasingly widespread throughout her whole ministerial career. It was also a decline which she and Joseph John hoped would be halted and reversed by their own combination of Evangelical enthusiasm and traditional Quaker piety, which they also believed reflected the beliefs of the Society in its early days of spectacular growth.

The night before the meeting, Betsy was overwhelmed by anxiety. When day finally dawned however, she felt ready to play her part in what she believed was a fight for the continued existence of the Society of Friends and for the Christian cause among young people in Britain.

To her delight, and her relief, the meeting was packed. Two thousand young people had come to hear the heroine of

Newgate speak, and apart from little Harry, all the Fry children were there, including Frank and Rachel Cresswell. It was to them, as well as to those around them, that Mrs Fry addressed her words. All who serve God by doing righteousness are acceptable to him, she told her audience. Indeed, she continued, our service is in fact a debt that is due to him for mercies to us, a debt that should be paid by our following a crucified Lord and ourselves taking up the cross. And by our so doing, she said, there would emerge from the church generally, and the Society of Friends in particular, a people who would be seen as a city set on a hill, whose light could never be hid. Later, after Joseph John had spoken on faith and doctrine, and Uncle Joseph prayed, Betsy concluded the meeting with a prayer, that the blessing of the Most High might rest upon them all, from generation to generation.

Anxiously, in the days and weeks that followed, she looked for signs of transformation in her own children, and when John announced his attachment to Rachel Reynolds, the third daughter of a grand Quaker family, it seemed as if her prayers had been heard.

The wedding took place in early August at Westminster Meeting House, itself a place of poignant memories for Betsy, and as she saw John and Rachel make their vows there, surrounded by their brothers and sisters, she began to hope that a turning point had been reached. Later, when the newly-wed couple returned from their honeymoon, she was convinced that her once wayward son was much improved. There was other good news too, that Frank and Rachel would move shortly to King's Lynn, where Frank was to take up a position at Gurney's Bank. On 19 August, as she celebrated her twenty-fifth wedding anniversary, Betsy looked with confidence to the future. *"Ah, may our last days be our best days,"* she prayed.

Almost immediately she set out with her sister-in-law, Elizabeth Fry, for Friends Meetings in Devon and Cornwall. Travelling westward, and relaxing to the steady drumming of hooves, she gazed on a late summer landscape that was lush and drowsy, and rich with the perfume of sun-warmed grass, while each glimpse of the distant sea showed it glassy smooth. Feeling that the journey was particularly blessed, memories of her first trip to the West Country in 1798 drifted through her mind. Sometimes that journey now seemed like a lifetime away, but although its images were often dim in her memory, at Devonport one of them jumped sharply into focus. "A concern that I first felt when a *girl*, travelling with my father," she remembered, "that if ever I was a minister, I must have a meeting there." Now, 27 years later, as she surveyed her audience of 1,500 people, most of them poor, she recalled her long-ago sight of the mean dockyard streets. "I longed to do them good," she had written of their inhabitants at the time. And she had done her best to do so, she reflected, and she thanked God that he had made her his instrument.

At Plymouth, as part of the campaign to restore young people to the Society of Friends, she held another huge meeting for Quaker youth. Later, in Exeter, she founded a branch of the British Society. It was a triumphant journey, with almost only one small sorrow marring the whole six weeks. At Bath, in cousin Priscilla Hannah Gurney's quiet announcement that she would no more go out, Betsy heard death's quiet footfall.

For a few weeks, the blessedness that attended her West Country journey seemed to linger. "Much peace and thankfulness, I may say, has been my portion, at being once more in my delightful home," she wrote at the beginning of November. Several years earlier, her daughter Katherine had taken over the reins of the household, and had proved a capable housekeeper, and returning once again to the neatness and order of Plashet, and anticipating a busy time ahead, Betsy allowed herself to relax.

Less than two weeks later, in mid-December, her family once again faced bankruptcy. The immediate cause was the devastating loss of large loans, but although Betsy recognised that even to have made them was imprudent for a bank in Fry's unstable condition, once again, Joseph Fry had been caught up in a much wider catastrophe.

A relaxed domestic monetary policy had encouraged him, like many other businessmen, to finance investments both in

Britain and in the newly independent states of South America. The enthusiasm had produced a stock-market boom, but early in 1825, as investors bid up the price of South American stock, some real and some imaginary, the boom became a bubble. The bubble burst in April, and by December, as the collapse of large London banks followed a wave of county banks' failures, the boom became a panic.[6]

In November, with the Bank of England surrounded by armed guards, it seemed that the country stood on the brink of ruin. From Mildred's Court, Joseph sent a note to his wife saying nothing now could save them except Providence, all other resources having failed. On reading it, Betsy was forced to face the unthinkable. Could it be, she asked herself, that although she had struggled so hard to obey God's commands and to do righteousness, that he was about to turn his face from her?

For weeks the precarious situation fluctuated, sometimes by the day, often by the hour. Fighting to maintain their own solvency, the Gurney bankers made agreements with Betsy which collapsed, were renewed, and then collapsed again. Joseph John and Sam Gurney, together with Fowell, were often at Plashet, suggesting as gently as they could that if Fry's finally collapsed, everything, including Betsy's beloved home, must be totally given up. In the face of the impending disaster, and after Betsy's investigations into the accounts revealed how much he had kept from her, Joseph became sulky and irritable. When the bills for John and Rachel's wedding and honeymoon arrived, and were far larger than anticipated, Betsy bemoaned to her journal the endless necessity for keeping up appearances. To act as rich, she said, when in reality the Frys were poor, constantly put them in an impossible situation. Later, she ripped out many of her furious pages.

The national uncertainty lasted until April 1826, by which time almost 60 British banks had failed. The Frys had been saved yet again by the Gurneys, but relations between them had changed. Even though Joseph John and Sam agreed with Betsy that their joint survival was evidence of God's grace to them all, they were in no mood for sentiment. They had shored up the bank and made the tea business safe for Joseph Fry and his sons, but they also made it painfully clear that this was to be the very last rescue.

Much as Betsy believed that God had provided, she was also more conscious than ever of being a burden to her relations. She was grateful to them all: even Louisa had sent a present of £100, and Uncle Barclay and Hudson had made it clear they would continue to fund her charities. And even though the shabby treatment she feared had never yet materialised, after this last disaster, she asked, would the Gurneys now despise her for her poverty?

At the annual meeting of the British Society, late in April, and at Yearly Meeting in May, she also wondered if any of the enthusiastic delegates suspected the true state of Fry affairs. Even if they did, she vowed, she herself would endeavour to concentrate on acting righteously in the sight of God.

It was during Yearly Meeting in 1826 that Betsy first began noting changes in her attitude to the Society of Friends. For no longer did Plain speech, Plain dress and Plain behaviour seem quite as important to her as they once had. Nor could she agree any longer that Quakers were a chosen people. Moreover, she confided to her journal, she was beginning to believe that while the Plain path had been right for her, and, she believed, for her children, it might not always be so right for others. "I have also had some fears," she said in July, "whether our peculiar views in bearing our testimonies in many little things much in the cross to young people, does not in measure turn them from religion itself." Was it not simply enough, she continued, that by any proper means possible they should come to know Christ? The differing religious paths of her own brothers and sisters, she admitted, that had once caused her such anguish, had finally taught her that even when Christians did not see entirely eye to eye, they could still be united in the Spirit and the bonds of peace.

In August, in the spirit of Christian unity, on her way to Friends Meetings in Kent, Betsy distributed Evangelical tracts aboard the Gravesend steam packet. Some fellow passengers found such fervour embarrassing, but even the cynics were filled with admiration when on her return journey, Mrs Fry disembarked in mid-river onto a small boat that took her straight to two female convict ships lying at Woolwich. "Their order, cleanliness and general appearance delighted me," she said of them, "and made me really struck with the wonderful change wrought since we first undertook them."

In September there were more ships to visit, this time with her sister-in-law Elizabeth Fry and William Wilberforce. Almost immediately afterwards, she went with Sam and his wife to Quaker Meetings in Bedfordshire and Hertfordshire, and to the prison at St Albans. But though she enjoyed their company, Sam and Elizabeth's unity also highlighted her own husband's absence and lack of interest. She was also concerned that the disaster of the previous year, which for a while she had believed was leading Joseph towards a spiritual path, had in fact made no appreciable difference to his religious state. "I have an awful fear as to spiritual," she said, "that in my dearest companion in life, there is a return to the world."

"I have for some weeks past, believed that I must accompany my beloved brother Joseph to Ireland in the Spring," Betsy wrote in December, "to visit Friends, and also the prisons."

It was a journey that had been on her mind for several years, and although continually sorrowful that her own Joseph failed her as a companion, she was encouraged that once again she would travel with Joseph John who would also fund their travels and help to produce a report. Despite her certainty that the trip was ordained, however, as her departure drew near, the thought of crossing the sea began to take on a momentous significance. Fearful that she might never see them again, in her anxiety she sent off a flood of letters to Kitty and Rachel, and to her own Rachel Cresswell. She wrote to Joseph and the children again from Bristol, and on reaching Dublin, early in February 1827, she was immediately overcome by homesickness and a guilty conscience.

Her reception in Ireland, however, restored and revived her. Once again, Mrs Fry drew the crowds; her public meetings were packed, with thousands filling the halls and hundreds more turned away, while sometimes more than 100 people called at her hotel each day. But, just as always, her fame roused conflicting emotions within her, both alarm and elation, and to her journal she expressed the hope that the eyes of her audience were focussed on God rather than on herself.

Back in Hampstead, Louisa Hoare sensed something of the attraction. Perhaps she even remembered the adolescent Betsy, who despite her melancholy had always captured so many masculine hearts. It was certainly an attraction that Betsy had never entirely lost, and although during her childbearing years it seemed overlaid by her view of herself as a careworn wife and mother, yet as she grew older, it appeared to be metamorphosing into something unique. At 47 years old, the mother of many children, and the figurehead of the prison cause, Mrs Fry seemed to represent something that although radically new, was also curiously primitive. The sight of her matronly figure in its Quaker costume, and the sound of her musical voice ringing out in preaching and in prayer, inspired feelings that were almost as reverential as they were admiring.

"Do you see the reports in the papers of Aunt Fry and her doings in Ireland?" Louisa wrote to her son Samuel.

> I wish you could see their letters. They are as entertaining and interesting as they are curious ... Catholics, Protestants, high and low, learned and ignorant, are drawn to your aunt by a sort of witchery; this witchery is, however, explained by the mighty power of the Gospel, manifested in a peculiar grace, combined with peculiar natural gifts.[7]

By mid-March Betsy, her sister-in-law and Joseph John had visited many Irish Quakers, both in their Meetings and as individual families, as well as nine prisons, three lunatic asylums, and a number of hospitals. Several new groups of prison visitors were also founded. They also called on Lord Wellesley, the Lord Lieutenant, and were entertained in splendour, and a nunnery of the Sisters of Charity, where they dined amidst austerity. Both a Roman Catholic and an Anglican Archbishop were among their own many callers. Rather to their surprise, when visiting prisoners on a day the Dublin court was in session, they were invited to join the judge on his bench. "Picture your uncle, myself, and some other Friends, in a crowded court, sitting beside the judges," Betsy wrote to her children. "I could but be reminded of the difference of our situation, to that of Friends formerly, taken into the courts in time of persecution, and so cruelly treated." The sight of a curious and beautiful collection of artifacts found in bogs made an interesting interlude, while the promise of Irish seashells, from the collection of John Humphreys, superintendent of an Institution for the Deaf and Dumb in Dublin, reminded Betsy of her family at home and cost her several sleepless nights. Everywhere they went, among Catholics and Protestants alike, Betsy was also mobbed for tracts.

Through the west and the south of the country, where they travelled on bad roads through a boggy countryside of strange and desolate looks, and huddled around turf fires in drab inns, there were more prisons and more asylums. To Betsy's delight, the latter, like those she had found in Dublin, were hives of order, comfort and industry, and far superior to anything she had seen in England. Less so, however, were the prisons. They were among the worst she had ever seen, especially in their conditions for debtors. She also encountered terrible cases of murder and cruelty in these desolate regions, including a woman nearly burned to death for angering her relatives. Earnestly she hoped that the new Ladies' Associations she left in her wake would rectify some of the evils.

At the end of their four-month tour, Betsy and Joseph John produced their report. Its publication coincided with that of Betsy's own book, *Observations on the Visiting, Superintendence and Government of Female Prisoners*, that described the system of the British Society, and also advocated a radical change in the status of women. Her introduction began,

> I wish to make a few general remarks, which have long impressed me, respecting my own sex, and the place which I believe it to be their duty and privilege to fill in the scale of society. I rejoice to see the day in which so many women of every rank, instead of spending their time in trifling and unprofitable pursuits, are engaged in

works of usefulness and charity. Earnestly it is to be desired that the number of these valuable labourers in the cause of virtue and humanity may be increased, and that all of us may be made sensible of the infinite importance of redeeming the time, of turning our talents to account, and of becoming the faithful, humble, devoted, followers of a crucified Lord, who went about DOING GOOD. (Appendix 3.)

Its publication, Betsy reflected, together with two joint reports produced together with Joseph John, as well as being yet another sign of the times, was a personal triumph for the child once dubbed as stupid.

She was back at Plashet in mid-May, and as on so many occasions before when she returned home triumphant, she was met by problems. To her dismay, her son John informed her that despite his Quaker marriage, he had decided that he would no longer wear the Quaker coat that proclaimed him a Friend. Experience told her that such a rejection of its outward attributes was only a short step from abandoning the Society of Friends completely. While she grieved for John, from Earlham came news of the worsening condition of her sister Rachel, who for several years had suffered symptoms of the illness that had earlier killed Priscilla.

In July, Betsy missed the wedding of Joseph John to his second wife, Mary Fowler, in order to be with Rachel in Brighton. Though the days of Betsy's confinements, at which Rachel had been her most regular comforter, had now passed, and Betsy's children, whom Rachel had helped mother, had grown, the ties between the two women had continued close. In 1821, Rachel had inscribed the cover of a new journal book she presented to her sister. "Given by her sister Rachel Gurney," it read, "who is to her and has been nearly as much as one mortal can be to another through life." Betsy thought so too. "In some other things there is nothing like husband and children," she said, "but my natural tie to Rachel is inexpressible, and if she is taken away one of my strongest interests in life is gone."

While in Brighton, however, she did find time to slip away in order to call on members of the Visiting Society. "Nothing of charity appears to me to effect so much as forming and helping these public charities," she wrote, "because so many are assisted by them. I think this Society last year induced the poor to lay by amongst them about £1,000, numbers of the distressed had been relieved and the visiting the poor appears to have been blessed to visitors and visited." Earlier, before leaving for Ireland, she had also been consulted by her own Rachel Cresswell, who intended to form a visiting society at Lynn. Proof, Betsy believed, that the example set in childhood had eventually borne fruit.

Later she nursed Rachel at Plashet, before reluctantly sending her home to Earlham at the end of July. "If she be taken, my friend near my own age" she wrote apprehensively, "I think it will in no common degree bring death home to my view." Early in August, she met with Secretary of State, Lord Lansdowne, and the Under-Secretary, T. Spring Rice, to discuss prison business. A week later, she was summoned urgently to Earlham where Rachel was dying.

To the watchers around the bed, it seemed that Rachel was changing before their eyes, and that despite her physical suffering, especially the consumptive's breathless bloody cough that racked her wasted body, she was taking on more of heaven as she left the world behind. "She has conversed very little," Louisa wrote, "but said to me, 'I have had trials of body, but do not know when I have been so free from trials of mind: they are turned or are turning into gold.'"

On Sunday 16 September 1827, a letter arrived at Earlham. It was to Rachel from Henry Enfield. In it he bade her farewell, and assured her that he had never, in all the 28 years they had been apart, passed a single day without thinking of her. Rachel pressed it to her heart as she died.

On the day after the funeral, Betsy went to Lynn where Rachel Cresswell gave birth to a boy. Next day she was at Runcton, nursing Dan's wife Harriet through the birth of another. Later, back at Plashet, a huge volume of correspondence, much of it from the Continent, waited to be dealt with. Dr Julius of Hamburg, M. Ducpetiaux of Brussels and Madame Potemkin of St Petersburg all wrote about prison reform; the Grand Duke of Baden requested information on the best methods of prison construction; while John Venning, an Englishman resident in Russia, forwarded correspondence from the Empress Dowager on the subject of lunatic asylums. Though she relished every letter, it was those from the Empress that Betsy found most moving.

A report had been prepared by Venning for the Emperor Nicholas on the defects of St Petersburg's Government Lunatic Asylum, and this had distressed the Empress Dowager so much that she began a correspondence with Mrs Fry that resulted finally in a new asylum.[8] After its construction, the elderly Empress liked to visit the inmates, eating with them at a neatly laid table where she listened to stories that often led her to respond to their needs – a comfortable chair, a basket of fruit, and often a priest to minister at their dying. On Betsy's advice, a system of rules was also instituted, that included treating the inmates as far as possible as sane persons, allowing them as much liberty as practicable, encouraging daily exercise in the fresh air, the wearing of personal clothes, and bringing to an end the custom of treating them as public exhibits.

How was she getting on in reforming the whole world? Hudson teased early in February 1828. Betsy seemed to be growing ever more zealous, he said. Even in his middle-age he could still remind her of the handsome man she once dreamed about at Earlham, and in her confusion, she answered him stiffly and later regretted it. She had already talked to his wife, Margaret, "pretty baldly", she admitted later, on the subject of theatres, and she regretted that too. It had followed her Friday Newgate reading, which had been crowded with a huge variety of people: magistrates, overseas visitors, a group of London Jews, aristocratic ladies, several Friends, and Samuel Gurney. Afterwards, she and Sam had called on the Bishop of London to reassure him that the religious services at Newgate were not at all denominational. She had also spoken too freely to the Bishop, she feared.

On leaving Hudson, the brother and sister went on to the office of Robert Peel. Betsy was encouraged by the government's recent assistance in improving conditions on female convict ships, although she was frustrated that the clauses in Peel's Act that still hindered prison visiting had not been revoked. "I had to speak my mind fully on many things, prisons especially," she said after her meeting with him.

Though it had been painful, she had finally convinced herself of the necessity for speaking out on the issues that troubled her. Nevertheless, at her meeting with Peel, just like those earlier in the day, she felt she spoke for too long, or else made her points badly. It was a fault she had suffered since childhood, she reflected, although she did also wonder if simply by being a woman in the unusual position of discussing major issues with persons of influence and power, she heightened the perceptions of all who came into contact with her. She had no doubt at all that it was that which the newspapers found so attractive, and why, she said, so often in their pages "I was made to say I do what I never did do."

Shortly after her meeting with Peel, she began to wonder whether she had also said too much in her journals. Hers had been no ordinary life, she had observed on several occasions, and she realised that one day her journals might be read by strangers. She had already removed many pages, but as she read back once again over her early illnesses with their convulsions and fainting fits; over James Lloyd and the terrible anguish he had caused; over her worst moments with Joseph and the family; and all the times she had doubted in God or been angry at him, she decided that over such things it would be wise to draw a veil.

Taking up her scissors, she removed whole pages, or sometimes just sections, while later, with a pot of ink, she carefully obliterated sentences and paragraphs. Finally, after holding her very first journals and the severed pieces close to her heart, and bidding farewell to all they contained, she laid them on the fire and watched them as they burned.

In April 1828 Betsy and Joseph Fry visited the Midlands. With them went their daughter Richenda and her Quaker fiancé, Foster Reynolds, and together they visited thirteen prisons, founded three new visiting committees and attended many Quaker Meetings where Betsy's fame once again drew huge crowds.

Later, on the last day of the month, she spoke at the annual meeting of the British Society. Her rough notes for her speech included observations on the good effects of ladies visiting prisons, workhouses, hospitals, lunatic asylums and other public institutions; they highlighted the need for classification of prisoners, for female officers and for employment; they stressed the vital need for religious instruction; they covered female convict ships and the need for better clothing for the women and their children; and they touched on District Visiting Societies, libraries for the blockade-men, and education in general.[9] A member of the audience recalled that the speech concluded

> with a heart-stirring appeal to the many present, gifted with influence and talent, wealth and position, on the subject of the increase of crime in this country, the responsibilities of all, the sphere of usefulness open to every individual, even to the tender and delicate woman ... as a wife to influence, as a mother to educate and train, as the mistress of a family to guide, control, reprove, encourage.[10]

The applause, when Mrs Fry finally sat down, was deafening.

Richenda was married in June, on a day that was gloriously fine, and as Betsy surveyed the Plashet lawns thronged with Frys, Gurneys and Reynoldses, all gaily attired in wedding clothes, she looked forward to her own twenty-eighth wedding anniversary and prayed once again that storms were over and done and that the Frys' last years would truly be their best.

The great storm broke in November. "Once more we are brought into perplexity and trial, through imprudence in business," Betsy wrote, "and it is believed that without some assistance we cannot get through this winter."

Throughout her journals Betsy makes it clear that in their early married life at least, Joseph Fry was a reluctant businessman. It is also clear that she sometimes helped with the business accounts. There are references to Joseph's extravagance: during years when the Frys were financially hard pressed major alterations were commissioned for Plashet. Though it is never stated explicitly, and though the Frys' financial problems always occurred at times of national financial crisis, the evidence does suggest that Joseph Fry contributed to his own downfall. In Betsy's correspondence with Joseph John there is also some evidence to suggest that between the Evangelical banker who consistently rescued the Frys, and his religiously indifferent and perhaps spendthrift brother-in-law, there was an animosity that sometimes resulted in argument.[11] It also seems significant that from the evidence of Betsy's journals, the Gurney bankers only ever dealt with her, never with her husband. And it was to her – though she makes it clear they did their best to be kind – that Joseph John and Fowell insisted that Fry's Bank cease trading. It stopped payment on 21 November 1828.

Finally it had come to pass, Betsy realised, the day she had dreaded for so long, when God turned his face from her. "How is it Lord," she asked him, with bitterness in her heart, "thou dealest thus with thy servant who loves thee, trusts in thee and fears thy name?"

Later, watching three bailiffs make inventories of the Frys' earthly possessions, Betsy knew it was only a question of time before Joseph Fry was disowned by the Society of Friends as a bankrupt, and that his wife, Britain's most high-profile Quaker and prison reformer, shared his disgrace. Dreading the inevitable exposure, she pleaded a cough, hid indoors, and covered pages of her journal with prayers and condemnations. Later, for the sake of the future, she cut most of them out and burned them.

When Betsy and Joseph Fry, followed by several of their children, made their way into Plaistow Meeting House, the silence grew uncomfortably expectant. Observing Joseph's pallor, and Betsy's red-rimmed eyes, the meeting wondered collectively if Mrs Fry would speak, and if so, what would she say? When she rose to her feet, however, she faced them dry-eyed. "Though He slay me," she began, "yet will I trust in Him."

"May it not be a mysterious dispensation of deep and sore affliction laid not only upon us," Betsy hoped, "but upon those who suffer through us, to draw us all from the things of time and to set us more on the undying riches of eternity." Despite her pious hope, however, few who suffered through the Frys' misfortunes, Quaker and non-Quaker alike, were prepared to regard it with anything other than anger. Meanwhile, in the world at large, rumour flourished. So closely had the secret been guarded that few people knew that for years the Frys had been underwritten by Joseph John and Sam Gurney, or that Betsy's donations to the poor had been maintained by Hudson and Uncle Barclay. Therefore, as news of the disaster spread, many people speculated on the possible destination of subscriptions made out via Sam's firm, Overend, Gurney & Co, to Mrs Fry's various charities, and on how she had maintained her children at school, kept up her house and servants and paid for her extensive travels.

It was comforting that not everyone joined the condemnation. "It is the strong only," William Wilberforce told her, "that will be selected for exhibiting those graces which require peculiar strength." Encouraging her to "bear the whole will of God, with cheerful confidence in His unerring wisdom, and unfailing goodness," he reminded her how richly provided she was with relatives and friends.[12] She very soon discovered that he was right, for together with the criticism and gossip, from all over the country came letters of support: from distant relatives, from old friends, from the British Society, and from many people she had never met but who had admired her for years, and who now that she was cast down, felt sympathy for her plight, prayed for her and wished her well. Some of them even made additional donations to her charities.

However, there were some things that even the goodwill of friends and strangers could not overcome. For the first three months of 1829, as the contents of Plashet were stripped for auction, Betsy and Joseph were forced to take refuge with John and Rachel Fry at Mildred's Court. There her son William suffered a breakdown, while Betsy herself took to her bed with fever and depression. When other members of the household went down with measles, as a final irony the entire company was evacuated to the empty shell of Plashet, which for several weeks served as a hospital.

Wandering through the empty and echoing rooms, Betsy finally confronted the reality that never again would she live as mistress of a great house, itself a community of family, servants and dependents. Nor, she realised, when she handed over responsibility for the Plashet school to the new vicar of East Ham, would she ever again be benefactress of her local poor and founder of village schools. For a moment her thoughts returned to Earlham, to her Norwich poor and the school in the laundry. What had it really led to, she asked herself, what had been the point? As depression overwhelmed her, she saw nothing but darkness.

"It to my mind partakes of the nature of a funeral," she wrote bitterly in her book, on the day she left Plashet for ever, "the Lord giveth and the Lord taketh away. Blessed be the name of the Lord."

CHAPTER FOURTEEN

Absolute duty

"**I** CANNOT FORBEAR OR DELAY assuring you," William Wilberforce wrote to Betsy in January 1829, "that I do not see how it is possible for any reasonable being to doubt the propriety (that is a very inadequate way of speaking – let me rather say, absolute duty), of your renewing the prison visitations."[1]

It was reassurance she badly needed. For years her life had existed behind a facade of appearances, but now, with everything brutally stripped away, the woman who so keenly feared the censure of the world was left naked and exposed. "It tried, not to say puzzled me," she said, still attempting to understand God's purposes, "why such a change is permitted me." But following her great friend's advice, she forced herself to maintain her public career.

At Newgate, where so much took place in the depths of the prison, her work went on largely as before. Only at her Friday public readings was she sometimes aware of an unsavoury curiosity somewhere in her audience. In June, at Yearly Meeting, she was surprised and reassured by the warmth of her welcome by Friends, and by finding that a way opened readily for her to play an active and prominent role. Almost the only thing that marred the whole two weeks was her inability to entertain in the old style. The Cedars in Upton Lane, the new home provided for the Frys on Sam Gurney's West Ham estate, was too small for the grand parties of former years.

Although Newgate and Yearly Meeting welcomed her, her fear that her own family would find her an embarrassment appeared to have become reality. They had rallied to help her – Sam with a home, and the Gurney fortune providing a regular allowance – but unlike Wilberforce, her brothers and sisters made it no secret that they believed it was time for Betsy to retire. In July, the whole family united to dissuade her from attending the General Meeting at Ackworth School.

Stubbornly, Betsy ignored them. Yet, as she sat squashed between other passengers on the public stagecoach to Sheffield, she did not much feel that in Wilberforce's words, she was "exhibiting those graces which require peculiar strength". She felt weary, cramped and lonely, and when she realised she had forgotten her travelling box of medicines, that also contained her brandy, she began quietly to cry. However, once again the welcome of Friends surprised her; that she was able to minister with authority and power, and then visit a prison, seemed not only a tribute to her fellow Quakers, but evidence of God's leading and providence.

Not all Friends, however, were so welcoming, and in November, after applying for authority to visit Suffolk with Joseph John and Mary, she was informed that her presence, in a region of many Fry creditors, was unwanted. "What a change," she wrote bitterly, of some former friends, "a family that used to be so glad to see me, so warm in pressing me to their houses, and not even the least wish for my company."

It was similar harsh reactions that also drove her family further from Friends. For as Joseph Fry's disownment loomed, it seemed to the Fry children that the father they loved was to be publicly humiliated by an organisation that in their opinion was not worth the admiration lavished on it by their mother. Their anger erupted on Christmas Eve when, with the support of her father, Rachel provoked a furious family quarrel with her criticisms of Friends. It was quite a shouting match, Betsy recalled, that reduced her to tears. Its effects were even more distressing when her son William announced that he would join his brother John in no longer dressing as a Quaker. It was a particularly savage blow, for over the years he had become Betsy's favourite son, and she had cherished hopes that one day he would follow in the footsteps of his uncle Joseph John.

Two months later, however, she abandoned her attempts to persuade him to recant. It was time to let him go, she said, and to leave him in God's hands.

At almost 50 years old, and with three of her children now abandoning the Society to which she had devoted her life, Betsy was continuing to question the views she had held for almost 30 years. "The longer I live," she said, "the more difficult do I see education to be; more particularly, as it respects the religious restraints that we put upon our children." Once again, she wondered if rather than insist that young Quakers conform closely to the particular scruples of Friends, it was not better to leave them to judge for themselves. Even when it came to parties, with music, dancing and late hours, she was ready to relax, and recalling her own turbulent adolescence that had led her finally to follow the Plain Quaker path, she decided that perhaps after all, it was better to let the effervescence of youth run its course. She also reflected on the differences that divided the various branches of Christianity. "It matters not what name we call ourselves by," she said, "or what outward *means* we may think right to use, if our hearts are but influenced by the love of Christ, cleansed by His baptism and strengthened by His Spirit."

In January 1830 Joseph Fry was formerly disowned by the Society of Friends. As she shared his shame and distress, even Betsy herself considered drawing her work to a close, but Newgate, the convict ships, and in June, the annual meeting of the British Society, all combined to dissuade her.

High on the British Society's agenda that year were the refuges for discharged prisoners, which since 1822 had greatly increased in number and attracted many private patrons. Among them was Robert Peel, to whom Betsy had written personally in 1824. The refuges had also inspired similar ventures in Europe, and many of the enthusiastic letters read out to the huge audience contained invitations encouraging Mrs Fry to see their work for herself. When she received another rebuff in England, this time from Liverpool Friends unwilling to receive her at farewell meetings for her America-bound cousins, Hannah and Jonathan Backhouse,[2] the notion of a welcoming

Continent was appealing. It was reinforced in August, after fourteen-year-old Gurney travelled to France with his tutor, Dr Pinkerton, and later regaled his mother with vivid descriptions of the Delesserts, her most longstanding French correspondents.

In October, Betsy received what she felt was a rebuff of a different kind, when during a visit with Sam to Sussex Quarterly Meeting, she was the subject of an embarrassing debacle in Brighton. Earlier in the year, after the death of the profligate George IV, formerly the Prince of Wales whom Betsy had once admired at the opera, his younger brother had been crowned William IV. Anxious that he should set a better example than his predecessor, Betsy felt called to speak to William's Queen. But although Mrs Fry was too weighty a subject to be ignored, Queen Adelaide had no appetite for weighty concerns, and in the exotic surroundings of the Royal Pavilion, Betsy was forced to recite her concerns to an embarrassed Lady-in-Waiting. She hoped and prayed that the King and the Queen would be strengthened by God to do his will, she told Lady Brownlow, and that they might support education for the poor, the general distribution of the Scriptures, the keeping of the Sabbath *seriously*, as well as discourage the parties among the higher classes that set such a bad example to the poor. After concluding with the hope that the royal family would support the abolition of slavery and capital punishment, she handed to Lady Brownlow the books by herself and Joseph John that she had intended to hand to the Queen. "Time was," she said afterwards, "when even the sight of me was sought after and now I feel the day of curiosity is passed."

Despite her depressing conclusion, and though the Queen of England ignored her, the ordinary folk of Brighton flocked to hear Betsy speak on the very same subjects. They also came to hear her preach the Christian gospel of salvation. "In the evening had a *very* large public meeting for the middle and lower classes," she wrote after one such event. "I had to preach from that beautiful scripture, the Spirit of the Lord God is upon me for the Lord hath anointed me to preach glad tidings ... " In November, the Quaker Meeting House at Bury Hill near

Dorking was just as full, with hundreds turned away, when she preached at the funeral of her generous Uncle Barclay.

Uncle Joseph Gurney died the following month, and with his passing Betsy became uneasily conscious that a whole generation was almost gone. On New Year's Day 1831, shortly after his funeral, she walked alone through the park at Earlham. "How did it remind me of days that are past!" she said, "hardly a tree, a walk, *or* a view, but brought interesting remembrances before me; how many gone! how many changes! and then how far was I ready for my great change?"

The thought of her death reminded her once more of her duty, and in April she arranged through the Duchess of Gloucester to visit the Duchess of Kent and her daughter, the Princess Victoria. In the heir to the throne, to whom she presented several books on the subject of slavery, Betsy felt she glimpsed a monarch who might at last provide the Christian example she and her colleagues yearned to see.

In the autumn, with Fowell and Hannah to help, and with Christian love and cooperation as her theme, Betsy held a series of evangelistic meetings at Barking and Dagenham in Essex. Most took place in rural barns, and just as in Brighton, they attracted huge crowds. The power that worked through her on such occasions, she said, was like "a *living* fresh spring, rising up and overflowing its banks," but as she reflected on it, she puzzled over why she had been so chosen to stand out from other women. Gazing at the hoards of agricultural labourers in smocked frocks, farmers in knee-breeches, clerks from nearby towns in trousers and top hats, and clergymen of all descriptions, she also puzzled over what it was about herself that drew such vast audiences. For at a time when most men, and many women, were repelled at the thought of a woman preaching, just as Louisa Hoare had observed earlier, there was a chemistry in Mrs Fry that drew them in their thousands. "As a poor frail woman, advocating boldly in the cause of Christ, I expected rather to be despised," Betsy said, "whereas, it is apparently just the reverse."

Her achievement bore a price, however, and fearing another

breakdown, Joseph Fry insisted on a holiday. For all his lack of religion, his poor business record and his extravagant habits, in his own fashion he had remained true to the promise he made Betsy before their marriage. He was always there at her need, content to take on a domestic role at a time when few other men would have done so, and solicitous over her health. Although he was perhaps not exactly what John Gurney and his brothers had in mind when they encouraged the marriage, in many ways he truly was the stable ground they had recognised.

Now that his eldest sons virtually ran the tea business, time weighed heavily upon Joseph, and he yearned for more of his wife's company. But, despite his pleas for rest and recreation, as they travelled to the Isle of Wight and then to the West Country, Betsy's fame travelled alongside them. And though during the previous year he had followed his two eldest sons in casting off the appearance of a Friend, he constantly found himself at Quaker Meetings as his wife ministered to the congregations along their way. At Exeter, she also felt obliged to visit the prison. She was also preoccupied, partly with a constant toothache that she relieved with laudanum and brandy, and partly with her son Joseph, who had fallen desperately in love with a young woman whose clergyman father objected to her marrying a Quaker.

In the end, young Joseph decided that Alice Partridge meant more to him than his Quaker heritage, and early in 1832 he entered the Church of England. His sister Hannah, also engaged to an Anglican, announced that she too would soon follow the same path. Although the two defections reduced Betsy to tears, she was beginning to reconsider her views on Quaker marriage.

I am of the opinion that parents are apt to exercise too much authority upon the subject of marriage, and that there would be more really happy unions, if young persons were more left to their own feelings and discretion. Marriage is too much treated like a business concern, and love, that essential ingredient, too little respected in it. I disapprove the rule of our Society, that disowns persons for allowing a child to marry one not a Friend; it is a most undue and unchristian restraint, as far as I can judge of it.

At the same time, she asked herself yet again if it had been her own insistence on obedience to strict codes that was driving her children away from the Society of Friends. "I see and feel the present to be a stirring time in our family," Betsy noted, regarding her children's defections. "And in our country also," she added. While Betsy worried about her sons and daughters, two huge issues concerned the country at large: a seemingly unstoppable outbreak of cholera which provoked such anxiety that the government proclaimed a day of fasting and penitence; and the Reform Bill, designed to extend the franchise, whose volatile passage over the previous years had sometimes resulted in violence. Betsy herself felt inclined to let the Reform Bill pass. She had lived through stirring times before, she said, and in her experience, although society changed, most people went on much as before. Instead she concentrated on the cholera spreading remorselessly eastwards from the London slums, "and although perhaps thought by some a busybody in it," she said, for memories of the Bible Society still rankled, she gathered together a group of women ready to nurse the sick if the disease should strike. As for the fast day, she doubted if any government could force its people to be god-fearing, and on 21 March 1832, the day designated for fasting and prayer, she was busy preparing for another appearance before a House of Commons Select Committee.

Making her way to Whitehall, Betsy reflected on how much London had changed from the city she first knew in 1798. The streets she recalled from those days, with their link-boys and sedan chairs, seemed a world away from the modern gas-lit thoroughfares full of hackney cabs and horse-drawn omnibuses, that since 1829 had also been patrolled by Robert Peel's blue-uniformed Metropolitan Police Force.

During his years as Home Secretary, between 1823 and 1830 Peel had also passed five statutes which together exempted 100 offences from the capital penalty. But, while most of those who escaped hanging were transported, by the early 1830s transportation was increasingly regarded in Britain as having little deterrent effect as well as being a huge financial drain. It was also bitterly resented by the free Australian settlers. It had also become evident that despite the Prison Act of 1823, rates of crime and of re-offending were continuing to rise.

With execution curtailed and the eventual end of transportation in sight, the government was forced to embark on a programme of prison building. At the same time, Mrs Fry was one among many experts called to a Select Committee charged with investigating what forms of punishment would most effectively bring about a reduction of crime. Even before the Committee commenced sitting, however, a number of factors were already being taken into account.

One of them was the "silent and separate system" currently in operation in America, in which the British Government believed it had found a scheme that would both punish and rehabilitate. An initial investigation had already been carried out by the government's agent, Mr William Crawford, who had returned to England convinced of its benefits. At his favoured model, the Eastern Penitentiary at Cherry Hill, Pennsylvania, inmates spent their entire sentence in solitary confinement, living and working in barren cells with only their Bibles for company, and exercising alone in individual compounds.

Another view maintained that while prisoners should not be left to spend their time in idleness, their labour should nevertherless be so wearisome and pointless that it would act as a deterrent to crime. For this reason the human tread-wheel had been developed specifically for prison use by the Lowestoft engineer, William Cubitt. It was widely endorsed. It was, said the Reverend Sydney Smith[3] "economical, certain, well-administered, little liable to abuse, capable of infinite division, a perpetual example before the eyes of those who want it, affecting the imagination only with horror and disgust, and affording great ease to the Government."[4]

Also a factor was that with most crime committed against property, that the large swathe of middle-class male voters enfranchised by the Reform Act, and possibly with an eye to the Exchequer, were likely to take a significant interest in penal reform.

Finally, due to persistent misuse of dangerous tools by convicts, as well as a lack of skilled supervisors, the experiment at

Millbank had largely failed, while since its opening, the prison had also been the scene of several disastrous riots.

Mrs Fry began her evidence by describing her work of nearly 16 years among female convicts in Britain and Ireland. She stressed the advantages of keeping women separate from men, under the control of female officers, and subject to regular visits by committees of independent ladies. Later, she produced letters from Australia confirming improvements among female transports. She also outlined her method of classifying prisoners by conduct and former character, and emphasised the importance of keeping prisoners on remand separate from the convicted. While she had no hesitation in agreeing that within her system there were relapses, she stressed that they were far outweighed by the overall reformation.

It was on that subject, however, that Mrs Fry and her questioners drew gradually apart. Did she feel that prevention of crime was the object of punishment, she was pointedly asked. Yes, she did, she replied, and went on to explain the link between the process of reformation, with education and employment playing a central role, and the reduction of crime. Could that really be described as punishment, her questioner continued, was it not, rather, enjoyment? After a while, another questioner asked if there were some convicts so incorrigible that they did not respond to her particular methods. It was hard to be certain, Mrs Fry told him, as so many convicts passed through prisons quickly, but even in the worst women she had seen, she thought there was always some improvement in manners and habits. But over 16 years, experience had taught her that great transformations did not always occur. "To say that they are really changed characters is going a long way," she admitted.[5]

Experience had also taught her that the issues surrounding crime were complex, and when pressed on whether "a right system of prison discipline together with religious instruction, might produce change",[6] she attempted to explain how environment and education also played a role.

I am of the opinion that the efforts made in the education of the poor, the circulation of the Scriptures, affording asylums for the profligate, with other establishments distinct from prisons, as well as the regulations made in them, enforced by the act of 1823, have produced an improvement in the morals in our gaols, and have had an influence in raising the moral standard of the worst class of women.[7]

On the issue of separation, to which her questioners returned constantly, Betsy also found it impossible to provide neat answers. The system was originally devised by American Quakers, who based it on their own habits of silent reflection, and while she agreed there could sometimes be benefits, she was also profoundly uneasy. At Millbank, where prisoners regularly spent long periods in isolation, she had observed that among young uneducated girls in particular, it often led to depression and sometimes to severe loss of mental faculties. "I think there is some reason to fear," she said, "whether the separation and strict discipline prepare for a return to social life."[8] On the issue of the treadmill, however, she was more forthright. It was injurious to women's health, she said, and although she was prepared to endorse the crank-mill, she stressed continually that education and employment should be a priority for convicts.

Caroline Neave, who had personally financed the first prisoners' refuges, and who continued to devote herself to the programme, also gave evidence. Only a small percentage of the young thieves, shoplifters and housebreakers who filled the refuges went on to re-offend, she told the Committee, but when she explained that part of the remedy lay in keeping them so busy they had little time for association, inevitably it led back to solitary confinement.

Mrs Fry also spoke on behalf of debtors, and although the subject was a painful one for her to raise, she felt bound to point out how their enforced idleness generally plunged them, and also their families, ever deeper into debt.

Finally, she made a plea for the British Society. Even prisoners themselves commented on the higher standards in gaols visited by ladies, she said, and she therefore urged government to bring pressure to bear on magistrates still restricting their prison visits. She also made a plea for additional financial assistance, pointing out that by the end of 1828, although government gave an allowance per convict, British Society ladies had spent between £1,000 and £2,000 of their own money on items for transports. They had also made huge personal donations towards refuges, she added.

While Betsy had misgivings about the separate system, other reformers endorsed it. Among them was her brother-in-law, Sam Hoare, who in his evidence to the Select Committee agreed with the view that it provoked reflection, remorse and subsequent reformation. In the end it was the view of Sam and his colleagues that prevailed, and from 1832 onwards, the separate system was increasingly introduced into Britain's prisons. At the same time, it was established that all women sentenced to transportation would first serve a term at Millbank, much of it in solitary confinement. Although the report of the Select Committee highlighted the beneficial effects of prison visitors, and recommended that every facility be afforded them, it fell short of also recommending that pressure be put on recalcitrant magistrates. Nor did government feel able to provide any financial assistance for the British Society.

Just as in 1823, Betsy was depressed by the government's unwillingness to endorse her ideas, both on education and training, and on solitary confinement, but, undaunted, in June she did her best to rally the spirits of the British Society. Given the extent of existing crime, she told her huge audience, and given that the higher classes almost inevitably influenced the lower, individuals should not shirk their personal responsibility. Failure to keep the Sabbath, keeping late hours, and vanity of dress all sent the wrong message, she claimed, while it was lack of thought or idleness on the part of mistresses which often led servants into temptation, and sometimes into crime. Finally, she encouraged her audience to assist with the education of the poor, watch over young girls entering service, provide libraries for hospitals and workhouses, and establish District Visiting Societies.

In the August of 1832 Betsy felt called to Ireland again, and before leaving home with her brother Sam and her sister-in-law Elizabeth, she informed the Home Office of her intention to visit that country's county gaols and to form Ladies' Associations. The reply from the Home Secretary, Lord Melbourne, was cautious. Reluctant to alienate either Mrs Fry and her powerful associates, or Ireland's judicial authorities, he provided her with a letter of recommendation that expressed admiration for her achievements, and also requested, that "as far as it could be done," Ireland's Visiting Magistrates should assist Mrs Fry in her benevolent objects.[9]

On the whole, they did so, and Betsy noted many improvements since her previous visit; she also vowed to persist in her campaign to remedy the deficiencies that remained. Meanwhile, as a preacher, she drew large crowds, both Protestant and Catholic, while for Irish Quakers she had a special message. External dependence was all very well, she said, whether it was membership of the Society of Friends, or following its particular practices, but, nevertheless, alone those things meant nothing. "Nothing," she emphasised, " unless the heart be really changed and cleansed from sin."

She was back home in time for William's marriage to Julia Pelly, the daughter of Sir John Henry Pelly, a Governor of the Hudson Bay Company.[10] But since once more a child was marrying outside the Society of Friends, Betsy and Joseph were again obliged to stay home. "Here am I sitting in solitude," she wrote as her favourite son married his bride, "keeping silence before the Lord, on the wedding day of my beloved son William." Yet, this time, though she prayed earnestly for William and Julia, she was conscious of how odd, and how unkind, her absence appeared to most other people. Later she reflected on her husband's lack of interest, and on her children's abandonment of Friends, both of which made her feel so isolated and so alone. As she contrasted it with members of her wider Gurney family, who were united in their faith, she felt herself overburdened by misery. "As for myself, I sit solitary in many things," she said sadly. But then, determined not to give way to self pity, she tried to be optimistic. "Have I not my Lord as my friend, and my comforter?" she asked, "and is He not as a husband to all the members of His church?" A month later, when Hannah married William Champion Streatfield, she too formally abandoned the Society of Friends.

Near Christmas, Betsy travelled to Norfolk with Katherine, who for all her rebellious youth had remained a Quaker, and who after the years spent managing the household at Plashet, now assisted her mother as secretary. There Kate also assisted as Betsy supported Richenda and Francis Cunningham in the formation of a District Visiting Society in Lowestoft.

The years had also seen changes in the Gurneys. Almost all of them had by now abandoned the reservations that followed Joseph Fry's bankruptcy, and Richenda spoke for many of them. "Our dear sister displayed much of her tact and power," she said, "and gave us the greatest assistance; how marvellously gifted she is." She also intimated just how much her view of the truculent adolescent who once so provoked her had also changed. "It is almost like having an angel visitor," she said of her sister, "so full of loveliness and grace is she."

But while Richenda saw gifts and loveliness, Betsy saw problems which were making her increasingly anxious. Since his marriage, her son John had been unable to live within his means, while William had more recently become the host of extravagant musical parties. In April 1833, as she struggled to pay John's debts, the tea business also seemed to be suffering once more. A host of new debts, arising from what she described as unexpected sources, were also beginning to mount. In the same month, she was struck by a violent influenza that caused her temperature to rocket and her pulse to race so fast that Joseph claimed he was unable to measure it.

Despite anxiety and sickness, however, there was to be no let-up in what was becoming a critical year. Since 1825, when William Wilberforce retired from politics, the movement against slavery had been led in the House of Commons by Fowell Buxton, and as the first months of 1833 passed by, he prepared to introduce the bill that would bring about its abolition in Britain's overseas colonies. His family and friends rallied to his support. In May, Sam Gurney chaired a huge abolitionist meeting at Exeter Hall, London's new Evangelical meeting-house in the Strand, and after another great assembly there, the delegates marched as a body to Downing Street. Britain's women, now increasingly involved in the affairs of the world, played a major role in the campaign; at the end of the month Fowell presented before the House of Commons a petition signed by 187,000 of them, begging their government to abolish slavery.

Within the Society of Friends too, momentous events were taking place. For years the various strands within the Society, – those who supported traditional Quaker piety and those who supported Joseph John's Evangelical views – had co-existed more or less peaceably. More recently, however, another strand had emerged of an extreme Evangelical persuasion bordering on Calvinism, and at Yearly Meeting 1832, the arguments had suddenly become bitter. By 1833, some Friends were forecasting a split in the Society before the end of the year. In June the divisions were disrupting London meetings, and as one of the Society's leading ministers Betsy began a relentless series of religious visits as she strove to calm the gathering storm.

In the preceding month, Joseph Fry had been overcome by what he later described, in the journal he suddenly felt inspired to keep, as a powerful visitation of judgement. Sadly he was a poor diarist, and his entries are sparse and details are few. But perhaps the experience was provoked by a sudden awakening to the reality of his business failures, embarrassment that during the previous year the Gurneys had felt obliged to pay his personal debts, and a recognition of how little depth there was to his life. Or perhaps it was a combined assault by his religiously inclined brothers-in-law, the formidable Gurney bankers, that shook Joseph Fry so profoundly and evidently drove him to his knees.

In the memoir they produced after their mother's death, Katherine Fry and Rachel Cresswell state that in the summer of 1833, "in consequence of the marriages which had taken place, and other circumstances, the press of interests and engagements had become more than the family could bear."[11] However, given the disownments, the financial problems, the drama of the anti-slavery campaign, the divisions in Friends, the effects on Joseph Fry of his visitation, and the after-effects of fever, it seems probable that there was another emotional collapse. However, for one usually so effusive on the subject of her illnesses, Betsy herself is curiously silent. Whatever the truth, when the Gurneys offered to pay for a long holiday, it seemed an ideal remedy.

When William Wilberforce died at the end of July, and when the Emancipation Bill became law in August, Betsy and Joseph Fry were far away, recuperating in the tranquillity of Caledonia Cottage on the island of Jersey. There in the benevolent climate Betsy wandered through verdant orchards, and admired swathes of carnation and·hydrangea in cottage gardens. She almost imagined herself back in Bramerton again, the paradise garden of her childhood, except that occasionally, as she glanced towards Katherine, Louisa and Harry, busily engaged in sketching the distant views, she couldn't help reflecting on the disappointment her children had caused her. As for Joseph, although he was now happy sometimes to pray and discuss the great things of God, more often he seemed to prefer dozing in the sunshine.

It was hard not to be bored, and before long she took herself off alone, with her bag of tracts, to proclaim the gospel in her halting French at cottage doors. The intrigued Jersey housewives drew her into their homes and sat her by their seaweed fires, where in blackened pots, *soupe à la graisse* or *potage* simmered for the family supper. In such unfamiliar surroundings, Betsy discovered how much two women could communicate, in a mixture of languages, signs and smiles, about families, losses and hopes, and about the gospel whose themes seemed to slip so easily into the language of everyday life.

Jersey, Betsy noted, had little poverty and few beggars. It did, however, have a tiny band of Friends, a lunatic asylum, a workhouse and a hospital, as well as a prison, which since Acts of the British Parliament had no power in the Channel Islands, remained completely untouched by reform. Such opportunities could not be overlooked, and when her sister-in-law Elizabeth Fry arrived, together with her friend, Rebecca Sturges, Betsy set about organising her team. She was full of purpose and feeling quite her old self.

With support from influential citizens, she eventually presented a detailed report to the island's prison authorities. She began by outlining what the reformers believed to be the object of imprisonment: not merely safe custody, but a suitable and legally defined measure of punishment that would both deter others, and also produce reform in the prisoners themselves. With the exception of safe custody, she pointed out, Jersey's prisons failed to meet the standard. She also produced a list of recommendations including suitable employment, classification, decent diets and the prohibition of alcohol, a uniform, proper payment for gaolers, and a code of regulations similar to those now in force in England. She also stressed the need for religious instruction and for education in general.

After the prison came the hospital, a subject in which she was becoming increasingly interested. As she toured the wards, all the knowledge gained from her years of nursing, and from personal sickness, began to coalesce in ideas taking shape in her mind. Some of them – the separation of men from women, the elderly infirm from the chronically sick, and special wards for children – she included in her report. Also, while acknowledging that efforts were already under way, she made a special plea for the insane.

On Guernsey, too, there was a prison to visit and a hospital to improve, as well as another District Society to found. On Sark, she felt called to heal divisions between the island's Methodists and Anglicans, while on Herm she helped found a school. She also felt that she was becoming quite a traveller, and after hearing from Captain Bazin, the evangelistic commander of the Channel Islands' steamer, of trips he made to St Malo with Bibles and tracts, her thoughts began turning to France. Just as she raised with Joseph the subject of Continental invitations still waiting to be fulfilled, however, bad news arrived from home. Sam and Louisa Hoare had suffered the death of their eldest son, while Betsy's own daughter, Rachel, lay gravely ill.

Leaving Joseph and the girls to travel on to France, Betsy and Harry set off for Southampton. It was a rough crossing, with mounting waves and shrieking winds that revived all Betsy's old fear of the sea. It also conjured visions of the convict ship, *Amphitrite*, which months earlier had sunk in a storm off the French coast, taking with her 120 women and several children, many of them known personally to Betsy. All night, as the wave-battered steamer shuddered and groaned, in her mind's eye Betsy saw the convicts' drowned faces sinking to the black ocean depths.

Immediately on reaching England, though unbearably weary, and travelling all the way by public stagecoach, she went straight to her bereaved sister at Hampstead. Then she went on to King's Lynn, where she spent six weeks nursing Rachel. While there, she wrote to another daughter with advice about the depressions she seemed to have inherited from her mother. "It is most important to look on them as much as possible like the toothache," said Betsy, who now had so much experience of both, "that it must be endured while it lasts, but is not dangerous in its nature." As for the discoloured view of life produced by depression, it was important to be very clear, throughout the whole episode, that such manifestations were not sound, and must neither be believed, nor taken heed of. And though it was hard, even for Christians, to deal with depression, she herself had learned through experience that the best remedy was to pray for help, while continuing with everyday work.

In April 1834 Betsy made a religious journey to Dorset, Hampshire and the Isle of Wight. With her went two nieces, Priscilla Buxton and Priscilla Gurney. Both found the experience a revelation, but Fowell's daughter, who had been nursed by Betsy through illness, and knew that softness hid behind the often over-anxious exterior, was particularly impressed. In long conversations with her aunt she discovered that there was virtually nothing – no weakness of body or mind, nor any view, feeling or wish – which could not safely be revealed, and also that Betsy had a way of transforming things so that whatever seemed hopeless or bitter began very soon to acquire the light of optimism. "Was it not the very secret of her power with the wretched and degraded prisoners?" Priscilla asked, "... The most abandoned must have felt, she did not despair for them, either for this world or another; and this it was that made her irresistible."[12]

Priscilla had received her insight after she confided her concerns over her forthcoming marriage, that her parents, who had lost so many children to death, would be unable to cope with her leaving the family home. Later, reassured by her aunt, she went forward joyfully to her wedding on 1 August 1834. The day had been specially chosen by Fowell himself, and by Andrew Johnston MP, Priscilla's future husband and one of her father's greatest supporters, for on that day, every slave in Britain's colonies was set free.

As the slaves were set free, and Priscilla Buxton was married, Betsy prayed for them all in a hotel near Loch Tay, during another holiday with Joseph. But just as on Jersey, she could not bear to be idle, and at Kenmore she invited a host of barefoot chamber-maids and blue-bonneted hostlers to her Bible readings where she also gave them all copies of Joseph John's book, *Evidences of Christianity*. Next day, she provided more copies for the local gamekeepers. In Glasgow, she met the newly wedded Priscilla and Andrew; seeing them so united in their support for Fowell, she recalled her own wedding, and wished once again that she and Joseph had more they could share. In Edinburgh, Glasgow and Dumbarton she also revisited the gaols she had first seen in 1818 with Joseph John and as well as leaving new Ladies' Associations and District Visiting Societies behind her, she also produced detailed reports of her visits and sent them to the relevant authorities together with her recommendations.

Early in 1835, as part of its continuing programme of standardisation, the government began a review of British prisons, and in May, on the day after her fifty-fifth birthday, Mrs Fry and other members of the British Society were called to give evidence to a Select Committee of the House of Lords. Following the recommendations of 1832, and the introduction of the separate system, the government was anxious to assess how far it was linked to a reduction in crime.

When pressed on whether prisoners at Newgate were contaminated by association, Mrs Fry was forced to agree, but she was also at pains to point out that the physical conditions of Newgate made it almost impossible to introduce a different regime. "We are doing the best we can with a very bad system," she said,[13] and went on to highlight how much had been achieved since 1818, much of it by dedicated bands of women throughout Britain who devoted themselves to the cause of reform.

She also highlighted abuses in the new system, where prisoners who broke the silent regime were punished by a reduction in an already meagre diet, and where men were forced to tread the wheel for up to ten hours a day. "In some respects," she said, "I think there is more cruelty in the gaols than I have ever seen before."[14]

Finally, she stressed the importance of religion. Though she had always held the Bible in high regard and reverence, she said, even she could not have imagined the powerful effect it had on even the worst criminals. It had strongly confirmed her own faith, and led her to believe that it should be the duty of government to promote the Christian faith in prisons in a manner most likely to lead to real reformation. "For though severe punishment may in a measure deter them and others from crime," she said, "it does not amend the character and change the heart, but if you have really altered the principles of the individuals, they are not only deterred from crime, because of the fear of punishment, but they go out and set a bright example to others."[15]

Later, making her way down Whitehall, she wondered how much of her evidence would be heeded. The tide appeared to be turning from the high ideals of the reformers, and their insistence that education, training, and a compassionate environment were the most effective catalysts for change, towards a system whose main focus was deterrence. Sadly she thought of her old dancing partner, William Frederick, the champion of prison reform, who had died the previous year. Many of her most ardent supporters were leaving her, she realised, and as she thought how much she missed them, she recalled William Wilberforce in 1829, urging her to remember the absolute duty of continuing the work she was appointed to do. Nearing the river, and drawn by a jostling crowd, she found herself overlooking the raw space left by a fire the previous year, when the Palace of Westminster, with both Houses of Parliament, had burned to the ground. What would rise in its place, she wondered,[16] and what did her own extraordinary life still hold in store?

CHAPTER FIFTEEN

Duty calls me that way

*I*N THE SPRING AND SUMMER of 1835 Betsy
began to feel almost that she was entering a golden age. "I
think I never knew Newgate go on so well," she said in July,
"several cases amongst the prisoners of real change." Her
Friday readings too, after an earlier falling-off, were also flourishing. "Such numbers come once more to hear me," she said
with satisfaction.

Almost the only event to cloud the early part of the year was
the disownment of her youngest daughter Louisa, after her
wedding in June to Julia Pelly's brother, Raymond. Yet even
Louisa's marrying out failed to provoke the distress of former
years, for by now Betsy was almost resigned to her children
abandoning Friends. She still felt unable to attend the service,
but instead of spending the day alone as before, when the
newly-wed couple returned from the church, Betsy and Joseph
hosted a party for 50 guests with a sumptuous wedding banquet at The Cedars. When she went to bed, Betsy also turned
an almost blind eye to the music and dancing that followed.

She was also beginning to feel that for all his musical parties, her son William was at last showing the promise she
longed to see. "The upright and circumspect man," she called
him in her journal. And though she grieved for Joseph John
when his second wife died of typhus aged just 32, she couldn't
help hoping that his resignation to the will of God would prove
a religious example to her children.

Full of optimism in the autumn of the year, with a new
Prison Act promising great changes, she arranged to make a

comprehensive tour of London's prisons. "As we certainly have the ear of the government," she said, "it is well to make such inspections as may be useful to the cause and therefore to know well for ourselves the real state of our jails."

The Prison Act of 1835 came into force with the express object of ensuring greater uniformity in the prisons of England and Wales. Already, many of the measures pressed for by the reformers had been achieved: in large towns especially, many of the old unsanitary and overcrowded gaols had either been replaced by purpose-built prisons or else entirely remodelled; classification had been widely introduced, and female officers were increasingly employed to oversee female convicts. The changes, however, had been piecemeal, and many prisons, particularly those in small towns and in Scotland, continued in their former state of neglect. As the government sought to bring the entire system under central control, the new Act replaced the previous autonomy of local authorities with partial government control, thus indirectly assisting prison visitors, while the Home Secretary received the power to create and enforce new prison regulations. He also received the power to create something the reformers had long argued for: a paid, professional Prison Inspectorate whose duty was to visit every place kept for the confinement of prisoners.

One of the new inspectors was William Crawford, whose American investigations had encouraged the introduction of the separate system, and towards the end of the year he carried out a review of Newgate. It was part of a wider investigation into London's prisons, and the introduction to its final report made it clear that the size of the task and the limited time available meant that it was less than comprehensive. However, its large body of evidence and many tables of statistics were proof that the reformers had succeeded in one thing: in future it would at least be agreed that British prisons should meet certain standards, and also be subject to regular professional inspection.

The report was highly critical of Newgate. In the men's wards, it said, prisoners of all ages, mental condition and degree of guilt were herded together with few facilities for education or employment. Dirt, drunkenness, disorder and brutal- ity were rife, food and clothing were inadequate, while the wardsmen, prisoners supposedly selected for good behaviour and appointed to keep order, were negligent and dishonest. Prostitutes as young as thirteen were often admitted, while the condemned had no seclusion and were treated with indiffer- ence by their fellows.

The report was more encouraging about the female section of the prison. It noted that matrons supervised the various departments, that female officers kept a check on visitors and the admission of alcohol, that there was a school, a wardswoman who doubled as schoolmistress who was paid by the Ladies' Association, and that ladies also visited the con- demned. However, by linking them to aspects of the regime over which they had no control, and by highlighting abuses in the areas where they did, the report also contrived to suggest, that although well-meaning, the Ladies' were less than compe- tent. In its implication that women who had sometimes worked at Newgate for almost 20 years were somehow unaware of the foul language, obscene material and sexual activity in the gaol, and of the mockery sometimes levelled at them by prisoners, it also made them appear foolishly naive. It also suggested that these hardened veterans would be over- come by embarrassment if these aspects, to which they had apparently been blind for so long, were to be suddenly brought to their attention.

At the same time, while acknowledging the transformation brought about by Mrs Fry, and the benefits produced by the Ladies' Association in terms of education and employment, other aspects of their role were more seriously called into question. In a professionally run prison, the report pointed out, no matter how long their service or wide their experience, it was unsuitable for amateur volunteers to receive and classify con- victs, or to use their influence for the mitigation of sentences.

It also reserved two major criticisms for Mrs Fry's Friday readings, and both concerned the constant streams of visitors. "They tend to diminish the necessary gloom of a prison, and mitigate the punishment which the law has sentenced a prisoner to undergo,"[1] it said, but more savagely it condemned the idea which Mrs Fry had so often maintained, that the visitors to Newgate took away with them some understanding of the prison cause. That, said the inspectors sternly, was not her function.

It was a bitter blow for Betsy, who had looked forward to the Inspectors beginning their work and to perhaps working in some capacity alongside them. Her reward, she now felt, was for the huge improvements she had made in London's worst gaol to be undervalued, and for years of experience and knowledge to be denigrated. And while she knew that she still commanded great influence, and that her readings remained too popular to be discontinued, it was becoming increasingly clear to her that their days were numbered. So too was her wider prison work in Britain. For new forces were in motion, that were motivated as much by present economy as by future social welfare, and which were ensuring that Mrs Fry, with her conviction that education, training and self-respect were the only certain measures for long-term reformation, was increasingly being sidelined. At the same time, like other reformers of her generation, she was being overtaken by the institutions and the professional men and women she had helped call into being.

While the Newgate Report depressed her, she was overjoyed that in another of her ventures her chief companion was her own husband. Perhaps at last, she reflected, they would work for the cause side by side. Equally encouraged was Joseph, who despite his spiritual experiences of 1833, always found it hard to talk about religion or deal with abstract things. In the coastguard libraries, however, he felt he had found a project which could flourish in his hands.

Its beginnings had been in Betsy's trip to the Isle of Wight with the two Priscillas, when she befriended coast guard families at Freshwater and left them with a promise of a library like the one founded earlier in Sussex. Later, the plan for the provision of similar libraries for every Coastguard Station in Britain was endorsed both by Robert Peel, during his period as Chancellor of the Exchequer, and by Captain Bowles R N,

Comptroller of the Coastguard. With 500 stations, housing a total of 21,000 men, women and children, it was an enormous task. Betsy suggested raising £1,000 by private subscription, and requested an additional £500 from the government, and it soon became clear that someone was needed who would make the enterprise their priority.

Now, two years later, after Joseph had worked almost full-time on the correspondence and accounts, the task was almost completed. As well as donations from individuals, far in excess of the original estimate, and additional sums from the government, grants had also been made by the Society for the Promotion of Christian Knowledge and the Religious Tract Society, while liberal donations of books had been received from booksellers. In all, a total of 25,896 books, comprising 52 different works, were finally dispatched; like the volumes on convict ships and those sent to Brighton, they included biography, books of travel and adventure and many volumes for children as well as Bibles and religious tracts. Later, similar libraries were provided by Betsy and Joseph for the steam packets that sailed out of Falmouth, for the Haslar Royal Navy Hospital at Portsmouth, and yet another for the shepherds who roamed Salisbury Plain.

In February 1836, during a religious tour of Sussex with Sam Gurney, several of the coastguards and their officers attended a public meeting at Hastings and stayed on afterwards to thank Betsy personally for her interest in their welfare. It was from that tour, as she returned home through Sheerness, that other officers of the Royal Navy invited her party on board a man-of-war. Stepping onto its decks, she was immediately reminded of another ship, in the days when Britain was still locked in conflict with France, when her Quaker opposition to war had prevented her from touring it with her sisters. So many years later, she reflected, she felt far more confident of her beliefs. "It was a fine sight, in a large man-of-war," she said, "instead of bloodshed and fightings, to see many naval officers, two chaplains, sailors, soldiers, ladies, numbers of women and children, all met to hear what two Quakers had to say."

Of course, by now, Betsy was more than accustomed to the

sight of people gathering to hear whatever she had to say. Yet with the new developments that were taking the momentum from her work in Britain's prisons, she was also keenly aware that she was unlikely ever to stand again at the centre of major events in her own land. And after almost 20 years on the stage of the theatre of action, with its excitement, its responsibilities and its rewards, the thought that it might soon come to an end was a depressing one. As she sought for a new cause, her thoughts began moving increasingly further afield.

In March, she planned another visit to Ireland, and after praying for Sam Gurney's daughter Catherine, and Fowell's son Edward, who were married on 12 April, she set out two days later. It was a journey with a special purpose, for at Grange Gorman Lane in Dublin, the first prison in the British Isles to be devoted exclusively to women was in its planning stage. Recognising its role as a future model, Betsy was anxious to ensure that it conformed as much as possible to the recommendations of the reformers. And despite the adverse Newgate Report, and the moves towards professionalism, almost every politician and prison governor knew that Mrs Fry's knowledge and experience of female prisoners was unequalled by anyone else in Britain.

Armed with a letter of introduction from the Home Office, she outlined her views to Lord Mulgrave, Ireland's Lord Lieutenant. He was a thoughtful man, anxious to install a system that was both efficient and merciful, and in Mrs Fry he recognised the voice of experience. Later, he asked her to select the prison's first matron. It proved to be a wise decision. Eleven years later an official report said:

> The visitor may see many changes in the faces and persons of the prisoners, but no surprise can ever find a difference in the high and superior order with which this prison is conducted. The Matron, Mrs Rawlings, upon whom the entire responsibility of the interior management devolves, was selected some years since, and sent over to this country by the benevolent and philanthropic Mrs Fry, whose exertions in the cause of female prison reformation, were extended to all parts of the British Empire.[2]

Mrs Rawlings herself gave the credit entirely to Mrs Fry:

> To her wise, judicious, and maternal counsel, I entirely ascribe the
> success that has attended our exertions. I never took any material
> step at the commencement without consulting her, and at her own
> request, at least every week, I wrote an account of my movements;
> and many obstacles that at first arose, she settled in her own quiet
> way, by her influence with the government.[3]

Returning to England in time for Yearly Meeting and the
Annual Meeting of the British Society, Betsy discovered that
Joseph had had her rooms at The Cedars specially altered, and
that all the children had decorated them with presents. Despite
the extravagance, it touched her heart. She also noted in her
journal how boldly she had spoken in Ireland, and when a delegation of elders arrived at The Cedars from Yearly Meeting, to
discuss some of the issues she had raised in the debates which
still remained heated, she felt quite confident in maintaining
her own particular views. What a change, she reflected, from
the timid young girl who once trembled so much at Norwich
Monthly Meeting that she could barely be heard.

Confident, articulate, knowledgeable and experienced, but
expecting the end of her journey in Britain, when another
opportunity arrived from across the sea, an invitation from
Jersey where a new House of Correction was proposed, Betsy
seized it immediately. Before leaving, she discussed it with the
Home Secretary, Lord John Russell, her old friend from the
heady days of June 1821. Later, if not exactly with his blessing,
but with the weight of his name behind her, she set off for Jersey
at the end of July with Joseph and Katherine in attendance.

She was there throughout August, discussing the new
prison with the island's governor, revisiting old friends, touring
the hospital and recommending a lunatic asylum. On Alderney
she also founded a Visiting Society, lent her support for a
Temperance Society, and promised a library. Desperate for rest
himself, the solicitous Joseph occasionally persuaded her to
join him at picnics in rocky coves among groups of summer

holiday-makers. "I believe our recreations are right," said Betsy, as she strove to assuage the guilt such leisure provoked, "as far as they fit us for our Master's service, and wrong, if they enervate and disqualify us for it."

She was also becoming increasingly certain that her Master's service was calling her to France, and on this trip to the Channel Islands she was certain that her feet would shortly step onto European soil. The thought of finally fulfilling some of her long-standing invitations left her almost breathless with excitement. Once again, however, it was news from home that frustrated her plan.

Louisa Hoare had never recovered from the tragedy of her son's death; she had been plagued by depression ever since, and more recently confined to bed by a series of burst blood vessels. By the time Betsy reached her, Louisa, the sister who Kitty still thought the most talented of them all, had all but lost the power of speech. "To see her place vacant – to miss her delightful influence and tender watchful care over all, is bitter," Betsy wrote to Hannah, after Louisa died in September. Suddenly she was conscious of death again. "I deeply feel, in the loss of my beloved sister," she wrote to Rachel Cresswell, "the shortness of the time that I may be with you."

Within two weeks, however, she was in France. Both she and William were anxious to reach Joseph, Kate, and their servant Mary, who had been thrown down a Normandy precipice after a carriage-wheel broke on a rocky road. To Betsy's initial relief, she saw Joseph waiting as soon as she stepped onto the Calais quayside, but as she went towards him, his worn face and weary expression told her just how much her husband was ageing. Once again she was reminded of how fast the years were slipping away.

Betsy herself didn't feel old. Although sometimes she felt downhearted or frustrated, the black depressions that had dogged her adolescence and her childbearing years had disappeared, leaving her more clearheaded than ever before and with a vigour that sometimes surprised her. After satisfying herself that although her party were shaken and bruised, they were not seriously injured, she immediately began looking for work. "William and I have not been idle," she wrote home, "we have already visited the Prison and Hospital."

At St Omar, they also visited a school and hospital run by Roman Catholic nuns. It put Betsy in mind of something she had written many years earlier when she had imagined that a nun's life consisted of little more than prayer and thanksgiving. In the nuns of St Omar, however, she quickly saw how wrong she had been. "The sacrifice that must be made to give up the whole life, as the Sisters of Charity do," she observed, "to teach and bring up the poor children and attend to the sick in their hospitals is very exemplary." It was a model, she thought, that might usefully be employed by Protestants.

When the time came to leave France, Betsy was reluctant to go. In a brief few days she had been charmed by its picturesque seaside towns and intrigued by its Roman Catholic charities. She also believed she had found the cause she was searching for, and as she shepherded her husband and daughter onto the home-bound steamer, she vowed that before very long she would be sure to return.

For a while, back in England, she wondered if rather than France, she would be called to America. The thought of travelling such a distance over heaving waters, however, was too much to contemplate, even to accompany Joseph John, who was already laying a concern to cross the Atlantic before his Monthly Meeting. Home duties, Betsy reflected, seemed presently to be her calling. They were not to prove very comfortable. In February 1837, Dan's wife, Harriet, died, leaving him with eight motherless children, and in April, after Rachel gave birth to another boy, Betsy was in Norfolk, ready to comfort the bereaved and welcome the new arrival.

Dan had never relented his views on the ministry of women, and while he valued Betsy's support for his family, he refused to let her either read the Bible to them or pray with them.

At Lynn, with the Cresswells, it was even more fraught. Though she was there ostensibly for Rachel's lying-in, when Hannah and Jonathan Backhouse invited her to preach at a meeting arranged by them in a local Methodist chapel, Betsy was unable to forgo the opportunity. When she returned, however, she was confronted by a near-hysterical Rachel. Not only had her mother left her again, Betsy's daughter accused, and at such a critical time, but by preaching in public she had also made an exhibition of herself before the Cresswells' Anglican friends and neighbours.

Miserably guilty, giving way to self-pity, and once again contrasting herself with others, this time Betsy looked enviously at Hannah Backhouse. "She appears built up on every hand in her friendly course," she said, "husband, children, near relations, friends." Whereas in her own life, she saw nothing but disunity and disappointment. "My poor spirit, had almost always had since I married," she said, "someone most near and tenderly beloved, a *real* wanderer from the path of holiness."

Weeks later, it all became much worse when the usually even-tempered Joseph Fry also exploded in frustration. "My dear husband really *feelingly* expressed his deep feeling of my constant engagements," Betsy said. The anger had come as a surprise, since she had imagined he was happy at home with the small amounts of administration still required by the coastguard libraries. She also liked to think that she did her best for him. "I make a point of always dining at home," she said, not quite truthfully, "and spending the evenings and mornings with him and my family." Later, when her conscience forced her to be more honest, she conceded just how much of her time was taken up elsewhere. "Yet my mornings are much occupied by public and relative duties," she admitted, "ministerial, public, children, brothers and sisters, their children, and others in illness, sorrow and death."

The unsettling outbursts by her family were almost enough to make her overlook the objections that prevented her travelling to America with Joseph John. She was swayed even more as she ministered beside him at the grand public meeting he called in Norwich in July to say farewell to its citizens, and yet again when she thought of his plans: to help heal a rift among American Friends where divisions had caused an open split, and then to assess the beneficial effects of emancipation in the British West Indies. In Liverpool, as she arranged flowers in her brother's cabin, and provided libraries for the crew and the passengers in steerage, she also noted with approval the presence onboard of Eliza Kirkbride, a clever, devoted and agreeable American Friend. Later, standing alongside Sam and Elizabeth, and watching Joseph John's ship hauled by its tugs into the Mersey, she wept; part of her wished she were going too, and another wondered if she would ever see her brother again.

Travelling home from Liverpool on one of the first stretches of railway line to be opened in Britain, she also thought, perhaps guiltily, about Joseph Fry, currently touring the spas of Europe with 20-year-old Gurney. Like his older brothers and sisters, Gurney's bad behaviour had caused Betsy many anxious hours, but more recently her journal entries had referred to his unstable mental health, which had finally threatened to collapse beneath the stresses of a love affair. Restoring Gurney to health, and smoothing his way with Sophia, the daughter of his old tutor, Dr Pinkerton, currently based at Frankfurt, had become Joseph Fry's latest family mission.

Back at The Cedars, uneasy about Gurney and uncomfortably aware of the rewards she would miss by forgoing the trip to America, Betsy threw herself into a programme of activity. In London there were official meetings to attend, concerning the prison now under construction at Grange Gorman Lane in Dublin, and others concerning The Factory, the female prison at Paramatta in New South Wales.[4] At Ratcliff, she also formed a Visiting Society, provided a library for the poor and helped found an infant school.

When Joseph Fry was reinstated as a Friend in October 1837, Betsy discovered to her surprise that her feelings were mixed. "I see some bondage attached to membership of any outward body," she observed. When she held a series of evangelistic meetings for the poor inhabitants of Ratcliff, in the style of those held in Essex in 1831, it also confirmed the liberating lesson she had learned earlier from the Gurneys, that even when Christians did not see entirely eye to eye, they could still be united in the Spirit and the bonds of peace. Almost immediately afterwards she set out on a religious visit to

Sussex. Throughout it all, she continued to worry about Gurney, and although John and William promised to make him a partner in the tea business, she covered pages of her journal with pessimistic thoughts. Later, she tore most of them out.

Though she did her duty in Britain, attending long and often highly detailed official meetings, and visited the Quaker Meetings that had become so familiar over the years, still she hankered for something as challenging as her first days at Newgate when everything was exciting and new. Shortly before Christmas 1837, after a party given in her honour by Joseph and Kate, where all her 20 grandchildren were in attendance, the opening came. In her eagerness to seize hold of it, she found her fellow Quakers' excessive attention to detail very frustrating. "If I had not come to a willingness, I should not have laid my concern before the Meeting," she said crossly, after it took days to reach a decision. At her age, Mrs Fry rather resented having to justify herself.

The French winter, and a view through a haze of January drizzle, at first cast a gloom over Betsy's warm memories of the previous year. The hotel at Abbeville was cold and the unusual diet, which she had scarcely noticed in the warm Normandy autumn, suddenly appeared alien and unappetising. Even having Joseph with her at last on a religious journey could barely compensate. Nor could their friend, Josiah Forster, an elder of the Society of Friends, and Lydia Irving, one of its more enthusiastic younger members.

But, with the fires built higher, a supply of additional warm coverings discovered, and more particularly the curiosity of the people aroused, the outlook began to change. "Picture us," Betsy wrote home to the family, "our feet on some fleeces that we have found, generally wrapped up in cloaks, surrounded by screens to keep off the air; the wood fire at our feet. We have just finished an interesting reading in French, in the New Testament, with the landlady, her daughters and some of the servants at the hotel."[5] Her audience, she assured her readers, "were very attentive and much interested."

The French were also awestruck. Even the Protestants

among them could hardly help seeing in the tall Englishwoman, her fair face dominated by her strange religious cap, and determined to read the Bible to them in her schoolgirl French, something of the saint. Combined with her reputation as the heroine of Newgate, whose story had filled the French newspapers in 1817, it was as if the chemistry that had provoked such enthusiasm in Scotland and Ireland with Joseph John, and which had so impressed Louisa Hoare, was beginning to work now in France. From the *fille de chambre* at the hotel at Abbeville to the governor of the prison at Montreuil, Mrs Fry began to attract a host of eager and bedazzled followers.

In Paris, although the weather remained cold, Betsy found that the apartments procured by her old correspondents, the Delesserts, were luxurious, and the city itself was cosmopolitan in a way she had never before experienced. News of her arrival spread rapidly, and through her door at the Hotel de Castille came a colourful host that to her mind represented the citizenry of the world. Urbane English diplomats were followed by rangy, republican Americans; dark-eyed Slavs with high slanting cheekbones mingled with jet-black Africans, while her letters of introduction from aristocratic friends in England also brought to her the cream of Parisian society. Through them, and through other letters from British government ministers, she found her path made clear to the Minister of the Interior and the Prefect of Police, and then through them to the hospitals, the schools and the prisons of France.

Entering the great female prison of St Lazare, with its 952 female inmates, was like Newgate all over again, Betsy thought. Gathered to meet her was a similar throng of half-reluctant women, too accustomed to rejection to appear eager and too ground-down to dare hope. Standing silently by, as the parable of the prodigal son was read aloud from a Roman Catholic Bible, she allowed her glance to rest on the convicts, and as she met many eyes, she tried to discern something of what lay within each woman's heart.

Slowly and carefully, waiting while each sentence was translated, Betsy began to comment on the parable. God yearns for sinners like us to turn to him, she told the assembled throng of women, he saved me, and now he longs also to save you. Briefly she then described the events at Newgate. Would you also like ladies to visit you, she asked, to read to you and listen to your troubles? Finally, after a long silence, a small voice came from the shadows. *"Oui,"* it said. *"Moi aussi,"* said another.

Next day, the newspapers were full of Mrs Fry; of tears shed by prisoners and jailors alike, and of how elegant French ladies in the accompanying party had immediately volunteered themselves as visitors to the unfortunate convicts. The miracle of Newgate had now become the miracle of St Lazare. So great was the sensation that when Betsy visited the *Prison des Jeunes Détenus* for young people, *La Force*, where male convicts were kept, the Military Prison at St Germains, the Central Prison at Poissy, and the Prison of the *Conciergerie*, that had once held the unhappy Mary Antoinette, crowds of curious onlookers lined her route.

At the Parisian schools the children regarded her as if she were an apparition come from another world and just as she had once done at the Islington Workhouse, Betsy smoothed her way by ensuring a plentiful supply of sugared buns. At a children's hospital, she advised the bemused nuns to loosen the babies' clothing and to open the windows. At the *Salpétrière*, a hospital for the elderly infirm and insane with 5,000 inmates, she was immediately struck by the humanity of their treatment. Nevertheless there was a cruelty, she protested. For notwithstanding their mental condition, it had often been proved that those who suffered in their minds were not only helped and soothed by the Scriptures, but were also capable "of feeling and appropriating the Christian's hope."

Throughout her stay, it was the Christian's hope that was frequently Betsy's central theme. Sometimes she spoke at meetings held at the homes of French Methodist ministers, sometimes among groups of Friends, and sometimes at the Parisian branch of the Bible Society. On one occasion she met with a large company of French Evangelicals who asked her advice on transforming their nation, mostly Roman Catholics or secular materialists, into Bible-believing Christians.

The Christian hope was also a subject she sometimes raised in the evenings during sumptuous dinners at the British Embassy with Lord and Lady Granville, the ambassador and his wife, as well as at the grand Parisian salons where she was guest of honour. When she did so, once again, her fellow guests often observed her with a mixture of curiosity and awe, as if she were indeed a saint come among them from a far-off world. At other times, Betsy found herself listening to conversations whose diversity reminded her of the long-ago dinner table of Earlham that had been home to all shades of ideas and opinion. She observed to herself wryly that in her old age she was enjoying such parties again.

Almost her final engagement, on 2 March 1838, was with the King and Queen of France and the Duchess of Orleans. To them, Betsy presented copies of her sister Louisa's tracts on education, several books by Joseph John and copies of a book of her own, written in 1830, where individual Scripture texts were followed by a brief thought for each day of the year. Princess Adelaide, the King's sister, promised to read it regularly. So too had hundreds of other individuals who had also taken copies of the book, that had been specially translated into French. However, she was not convinced that her small book, no matter how well thumbed, was enough to transform the French nation. "Such a nation," she said, "such a numerous and superior people, filling such a place in the world, and Satan appearing in no common degree to be seeking to destroy them, first, by infidelity and so-called philosophy, secondly by superstition." As she boarded the packet for Dover, she decided that there was no doubt that she was called to return.

France remained at the forefront of her mind when she described her continental trip to the Annual Meeting of the British Society in May. The turnout was the largest in the organisation's history, with many hundreds present, of all ranks of society, and as the women of Britain listened to their founder's adventures, their horizons grew wider. The meeting also discussed the transformation that had taken place in prisons throughout the British Isles since 1817, and how much it had been the result of the unremitting work of the British

Society and the Prison Discipline Society. It also noted that since the Act of 1835, imposing greater government control on local authorities, many obstacles to prison visiting had finally been removed. The breach with the Inspectorate that had followed the Newgate Report had also been healed and replaced by co-operation.

"Tomorrow I am 58," Betsy wrote on 20 April 1838, "an advanced period of what I apprehend to be not a very common pilgrimage." Earlier that same day, she had been very open with Dr Pinkerton about Gurney, and later feared she had revealed too much about her wayward and difficult son. Gurney had also informed her that in order to marry Sophia, he too would be leaving the Society of Friends for the Church of England. He left for Frankfurt in June and was married there on 12 July.

In that month, Betsy preached before a huge gathering at Westminster Meeting House, organised by Hannah Backhouse for high-ranking foreigners and British nobility. Among them were Lord Morpeth, Secretary of State for Ireland, the Chancellor of the Exchequer and the Duchess of Sutherland, the leading Lady of Honour to Victoria, who had been crowned Queen the previous year. Preparing for the meeting, Betsy was forced to recognise that even though she was not the main speaker, she was, nevertheless, the main attraction, and it revived all her conflicts about women's ministry. God is no respecter of persons, she reminded herself sternly, and the point was surely that the crowds who filled the wooden benches should hear the gospel preached. Nevertheless, she couldn't also help noting that she was a far better speaker than Hannah.

In August, so great was the crowd of women who arrived at an Aberdeen drawing-room meeting, all eager to hear Mrs Fry and to offer themselves for a Ladies' Association, that a large public assembly room was substituted at short notice. There, to the assembled throng of eager volunteers, Betsy also raised her concerns about the separate system, that with the passing years was causing her increasing anxiety. Later, after visiting Aberdeen's prison, and sending a comprehensive report to the provost and magistrates of the city, and to the two sheriffs responsible for the county, she raised her concerns again. "The system of separate confinement, although it has many advantages" she said, "requires great care in its administration, in order to make it productive of good effects on the mind of the prisoner, who should frequently be visited by serious, judicious persons, to read the scriptures, and carefully mark and cherish any returning good impressions." Just how much care was needed, she pointed out, was highlighted by the fact that two prisoners at Aberdeen, both of them kept in solitary confinement, had attempted suicide.

Taking a break from her punishing schedule and relaxing at Renny Hill, the ancestral home of Priscilla Buxton's husband, Andrew Johnston, she discussed with the young couple the forthcoming Prison Bill for Scotland, and the many changes that had taken place over the previous 20 years. While not always conforming to the highest ideals, theirs was a reforming century, they concluded, and when the subject arose of Joseph John's research in the West Indies, Priscilla and Andrew asked Betsy whether she planned to join him in America. Since his departure from Liverpool he had several times repeated his invitation, and the knowledge that he missed her, and valued her ministry so much that he now urged others to persuade her, brought her to the verge of tears. In her heart she still yearned to go, and for Joseph John's sake she might even overcome her old fear of the sea, yet she knew she could never justify leaving her family for the year of absence required. She felt it as a terrible sadness, for she knew how significant the work was, how rewarding it would be, and that the opportunity would never come her way again. Had she gone, she reflected, she would dearly have liked to visit Philadelphia, and to have stood by the grave where William Savery had lain since 1804, when he was struck down while tending the victims of the yellow fever then ravaging his city.

Unable to join Joseph John in America, but increasingly eager to travel overseas, Betsy had no intention of abandoning her campaign against solitary confinement. In Edinburgh she was allowed into the solitary cells for women, recently installed in the city prison, and what she saw there left her deeply troubled. Later, at a meeting of magistrates, lawyers and reformers called to discuss the new Scottish Prison Bill, she drew a picture for them of the reality of solitary confinement. Many of the isolated captives, she said, were simple women, with few inner resources, and weeks spent in silent cells with their fears, bitterness and regrets, rather than encouraging pious reflection, often left them hovering on the brink of insanity. Surely, she continued, the evidences of both reason and religion proved that humanity was intended by its creator for social life. While association might be denied for specific purposes and periods, to deny it entirely could only warp creatures who both grew and were transformed and reformed through fellowship.

During her remaining meetings in Scotland, and all the way back home through Westmoreland and Lancashire, when she visited prisons or spoke for the prison cause, alongside her continuing campaign to see female officers entirely in charge of female convicts, Betsy also spoke out against the separate system.

There would almost certainly be opportunities to raise both subjects in France, she thought, when in December 1838 she requested another travelling minute from her Monthly Meeting. This time she envisaged a much longer trip, something more adventurous, that would take her further afield and into regions quite unlike any she had ever experienced – perhaps almost as strange as those Joseph John would soon see in the West Indies. As she began to make plans, she noted down a few concerns. Foremost among them were the Fry finances: once again, the account was overdrawn, and since Joseph had extravagantly embarked on a massive series of alterations at The Cedars, the deficit was growing daily. However, with the three older boys now actively supporting their parents, by adding their contributions to the regular Gurney income Betsy thought she could manage. Another concern was her health, which had suffered, she believed, from the painful shortage of malt liquor in France. "But, if the Lord calls me there," she said, "I must be willing to suffer for His name's sake, and my belief is that He will supply my needs."

CHAPTER SIXTEEN

A city set on a hill that cannot be hid

*B*ETSY ARRIVED IN PARIS in March 1839. With her were Joseph, Kate and young Harry, Josiah Forster, and Mary, her maid. Waiting for them they found a grand apartment filled with scented flowers by Madame Pelet, an admirer from the previous year, and a city waking to the spring and alive with anticipation.

With the success of the previous year still echoing in her mind, and hopes for the future stirring her soul, Betsy was full of confidence and eager to begin work. It was also a very satisfactory feature of the French, she told her journal, that they appeared to favour the more mature and matronly woman. How appropriate it was that as she approached her sixtieth year, the inner voice that moved her had guided her in their direction.

The journey from Boulogne was memorable. Every town on the route to the capital had fond memories of the Englishwoman of the previous year, and wherever she stopped, whether it was to address prison visiting committees founded earlier at Abbeville or Montreuil-sur-Mer, or simply to change horses on the road, she was besieged by enthusiastic crowds. Even hotel servants beguiled her into the kitchens to request more copies of *les petits livres de matin*. "The people here are craving Testaments, Ma'am," Mary observed, as the party learned how Betsy's book of daily readings had made its way through almost the whole of France, passing from friend to friend and from family to family. The news convinced Betsy that France was ready to throw off infidelity and superstition, and that the day of the gospel was at hand. It also reinforced her own sense of mission.

In Paris, a visit to the Prefect of Police reinforced it even more. "He allowed us to visit all the prisons," she noted, "say what we liked in them, and give Testaments in them, through him." More Testaments were distributed at a French Methodist school where the children were principally Roman Catholics, and at the hospitals she had visited the previous year.

To some of the aristocratic ladies who called on her, Betsy described the hugely successful British Society sale at Crosby Hall, held shortly before she left England, that had raised over £1,000 for the expenses of refuges and convict ships. Hearing how Mrs Fry's daughters and 15 of her grandchildren had taken part in the effort, the Frenchwomen were enchanted. They could just picture the charitable bustle among rows of trestle tables loaded with prison-made goods, the chattering scampering children collecting money and wrapping parcels, a bookstall selling Evangelical pamphlets, and a quiet corner set aside for tea. It was all so charmingly English, they thought. It also increased their admiration for Mrs Fry, who within the space of a few hours could engage in rapturous prayer, preach from the Bible, explain the ordering of charity sales, and hold detailed discussions on the subject of fresh air and ventilation.

Both at the hospital of the *Hôtel Dieu*, an ancient foundation with 1260 beds, and the hospital of St Louis, founded originally for plague victims, Betsy recommended more space between the beds and a better flow of air. Once again, just as at St Omar three years earlier, she was impressed by the devotion of the Roman Catholic nuns. If a commitment to mental occupation and spiritual welfare were added to physical care, she said, there could surely be nothing better for hospital patients than to be nursed by a devoted and properly trained band of women.

She was still thinking about it when she spoke to a huge public meeting called for her final evening in Paris. She began by telling the assembled crowd how impressed she was with the piety and charity of French Protestants and Roman Catholics alike. Describing her meetings with many Christian organisations, where she had spoken on evangelism, on slavery, and how the conduct of the higher classes influenced the lower, she said that in all of them she had seen enthusiasm and commitment. Then, finally, she spoke of the city's hospitals, schools and prisons. In the prisons, she said, she had frequently been asked her views on solitary confinement, and in response she had expressed the concerns she was consistently raising in Britain. The thought that the separate system would soon be introduced into France had depressed her, she said, but other prison issues had provided much satisfaction. At St Lazare, where she had gone from ward to ward, speaking to all the prisoners, she had seen some important improvements since her previous visit there. Chief among them was the introduction of female officers, an innovation which she believed would soon be seen throughout the whole of France. In conclusion, she referred to the days when she first entered Newgate, to the changes that had taken place since, and to what had motivated the men and women at the forefront of the movement for reform. "Improving Christian *principle*," she told her audience, "*is the only sure means of improving practice.*"

Leaving behind her a report of her prison visits for the Prefect of Police, several Protestant ladies' visiting committees, and a host of new admirers, Betsy left Paris at the end of April. For Joseph and Kate, it was an enormous relief. During their first weeks in the city they had spent long days sightseeing, and their evenings either at Betsy's meetings or the dinners to which she was constantly invited. As time passed, and the novelty of Paris wore thin, they found that increasingly they had nothing to do but entertain ladies with no English who called unexpectedly in the hope of spiritual advice or a prayer from Mrs Fry, or else grapple in French with callers intent on discussing the finer points of prison reform or theology.

Betsy, although loath to admit it, also found their presence frustrating. "I feel the comfort, and may say the blessing, of having my dearest husband and children with me," she said, "but it is at times difficult to perform all my duties." When

Kate suddenly began complaining of faintness and stomach cramps, her mother was in no mood to be a nurse. The Duchess of Orléans, now a close friend, had assured her that her visits had been a blessing to Paris, while the Prefect of Police had granted her permission to visit all the prisons in France. At the same time, a Roman Catholic Archbishop had criticised her visit, her books, her suggestions for St Lazare, and his co-religionist, the Baron de Girando, her main supporter at the Parisian hospitals. The heady combination of adulation, encouragement and virulent censure had fired Betsy with Evangelical zeal, and brushing Kate's complaints aside, she began planning her crusade through France.

Travelling south on long, straight, tree-lined roads, Betsy's optimism increased. It was reinforced further by the respectful welcome she received at prisons in Melun and Lyons. As she approached Avignon, where the skies grew steadily brighter, and warm breezes wafted scents of rosemary and lavender through her carriage windows, her spirits rose even higher and she felt a new energy flowing. At last she had reached a land that was quite unlike anything she had ever known. Everything about it combined to enchant and intrigue her: the black-clad peasant women at the roadside whose eyes followed her passage; the sunny orchards planted with olives, mulberry and figs; the vistas of distant vine-clad hillsides and snow-capped mountains; and the Roman Catholic religious orders who devoted themselves to so many prisons, hospitals and asylums. Even the growing discord among her companions could barely quench her enthusiasm. With so many people travelling together, she reasoned, frequent disagreements were inevitable, and ignoring Joseph and Kate, who pleaded for a slower pace and for rest, she threw herself into a relentless round of prison visits and evangelistic meetings.

On reaching Nîmes, Betsy found herself in a stronghold of French Protestantism, where the people had maintained their faith during the persecutions that followed the revocation of the Edict of Nantes in 1685, when religious liberty in France had come to a bitter and bloody end.

Emilien Frossard, Nîmes' leading Protestant pastor, became her interpreter and guide, and it was he who translated when she addressed the male prisoners at the town's great Maison Centrale. There, after expressing a desire to visit the *cachots*, the prison's punishment cells, she encountered in them men chained by their hands and feet and kept in total darkness. She had seen others in their condition, she told them, but after giving their word for future good conduct they had been allowed to rejoin their fellows. She urged the men to think hard on their misdeeds.

Using the story of Mary Magdalene as her theme, she went on to preach to a mixture of Protestant and Roman Catholic prisoners, and as she heard her words translated into French, and saw tears trickle from the eyes of prisoners and turnkeys alike, she reflected on how powerful was the message of the Bible to transform lives that were lost. Later, as she made her way out of the gaol through workshops where men sat labouring in silent rows, a gendarme brought two prisoners to her. Both were men she had met earlier in the *cachots*, and after their own promises had been obtained, and Betsy's subsequent intercession, their chains had been struck off and they were reunited with their fellow prisoners. Never, they assured Mrs Fry, would they cease to pray for her and bless her.

At the beginning of June, Betsy succumbed finally to family protests and for two weeks she lived the life of rural France in a village house at Congénies. Joseph and Kate loved the lazy days where nothing disturbed them but the cooing of doves and the clucking of chickens, and occasionally a passing donkey loaded with produce, but Betsy was impatient and restless. Immediately on arriving at Marseilles, she threw herself into a round of visits, to the prison, the schools and the hospitals. At one of the latter, Kate remembered later, an English sailor, who had once seen Mrs Fry on a convict ship in the Thames, greeted her mother as though she were an old and valued friend, and then went on to tell the story of Newgate in his broken French to anyone who would listen.

Later, back once more in Nîmes, and resuming her campaign for the soul of France, together with Emilien Frossard and his wife, Betsy embarked on a series of evangelistic meetings for the Protestant community. "I felt it my duty to show them, as Protestants," she wrote later, "the infinite importance, not only in France, but in the surrounding nations, of their being as a city set on a hill that cannot be hid. I showed them how the truth is spreading, and how important to promote it, by being preachers of righteousness in life and conversation, as well as in words and doctrine."

At the village of *Codognan*, however, when the local pastor insisted that truth included the injunction contained in St Paul's letter to the Corinthians[1] against women speaking in churches, Betsy was intensely irritated. Despite having for years expressed her own fears and reservations on the subject, when finally confronted, she discovered that she had no inclination for submission. Flouting the minister, and overlooking the pages of anxieties committed earlier to her journals, she simply held her meeting in the open air. The novelty of it entranced her, and standing in the shade cast by almond trees, and with swallows dipping through the sunny air before her, it was to the background chatter of insects that she proclaimed her gospel message to the enormous crowd that surrounded her.

She preached again at Montpellier, where she founded a Protestant Ladies' Association to visit the women at the *Maison Centrale*, and also arranged for several female convicts there to be freed from solitary confinement. At her final evening meeting in the town, the press in the room was so thick that even the ledges of the open windows were crowded, while swarms of small boys, all eager to glimpse the extraordinary sight of a lady priest, perched in the trees outside. Five days later, after a brief interlude at a pretty vine-swathed hotel on the shores of the blue Mediterranean, she was at Toulouse, where as well as reading the Scripture with men from a British regiment quartered there since 1814, she found another two prisons to visit.

It was from the cooler regions north of Toulouse, their base since Joseph declared he was ready to collapse from the heat and constant activity, that Betsy planned to take her message to Montauban, home of the college that trained the Protestant ministers of France. But as she did so, the differences within the party, that had prompted the two week rest at Congenies, began threatening to disrupt the entire enterprise. When she rose before five in the morning, ready to begin the long mountain journey, both Joseph and Kate flatly refused to be moved. A furious argument followed, and after ignoring her husband's insistence that she abandon her plans, Betsy left in a temper.

Throughout the subsequent journey, with only Josiah for company, and the mountain landscape growing gradually harsher, Betsy brooded on her fraught relationship with her husband. Despite all her constant hopes and prayers, he still failed to be the partner she longed for him to be. She also wondered if he was right, that the hectic pace was wearing everyone down, and that she herself was too old to be setting out on adventures before daybreak.

On reaching Montauban, however, she knew she had been right to come. "What was my surprise," she wrote later, "when we approached the college, to be met in a formal manner by the professors, the students and the Dean." Ushered by her hosts into their chapel, Betsy also realised that not only was she the honoured guest of the college, but that virtually the whole town had turned out to hear her. "Only a poor woman," she wrote later, wryly recalling the Pastor of Codognan, "only speaking through an interpreter, I felt it very weighty indeed." She couldn't help noting later, however, that she was more effective than Josiah, who spoke in French and often seemed flustered. Her talk was weighty too, and ranged from the prison cause and the power of the Scriptures to change lives, through the specific conditions in French gaols, to the political and religious state of France in general. She also especially encouraged the students. "I endeavoured to show them," she said, "the extreme importance of their being sound in doctrine and practice."

"I have seldom felt sweeter peace in leaving a place than Montauban," she wrote, when several days later she and Josiah headed back towards Toulouse. But on reaching their party, the rebellion that had been brewing now erupted, as a tearful Kate insisted that rather than being refreshed by visiting the south of France, and having time to see the sights, she was physically worn out and heartily sick of prisons and religious meetings. And as far as he was concerned, Joseph added, his relationship with his wife was on the point of complete breakdown. After years of acceding to the demands of her ministry, her commitment to reform and her fame, he had finally reached breaking-point.

Betsy was dumbfounded. She really couldn't understand how, on the one hand, her family could be so uninterested in what she believed was so critically important; and why, on the other, even if they were so dissatisfied, they couldn't subdue their feelings for the sake of the cause. "This journey, that I had entertained a hope would have been so much blessed to us," she said, "and laboured so to take my beloved family with me, for their own good, my heart was *pained* within me." So stung was she by their ingratitude, that tempestuously she decided they all should go home at once.

"I very seriously lay before my husband and Kate my doubts how far I could go on with this journey unless there was more peace," she said. As she did so, an exasperated Josiah Forster intervened to denounce the whole company, who though calling themselves Friends, were currently behaving like the bitterest of adversaries and setting an appalling example to their hosts.

Exacerbated by the summer heat, the wounded feelings continued to simmer, until eventually, at the beginning of July, a compromise was finally concluded. A short break in the Pyrenees would allow everyone to relax, as well as enabling Joseph and Josiah to assist Betsy with two reports on French prisons, one for the Minister of the Interior, and a shorter version for the Prefect of Police. Then, when that was done, the party agreed that it would make its way home, quietly and slowly, by way of Switzerland.

Almost immediately, a quarrel with Josiah over Christian doctrine threatened to disrupt the carefully engineered harmony. Her friend was quite unable to separate his peculiarly Quaker views, Betsy decided, from the Evangelical principles she believed lay at the heart of Christianity and which also formed the basis of the message she preached. She also questioned her reasons for encouraging Josiah to travel with them. "My fear of women coming too far forward," she said, "has led me to be too anxious to have a man with me who I really esteemed as I do J. Forster, and who takes part in the service of meeting."

Later, as they headed out of France and into Switzerland, her own inability to ignore prisons and evangelistic opportunities continued to cause friction. It was only when they reached Geneva in August that the presence of Swiss friends, and many others from Paris, allowed the party to separate and the tensions to disperse. The Baroness de Stael, the Duke of Broglie, and Betsy's old friend Sophia Delessert entertained them to grand outdoor banquets on the shores of the lake, and to all outward appearances, friendliness once more reigned triumphant.

In Geneva itself, where the prison governor was the brother of her old friend Stephen Grellet, Betsy saw a prison that almost entirely exemplified the ideals of the reformers. After being classified into four groups, prisoners spent their sentences working and exercising within them, while sleeping alone in individual cells furnished with a bed, a table, a chair and a shelf filled with books. To her dismay, however, at the city's second gaol, the Roman Catholic priest refused to allow his own flock either to hear her or to meet her.

For a while, it seemed that the urgency that had driven her through France would continue through Switzerland and the provinces of Germany. At Lausanne there was another prison to visit, and another at Berne, together with a large school for boys. Later, there were still more at Zurich, Stuttgart and Ludwigsberg, and in early September, on reaching Frankfurt, and a welcome at the home of Gurney's father-in-law, Dr Pinkerton, there were yet more. "I also visited the prisons," Betsy noted, "all sad (with one exception). I hope the prisoners will be visited in consequence, and a stall opened in the town for the sale of Bibles and tracts."

Then, after almost seven months, it was over. "Probably my

next journal may be written in our sweet dear home," Betsy wrote at Cologne in mid-September. She did not feel called to travel further, she said. Since leaving Geneva she had found herself daydreaming more and more of The Cedars, while Joseph and Kate, who both seemed to be almost continually unwell, tried her severely. Kate had also developed what her mother regarded as a very foolish fear of railways.

But though she chided Kate for her fears, as the party made the crossing from Ostend through a thick fog made more ominous by the eerie moaning of the packet's horn, Betsy had done little but gaze apprehensively at the restless black waters. Stepping onto English soil, it was a huge relief to see Sam's olive-green coach and its neat footmen waiting for her, and Sam inside, looking reassuringly solid and prosperous.

"Our house and garden looking lovely," she wrote on 22 September, "everything that we can require, or should I say, desire."

As the Christmas of 1839 approached, Betsy felt she had many more reasons to feel satisfied. From the continent came dozens of letters each week, all filled with news of the prison cause, the Christian cause, or simply with tidings of friends. At a meeting with the Home Secretary, Lord Normanby, she discovered that recommendations she had made earlier concerning the female transports serving time at Millbank were likely to result in their being educated and instructed in trades rather than abandoned entirely to solitary confinement. With assistance from Sam and Joseph John, the tea business was also buoyant once more and the three eldest boys were not only more settled, but were prospering. In October, Rachel had produced another healthy boy, adding to one born to Hannah earlier in the year, and in November, Julia produced a girl, just as Alice had done months earlier. There was also the exciting news from Buckingham Palace that the Queen was to marry the earnest Prince Albert of Saxe-Coburg-Gotha, while from Victoria herself came a gift of £50 for the discharged prisoners' refuge at Chelsea.

Shortly before the turning of the year, Betsy's old friend

John Pitchford died. For many years he and his wife Susan had lived at Bow, where John worked as a manufacturing chemist, and their proximity to West Ham had led to a deepening of the friendships that had begun long ago at Earlham. In 1830, shortly after the Catholic Emancipation Act gave Roman Catholics the right to vote, sit in Parliament, and hold public office, Betsy had ministered at the deathbed of the Pitchfords' eldest son, and as she comforted the bereaved parents, she had reflected that if the Christian's hope was firmly established upon the Rock of Ages, then with or without ceremonies, all would be well. Now, however, with the emergence of the Tractarian Movement and the growth of ritualism in the Church of England,[2] she was no longer so certain. At the same time, she was also concerned that just like many of the extreme radicals of her youth, the followers of the socialist movements now springing up all over Europe made no secret of their hostility towards Christianity. Both issues were clouds on her horizon, and she reflected that although the world changed, in some ways it seemed to move in cycles, rather than steadily forward.

The death of John Pitchford, and the changes in the world around her, reminded Betsy once more that her own great change was drawing inevitably closer. Would her faith carry her through the storm, she wondered anxiously, or would her old scepticism overwhelm her at the last, leaving her bereft and sinking for ever into the ocean of darkness of death? But as she sensed the grim presence at her back, she also felt the urgency that had carried her through France gathering momentum once more and driving her on. Early in 1840, as she also made her will, together with her brother Sam, she planned another European journey.

Though she had not reached America, she was nevertheless quite a traveller, Betsy concluded, and early in February, when she and Sam were presented to Queen Victoria, she yearned to share her enthusiasm and her plans with her young monarch. Protocol, however, dictated otherwise. "We were only to reply to the Queen's questions," Betsy said disappointedly, "and not to say what we liked. This was very cramping." She did, however, leave copies of the various books written by herself and Joseph John, and as she did so, she prayed that there might be future openings into the royal household.

Reflecting on her forthcoming departure, and recalling the great Norwich meeting that had preceded Joseph John's trip to America, Betsy felt called to hold something similar in London. It forced her, finally, to confront the issue of women's ministry.

Since Codognan she had grown increasingly concerned, for although she had flouted him, the minister's attitude had brought into sharp focus the conflict that had troubled her for years. Deborah Darby and Priscilla Hannah Gurney, the women who had so inspired her youth, had ministered largely within their own Quaker community. Betsy, on the other hand, had not only become Europe's most well-known prison reformer, but had also preached as an evangelist to thousands of non-Quakers. And although it was her fame as a reformer and her authority as a Quaker minister that provided the openings, much of her impetus was the Evangelical Christianity she espoused. In that, however, lay her problem. The Evangelical view of faith maintained that Scripture constituted a divine authority, and she was constantly and uncomfortably aware that Jesus had apparently only chosen men to be disciples; there were also St Paul's strictures against the public ministry of women.

She struggled to find a solution and also a justification for her own years of public preaching. She finally found it in her own powerful sense of calling and the anointing that fuelled her ministry.

I am sure the Scripture most clearly and forcibly lays down the principle that the Spirit is not to be grieved and quenched, or vexed or resisted, and on this principle I act under the earnest desire that I may not do this, but whatever the Lord leads me into by His Spirit, may be done faithfully to Him, and in His name. I am of the opinion that nothing Paul said to discourage women speaking in the churches alluded to their speaking through the help of the Spirit, as he clearly gave directions how they should conduct themselves under such circumstances when they prayed or prophesied.

Betsy was not alone in her conclusion. It was a view shared by many others, including her brother Joseph John who in 1838 wrote in a letter to his children, "I do not approve of ladies speaking in public even in the anti-slavery cause except under the immediate influence of the Holy Spirit. Then and only then all is safe."[3]

Reassured that she had overcome her dilemma, Betsy stood confidently before the crowd of 1,500 people who flocked to hear her, led them in worship and prayer, and preached to them with power.

In a letter written a few days later, a woman in the congregation described Mrs Fry's charismatic appeal:

> She began by entreating the sympathy and supplications of those present, I cannot tell you how mine flowed forth on her behalf. After her prayer, we sat still for some time, ... and then she rose, giving as a text, "Yield yourselves unto God, as those that are alive from the dead", and uncommon fine was her animated yet tender exhortation to all present, but more especially the young, to present themselves as living sacrifices to the Lord, – to be made of Him new creatures in Christ – the old things passed away, and all things become new as those alive from the dead. This change she dwelt and enlarged on much; its character, and the Power that alone can effect it; the duty demanded of us – "Yield yourselves", and its infinite and eternal blessedness. I was astonished and deeply impressed. The feeling was, "surely God is amongst us of a truth."[4]

When Mrs Fry finally sat down, many of her audience were in tears.

The voyage to Ostend in February 1840 was uneventful, and as Betsy sat with Sam, his daughter Elizabeth, her old friend William Allen, and William's niece, Lucy Bradshaw, she gazed thankfully at a placid sea.

European travel with Sam, she soon discovered, to her

relief, was quite different from her previous trip through France. Not only were there no family tensions, but Sam's enormous wealth smoothed the way; even the sight of his carriage drawing towards the portals of a grand hotel was enough to bring not only porters flying, but eager and deferential proprietors too. It reminded Betsy of her first trip to Scotland with Joseph John.

The Belgian government was eager to welcome Mrs Fry, too, and to her letters of introduction from influential friends in Britain they added a permit to visit all Belgian gaols. Betsy's enthusiasm, her certainty in her calling and her sense of destiny were all reinforced and increased. The powerful fascination that she had earlier held for the French, also began to work its chemistry on the Belgians, and during days spent in prison visits, or in admiring some of the country's well-conducted lunatic asylums, she found herself the centre of an enthusiastic throng of admirers. The Belgian nobility, like their French counterparts, were also eager to meet her, to welcome her to their homes, and to be seen in her company. Among them was the Count Arrivabene, a visiting Italian nobleman who conducted her through the city's Vilvorde prison, and the Baron de Bois, who insisted she visit his priceless collection of Dutch and Flemish masters. Even the King was eager to participate, grasping Betsy's hands in his own as he welcomed her to his land, and then later listening carefully as she and Sam outlined their views on penal reform. It was all rather different from what she had been used to from the royalty of Britain, she reflected. Afterwards, the palace servants sent a petition, begging that they too might hear from Mrs Fry.

After days filled with official visits and religious meetings for Brussels' Belgian population and its large expatriate English community, the evenings were devoted to "philanthropic parties" and grand dinners. "Had I a hundred times more power of writing," said Betsy's niece, Elizabeth, who herself constantly reflected on the extraordinary fascination her aunt held for people of every walk of life, "I could not initiate you into our life here." On their last night in the city, surrounded by leading Belgian families, and with the Dean, "the head of the church here, under the Bishop of Malines," at her side, Betsy was invited to speak freely to the company about her religious views. "She began on the prisons," recalled Elizabeth, "prevention of crime – how much the upper classes are often the cause, by example, for the sins of the lower."[5] Betsy herself recalled how she "spoke very seriously about the Scriptures being read in prisons, and endeavoured to show in a few words what alone can produce change of heart, life and conduct."

"These are extraordinary times," Betsy observed to her journal as the olive-green coach flew over the flat landscape of Belgium, and on into the strange country, "half water and half land," that was Holland. The sense that every door along her way was being opened for her reinforced her conviction that she travelled at God's command, and that perhaps he was making it clear, as her last days approached, just how enormous and widespread had been the effect and inspiration on others of the task he had given her to do.

The refuge for poor girls at Amsterdam, she thought, was just such an example. "It was in the most beautiful order," she said, "kept by ladies, who give up their time and their fortune to attend to this Christian duty." At Rotterdam, there was a huge prison for boys, "capitally taught by gentlemen, who daily visit them." Later, at Gouda, at the end of a long journey by land and water, she found herself in one of the oddest prisons of her whole career. "Such a curious place I never saw," she said, "we had to ascend story by story, by stairs little better than ladders, and at the very top we found three great rooms in the roof." There, overlooking a watery landscape, where farmhouses sat on islands connected by swing bridges, she held a meeting for the female prisoners who once again wept at her words. She also spoke with their female officers, newly introduced after the lobbying of a local Ladies' Association.

"How curious is the variety we meet with," Betsy wrote at Hamelin, shortly after entering Germany, "and the different things there are to occupy our attention." At her public meeting earlier in the day, she had observed that sitting beside members of the town's leading families were also the proprietor of her hotel and his wife, the local doctor, the post-master, the bookbinder, the shoe-maker and many, many more, all of them equally eager to hear Mrs Fry's words translated for them into German. It was also curious, she thought, that the town had no tradition of visiting the poor. "I hope and expect our coming will be useful in this respect," she said.

It was useful indeed. During her stay Betsy befriended a Jewish shopkeeper, a woman of some stature, from whom she bought a little gift for a grandson. In the pleasant exchange of family information between two women that followed, an invitation to Meeting later brought not only the shopkeeper herself, but several of her friends too, who all later called on Betsy at her hotel. "The following day," she said, "we agreed to form a District Society, to attend to the deplorable state of the poor."

At Hanover, Betsy also found the prisons in a deplorable state, with untried prisoners held in chains until confessions were extracted – even, she said, if they were innocent. Days later, she raised the issue with the town's chief magistrate and his colleagues. In her audience with the Queen of Hanover, who had also been eager to meet her, she raised one of the concerns that had always been so central to her ministry. "We had very interesting and important subjects brought forward," she said, "the difficulties and temptations to which rank is subject, the value of example, the objects incumbent upon people of influence, Bible Societies, Prisons &c. We then read our address to the Queen, wishing her to patronise ladies visiting the prisons."

Berlin offered more opportunities, and the prospect of influencing yet another royal family, when early in April the Princess William, sister to the King of Prussia, held a reception for Mrs Fry. The venue was the magnificent *Hôtel de Russie* where, flanked by marble columns and surrounded by greenery and scented bouquets, and beneath crystal chandeliers sparkling with candlelight, Betsy addressed a gathering of 200 members of Prussia's elite. "It is impossible to give an idea of the intense eagerness and interest when our aunt arose," wrote Elizabeth. Enthralled, the vast audience were barely able to take their eyes from the tall, matronly woman, in her white muslin cap, whose passion glowed so brightly that it seemed to reflect a light burning deep within her soul. "Even those who could not understand English," said Elizabeth, "seemed to gather something by watching her and listening to her voice."

Afterwards, the chamber buzzed with questions. "'Everyone wants to know about our aunt's history. Where does she live? Is she married? And their astonishment is great," said Elizabeth, "when I tell them of five-and-twenty grandchildren, though it seems only to add to the respect paid to her."[6]

Later, when Princess William led the call for a Ladies' Association, she arranged for its first meeting to be held at her palace.

Betsy, Elizabeth and Lucy arrived together to oversee the foundation of Berlin's Association for the Improvement of Female Offenders, and as they did so, extraordinary scenes awaited them. Many of the potential members were close friends of the Princess, and their carriages, most of them far grander even than Sam's, were drawn up behind impeccably groomed horses on a sweeping gravelled drive. Waiting inside, in an exquisite suite of rooms, stood 40 women, all of them dressed in the latest French fashions, and all sipping chocolate from a bone china service. "I could not but long for a painter's eye, to have carried away the scene,"[7] said Elizabeth. Presently, the Crown Prince and Princess of Prussia arrived to usher the assembly into an elegant ante-room overlooking a sunny formal garden.

With the Crown Prince and Princess, and the Princess Charles on her right, and the Princess William, the Princess Marie, and the Princess Czartoryski on her left, and with the Count Gröben to interpret, Mrs Fry opened the proceedings. She wore a plain dark satin gown and a new fawn-coloured silk shawl she remembered later. Before her on an elegant table stood a silver inkstand and pens, and after the rules, exactly as they were in Britain and elsewhere, were read to the assembly and agreed, Mrs Fry was the first to sign to her name. Finally, with the permission of the Crown Prince, in the midst of the elegant throng she knelt on the ground in prayer. "She offered one of her touching, heartfelt prayers for them," said Elizabeth, "that a blessing might rest on the whole place, from the King on his throne to the poor prisoner in the dungeon, and she prayed especially for the Royal Family. Then for the ladies, that the works of their hands might be prospered in what they had undertaken to perform."[8]

"My spirits were so unusually low yesterday," Betsy wrote in Frankfurt, on 3 May, "that I could have wept for nothing." After the formation of the Berlin Ladies' Association, she had been received privately by the Crown Prince to discuss the persecution of the Lutheran Church. It had been followed by more hospital visits, then another to a workhouse, and then still more to prisons. But ever since the last of them, she had felt unusually weary, and at Leipzig she had spent two days resting alone while the party went on to Dresden. By the time she joined them again, she was feeling delicate and in need of the devoted attention showered on her by Sam and the two girls.

Devotion was at the forefront of her mind soon after she reached Düsseldorf. Chief among her objects there was Theodor Fliedner, a German clergyman who had first heard her speak at Newgate six years earlier, after which he had visited her personally and then joined the ranks of her correspondents. So impressed had he been with all he had seen and heard, that almost immediately on returning home he founded the Association for the Improvement of Prisoners in the Prussian Provinces of the Rhine and Westphalia. In his parsonage garden he had also founded a refuge for discharged female prisoners. From small beginnings, he told the woman who had been his inspiration, his society had developed five major branches throughout the region. He also welcomed her to another of his foundations, an institution based at nearby Kaiserswerth, on the Rhine, where Protestant deaconesses were trained to tend and nurse the sick.

Later, as Betsy wound her way back through the Prussian mountains, and then crossed the wet lowlands of Holland and the flat fields of Belgium, her thoughts were full of Kaiserswerth. They were still there at the beginning of May as Sam's coach was guided onto English soil and then made its way through familiar English villages to West Ham. And when Joseph greeted her at The Cedars and chided her for not answering his letters sooner, she barely noticed the tone of sad reproach in her husband's voice. "It would be truly kind of thee my love, to tell us not only where *you have been*," he had written in a letter sent to her in April, "but when and where you expect to be for about ten days ahead – thy last letter had not even *a date* of either place or time."[9] At the end of another, he had signed himself, "From thy very affectionate but rather widowed husband".[10] But, though safely back at home, in her mind, Betsy still walked the wards of Kaiserswerth, beside the neatly uniformed students who went about their caring work with quiet efficiency, and whose eyes shone with purpose as they spoke of the years ahead. And already, she was making plans.

CHAPTER SEVENTEEN

❧ ❦ ❧

My dear love to all
our sisters

*L*ATE IN MAY 1840, shortly after her sixtieth birthday, Betsy updated her will. Ever since the weariness that had overtaken her at Leipzig, she had felt unwell in a way that was new to her, and after arriving home, she had been very ill. "I query whether a step downwards is not taken," she said apprehensively, "that I shall never fully recover. At all events, I have been poorly enough to have the end of life brought closely before me, and to stimulate me in faith to do *quickly* what my Lord may require of me."

One of those things, she believed, was to found something similar to Theodor Fliedner's training school at Kaiserswerth. It was yet another radical idea for Britain. For while nursing the sick was generally considered to be the preserve of women, and something they were by nature inherently fitted to do, the women who worked in Britain's public hospitals were renowned for their low breeding, their drunkenness and their immorality. The hospitals in which they worked were also generally filthy, and since the middle-classes were almost exclusively cared for at home, their patients were largely the poor and the armed forces. In her book, *Observations on Visiting*, Betsy had called on ladies to visit the hospitals, but the idea that respectable women might also work in them was novel. When she raised the issue at the annual meeting of the British Society, a tremor of nervous excitement gripped her audience as they struggled to comprehend the very idea.

Days later there was excitement of a different kind, when Betsy arrived at Exeter Hall, at a huge meeting convened by the British and Foreign Anti-Slavery Society, with the Duchess of Sutherland as her guest. It immediately followed the two-week-long World's Anti-Slavery Convention, and it had been something of a triumph, Betsy thought, to have successfully encouraged the influential aristocrat to attended. "When we got to the meeting," she said, "we could have no suitable place but the front seat of the platform, close where the Duke of Sussex was to sit." Her fame as a reformer, as an Evangelical preacher, and as someone who had spoken widely for abolition, ensured that the huge gathering of over 3,000 people clapped Mrs Fry enthusiastically when she arrived, and treated her to an ovation when she left.

Among the few who did not join the applause were the conference's resentful female delegates. From its beginnings, women supported the anti-slavery movement in their thousands and their personal financial contribution had been massive. Yet, despite it, and despite making exceptions for Hannah More and Elizabeth Fry, many of the movement's leaders had sought to undermine women's involvement, and in some cases prevent it entirely. Even as she led the Duchess to their prominent seats, Betsy was well aware that not only had attempts been made to restrict women's attendance at the conference, but that two American women, Elizabeth Cady Stanton and Lucretia Mott, both of them delegated to speak by their American colleagues, had been refused permission to do so by the conference organisers, the British and Foreign Anti-Slavery Society.

Later, at a large party in Sam Gurney's garden, Betsy apologised to Lucretia for her prominence in the face of such discrimination. Lucretia, herself a recorded minister of the Society of Friends, replied with a mild observation that the event had certainly highlighted inconsistencies in the policies of the British and Foreign Anti-Slavery Society. But though Lucretia was unwilling to share the harsh opinion of Mrs Fry that Elizabeth Cady Stanton took back to America, the events of 1840 were significant for both women. Years later, as pioneers in the American movement for women's suffrage, both quoted their rejection by the 1840 conference as marking the moment they became convinced that women should play a full part in the democratic process.[1]

That Mrs Fry did not stand up for the rejected Americans is perhaps not surprising. For years she had shared the view of her brother Joseph John and of William Wilberforce that the rich and powerful were to be courted for the influence they could bring to bear on others. In the case of the Duchess, who went on to oppose slavery, Betsy's actions of 1840 bore fruit.[2] At the same time, although she urged women to involve themselves in works of charity, and had found a solution to Christian arguments against the public ministry of women, her own public role was perhaps too intimately linked with the guilt she experienced over her family for her ever to be truly objective.

Besides, at 60 years old, and with the conviction that her last days were approaching, Betsy was intent on continuing the work she believed she had been called to do.

Among her many continental letters, news came from Prussia announcing the achievements of the Berlin Ladies' Association, and also that following the death of Prussia's King in June, the Crown Prince had assumed the throne. Another arrived from Denmark bearing an invitation from the Queen who had corresponded with Betsy since their meeting in 1822. "If I am called still to go, may my Lord make my way plain before me," said Betsy. Anxiously she hoped that she might be.

Early in August, as she visited Parkhurst, a new prison for boys on the Isle of Wight, she wondered if a future visit to the continent might be made with Joseph John. He was expected home from America later in the month, and her eagerness to see him was intense. At the same time, she was apprehensive. The Fry account was still overdrawn, and she was also concerned that after a three-year absence, their relationship would have lost its old intimacy.

"I think I never saw anybody in so perfectly peaceful a state," she wrote later, after she travelled back to Earlham beside her brother, with so much to say that she could barely contain herself. Fowell had been made a baronet, she told him, in recognition of his long years of public work; a Patronage Society for discharged prisoners had been founded, whose supporters could assist former convicts to find jobs and decent housing; so had the Protestant Sisters of Charity, whose patron was the widow of William IV, and who were already known as Fry Nurses. She went on to explain how detailed plans and rules had been drawn up for a specially selected group of women who would be trained at Guy's Hospital and then live in a nurses' home in the City. There they would tend the poor in their own homes, and even stay with those who needed long-term care. They would also be distinguished from the despised regular nurses by a neat uniform, a regular small stipend, and their devotion to the Bible and to prayer.

In return, Joseph John described his long journey, particularly his visit to the British West Indies where he had observed the beneficial effects of emancipation. It had inspired him, he said, to visit Holland, Denmark and other European nations that still permitted slavery in their overseas colonies. He also felt that he and Betsy should travel together.

"In what a flowing capital state he found his money matters," Joseph John said later, as he pressed a cheque for £200 into Betsy's grateful hand.

Planning to leave England once more, Betsy was uncomfortably conscious that her health was growing worse. Late in November she had become aware of a disturbing pain in her chest, while during a meeting in Birmingham, her voice almost failed her and she was forced to sit down in mid-sentence. "This was humbling and rather painful," she said. The visit was painful in another way too, for when an elderly James Lloyd welcomed her to his home, old memories crept from their hiding places and made her feel somehow child-like and naked. James, however, was charming. "After all the changes of life," Betsy said, "to partake of a spiritual unity is striking and highly satisfactory."

During her railway journey back to London, it was impossible not to muse on what might have been had she married James Lloyd. She would almost certainly have been richer, she reflected, but whether life would have been so full or so rewarding, it was impossible to tell.

She left England again in July 1841. With her went Joseph John, his daughter Anna, and Sam's daughter Elizabeth, and despite the realisation that the schedule would be punishing, Betsy looked forward to the journey. The packed meetings, the eager crowds and the royal courts of Europe would be a welcome relief from a year which up to that point had been an anxious one. In February, Sam Hoare had suffered a stroke, while Aunt Jane Gurney at The Grove was declared incurably ill. Betsy's daughter Louisa had also been desperately unwell after producing a baby boy, and for the first time in her nursing career Betsy had administered the wrong medicine. There was no damage, but the incident was disturbing. It was yet another sign of her failing powers.

She was also depressed by the government's continuing partiality for solitary confinement. In the early summer, during a visit with Fowell to a convict ship, she had met a young woman whose mental breakdown had begun after being taken straight from a solitary cell at Millbank. "This must lead me to make further and stronger efforts for an entire change of the system adopted with them," Betsy urged herself. Stronger efforts were also needed at the new model prison under construction at Pentonville; during a visit there with Sam, it had been horribly clear that if the plans were not altered, there would be an increasing number of similar breakdowns in Britain's gaols. She wrote urgently to Colonel Jebb, the official in charge.

"We think the building, generally, does much credit to the architect," she began diplomatically. Later she listed her concerns. "I consider it a very important object to preserve the *health of mind and body* in these poor creatures,"[3] she said, and went on to stress that in her view, the dark cells and the thick window glass that obliterated the sky should never exist in a Christian and civilised country. Too easily, she said, did the darkness give rise to a gloom which eventually led to depression. She also made clear that while objecting to the physical and mental deterioration caused by solitary confinement on health grounds, she also objected to it on others. The despairing and stupefied state it produced, she said, would no more lead convicts to recognise their need for God's pardon and for salvation, than it would encourage them to live useful and productive lives.

She also hoped to encourage more useful and productive lives throughout Europe, and as she left Ostend behind, she tried desperately to overcome her growing weariness. It was a relief, she reflected, that once again the Gurneys travelled in style, and although this time much of it was by railway, at each destination there were grand hotels to welcome them where no expense was spared.

But, unlike Sam, who often seemed happy simply to smooth the way, Joseph John was a man on a mission, and Betsy couldn't help thinking that sometimes he overlooked important little details of his companions' welfare. Still, she was anxious to encourage his cause, and trying hard to banish a fear that daily grew stronger, she introduced him to the extraordinary range of people she already counted as friends.

Among them were the Gentlemen's Visiting Committee at Rotterdam, the female officers at Gouda, and the King and Queen of Holland, to whom Betsy and Joseph John presented a letter of introduction specially prepared by Victoria's Prince Albert. Writing home, Betsy described the royal couple, the King in his regimentals, and the elegant Queen, a sister to the Emperor of Russia, in a dazzling white silk morning dress. After introducing Joseph John to them, Betsy had explained the purpose of his visit. "I then said," she recounted, "that my brother had visited the West Indies, and would be glad to tell the King and Queen the result of his observations in those islands."

At Amsterdam, Joseph John spoke on slavery again, this time directly to the hearts of merchants and businessmen. "I addressed them for about an hour," he said, "in order to prove to them from facts which I had myself witnessed, the agricultural, mercantile, and pecuniary advantages of the abolition of slavery. It was a thorough man-of-business operation, adapted to Dutchmen attached to their ledgers."[4]

At Bremen, it was his turn to watch as his sister spoke directly to the hearts of ordinary people. "Your name has long been to us a word of beauty," a local clergyman told Betsy, and after he publicly blessed "the missionary brother and sister", their coach was surrounded by an enormous crowd of people demanding to shake Mrs Fry by the hand and to receive a tract. Just miles further on, after encountering a similar throng returning from the market at Harburg, the whole good-natured procedure was gone through again.

Crossing the Baltic to Copenhagen on a brilliant moonlit night, the party were welcomed to Denmark by Peter Browne, Secretary to the English Legation. Later they were entertained royally by the Danish Queen, who begged her guests to bring pressure to bear on the King regarding the country's brutal prison system, the slaves that worked its West Indies plantations, and the persecution of its own Baptist minority.

During a prison visit, the party witnessed the persecution for themselves when they discovered two ministers, Peter and Adolph Munster, held in solitary confinement for their religious beliefs. Determined to raise the issue with the King, Betsy rehearsed over and again the words she would use. However, when the day came, before she could speak, the monarch secreted himself away to discuss slavery with Joseph John. Hours passed until, with images of the wretched Baptists filling her mind, and her heart racing, she burst through the door and confronted them. "I did my best, in a few words to express my mind," she said, recalling the monarch's astonished face, "and very strongly I did it." Later, before she left Europe, at her request, the two captives were set free.

By mid-September the party had been travelling for six weeks; since leaving Denmark they had returned to Hamburg, and then gone on to Hanover, Berlin, Dresden and Halle. At almost every stop there were schools, prisons and asylums to visit, visiting associations to set up, and public meetings to address. There were also innumerable calls to almost every member of the Prussian royal family who often seemed as anxious for Mrs Fry to admire their babies and to pray for their welfare, as they were to hear about her prison visits and her deep Christian faith. Betsy found even those meetings draining, for despite the comfort and the domestic good cheer, she still chose her words carefully, so that eventually they would play their part for the causes that were her life's passion.

At Hamelin she confessed herself completely worn out. Then, one morning near the end of the month, at a hotel deep in the heart of the mountains of Silesia, she woke up barely able to move. To her disgust, it was also obvious there was a serious problem in her bowels.

Uncharacteristically, Joseph John began to panic. Not only did he suddenly realise the international consternation likely to occur if Mrs Fry were to become seriously ill, or even die, so far from England, but in less than three weeks he was to marry his Atlantic travelling companion, Eliza Kirkbride, and at Earlham the arrangements were already underway.

In a coach drawn by six horses refreshed at each stage, and often lying prostrate on a board made soft with pillows, Betsy was carried across Europe. When they finally reached Dover, as Joseph Fry became distraught over his wife's condition, all Betsy's pent-up resentment at Joseph John's lack of attention spilled over into harsh words. "We parted," she said of her brother, "after this most extraordinary journey, under a cloud. I could have wept all day!" Joseph John himself also left the scene in tears.

By his wedding day Joseph John had apologised and the cloud that had cast such gloom over their journey seemed swept away. Betsy's illness, however, lingered, and as she was cared for by several of her children in turn: in Ramsgate by Kate, at Upton Lane by William and Julia, and in Norfolk by Rachel and Frank, once more she entered a state of denial. "The day appears come," she said, "that my beloved children (for whom I have passed through such deep travail of spirit and for whom I have exercised such tender care and felt such wonderful love), are to take care of me."

Back home in November, with no lessening of the pain in the bowels, and with her ankles beginning to swell, she began keeping a detailed record of her medication. "Seldom in 24 hours more than 1/2 grain opium," she wrote, while noting that as well as easing her pain, the drug also slowed her racing pulse. Wine and brandy were also included among her medicines, and despite reassuring herself that Christians could safely use them as remedies, she remained uncomfortably aware of her own weakness for them.

Later in the month Elizabeth Pryor died, and as Betsy grieved for her old friend, in her mind she also re-lived their work on the convict ships. In the 20-year period up to 1839, Elizabeth had visited every female convict ship leaving London, a total of 69 ships and 8,476 prisoners,[5] many of them in the company of Betsy herself. She also recalled the many times that after hours spent classifying convict women, she and Elizabeth went on to Whitehall together to plead that children be reunited with mothers bound for Botany Bay. As she thought of Elizabeth, she also sensed that her own illness was growing worse, and during long sleepless nights spent gazing into the darkness, she heard once again the rush of the sea and the roar of the wind.

"No day passed since I was at Berlin," she wrote in December, "without needing small portions of opium." In the same month, Aunt Jane died and left Betsy £100.

"One grain in day, 3/4 at night," Betsy wrote in January 1842. "Tumbler of porter or ale twice a day, at luncheon or dinner. Port wine as required." Her mind, she noted, felt extraordinarily clear, and after three months' absence from Meeting, whenever she felt well enough to attend she found the anointing rather unusually poured out.

During the day she often dictated to Kate the answers to letters that continued to pour in from all over Europe. Although her opening words often expressed how short was the human span on earth, the correspondence itself reminded her that she still played a role in the Europe-wide prison cause.

So too did a visit from the Chevelier Bunsen, the Prussian Ambassador, on behalf of his King, and also several visits from Lady Pirie, one of Betsy's most long-standing supporters at Newgate, whose husband had recently become Lord Mayor of London. "The Lady Mayoress has been here again today,"

Betsy wrote in January 1842, "to see if there is any prospect of my going to the Mansion House, alluding to the warm desire they have expressed for me to meet Prince Albert, the Duke of Wellington and our different ministers."

The invitation to the banquet, designed to mark the commencement of a new Royal Exchange,[6] immediately made Betsy feel better. So too did the prospect of a meeting with the Prince. Reports of the royal domestic life, of the young couple's Bible readings and family prayers, all of which Betsy had noted enthusiastically in her journal, had convinced her that her intuition about Victoria had been right, and she was anxious for an opportunity to encourage her Christian example.

The event, however, did not begin well, and after arriving at the Mansion House on a wet January evening, Betsy found herself at the centre of a jostling mob, in mud up to her knees, and later forced to keep the Lord Mayor waiting while she scrubbed at her gown. Yet it was extraordinary, she noted later, that as she entered the room on her host's arm, the pains that had plagued her for months immediately disappeared. As she discussed the Patronage Society and the British Society with Secretary of State, Sir James Graham, the state of Europe with the Foreign Secretary, Lord Aberdeen, and penal settlements in Australia with the Colonial Secretary, Lord Stanley, she felt quite like her old self.

Later she walked into dinner on the arm of the Prime Minister, Sir Robert Peel, and sat between him and Prince Albert. To her delight, the Prince was not only fascinated by her traveller's tales, but he charmingly agreed to pass on to the Queen her views on the importance of religious life in families, the arrangement of the royal nursery and the solitary confinement of female convicts. With Sir Robert Peel, she raised her concerns about Pentonville. With both men she shared her reservations over toasts, a mode of rejoicing that she could not approve; although she stood for "God Save the Queen", which was a hymn, she said, she made it clear to the Prince that neither did she approve of praying for victory. She longed only for peace.

When Robert Peel reached the end of his speech, he turned

to Mrs Fry. As he did so, every eye in the room followed his gaze. There was not a table in Europe that would not be honoured by her presence, he said, and many nodded their agreement.

But, when the newspapers reported Mrs Fry's attendance at the lavish event, where despite her observations there had been toasts in abundance, Betsy's Quaker colleagues were less than impressed. It would only encourage others, they maintained, to follow her worldly example. Betsy, however, chose to regard their reaction as a misunderstanding, and her invitation as yet another providential opening for the cause.

At the end of January, she believed she was presented with another when the new King of Prussia arrived in England for the christening of the Prince of Wales.

"Yesterday," she wrote on 1 February 1842, "was a day never to be forgotten while memory lasts."

It began with Meeting at Gracechurch Street, the spiritual home of her early married years. Later, in the grandeur of the Mansion House, and before all the assembled dignity of the City of London, the King of Prussia took Mrs Fry by the hand and kissed her in the manner of a close friend. Then, together with Sam and Elizabeth Gurney, Lady Pirie, the sheriffs, and a procession of aldermen, she led him to Newgate, where gathered around a table set with wine and delicate spicy cakes, she recalled for him the first time she had entered its walls. On the royal arm she then led the procession into the depths of the gaol, where 60 female convicts and many members of the Ladies' Association waited to greet them.

"Remember," Betsy told the assembly before her, "that the King of Kings and Lord of Lords is present, in whose fear we should abide." Kneeling down, with some following her example and others bowing their heads, she prayed for them all: for prisoners, for those in authority, the King and his Queen, and for his kingdom "that it might be more and more as a city set on the hill that could not be hid."

In the afternoon she entertained the King at The Cedars. Initially it had caused a huge furore that a relative of the British royal family should lunch in a bourgeois lodge with the family of a bankrupt, but the King himself had insisted, and as

Betsy led him into her drawing room, she felt an enormous glow of satisfaction. Waiting to greet him were all her daughters except Rachel, who was away, and her five sons together with Frank Cresswell and Raymond Pelly. Fowell and Hannah Buxton were there too, as well as Sam and Elizabeth Gurney, Sir John Henry and Lady Pelly, and Betsy's sister-in-law, Elizabeth Fry. Joseph Fry was there too, flushed and almost overwhelmed by honour and the grandeur. The room itself was heavy with the scent of flowers, while from a distant chamber came the excited chatter of 25 grandchildren, who all waited their turn to be presented.

The King was enchanted. It was exactly as he had imagined it, and nothing, he assured his friend, not even his own Berlin palace, could be more gracious and welcoming than the home where Mrs Fry reigned at the centre of her loving and devoted family. Betsy smiled with satisfaction. It was exactly as she liked to think of it herself. "He wept aloud at parting," she wrote after the King had gone, "and hardly let me leave hold of his arm the whole time he was here." When he left, she watched as his carriage passed through a West Ham crowd as eager to shake his hand as the continental crowds had been to shake hers. When her front door closed, she was immediately convinced that she would never see him again.

The following month, stung but not surprised by Friends' criticisms of the King's visit, Betsy and a niece paid a religious visit to Brighton. While there she attended to the Visiting Society, gathered strength for a forthcoming British Society sale at the Mansion House, and grieved at the prospect of Rachel's second son, Gurney, entering the navy.[7] Earlier, her intervention had kept his older brother, Frank, from the army, but as Midshipman Cresswell headed with his father for Devonport, she admitted that despite all her urging, she had been powerless to dissuade him.

She also admitted that she was frequently unable to rise early enough for the morning Bible reading that had been part of her life ever since George Dilwyn's residence at Mildred's Court so many years before. Meanwhile the pain that had so briefly disappeared had returned with a vengeance, and Dr

Elliot, who had replaced the ageing Dr Sims, advised an increase in opium and wine.

In the same month, she visited the Queen Dowager and the Duchess of Gloucester, both of them patrons of her societies. "I had fears for myself visiting palaces rather than prisons," she wrote afterwards, her mind still echoing to the criticisms of Friends, "and going after the rich rather than the poor." Yet, how else, she reminded herself, but by following such openings, could she convince those in power to support her cause? "I trust I have been at times enabled to throw a little weight into the right scale with some of them," she said.

With her health deteriorating, Betsy spent the latter part of 1842 at the country house near Cromer bought by the invalid Sam Hoare. There she reminisced with Kitty, and assisted Fowell and Hannah to provide a library and a coffee room for local seamen. She also wrote to her son John, shortly to become a magistrate, advising him to become well acquainted with the law, to lean on the side of mercy, and to be aware of a new Act of Parliament that provided for more lenient sentencing for young people.

Among her mountain of correspondence came news of prison reforms in Denmark, and of new model penitentiaries and a discharged prisoners' refuge in Prussia. From the Colonial Office in London also came the announcement that after years of petitioning by the Convict Ship Committee, and eight years after the first experiment, female matrons were at last to sail with the ships to Australia. Betsy wrote to Miss Fraser, who had supervised the committee for years, asking her to convey a message to two of the first matrons, who were to sail on the *Garland Grove* to Van Diemens Land. "My dear love to all our sisters in this service," she concluded.

Later, her thoughts went with them, just as they had once followed the *Maria*. They went too with Gurney Cresswell, on board HMS *Agincourt* in the South China Sea, and to his brother Frank, who to Betsy's deep distress, had finally entered the army.

The year closed with sorrow. In December, Betsy's eight-year-old granddaughter, Harriet Streatfield, died after weeks of terrible suffering, and just as after the deaths of little Betsy and Fowell's four children, Betsy struggled to maintain her faith. Joseph John was also diagnosed with diabetes, and as his doctor advised against alcohol, the man who had once recommended the fourth glass began a campaign for abstinence, replacing Earlham's brewery with a coffee tap, and publishing a pamphlet entitled *Water is Best*. His new ardour added to Betsy's unease. "A small portion of opium and a rather free use of port wine," she wrote, "are essential to keep me in the degree of health that I am favoured to partake of."

"I cannot but believe it is the call of the Lord," Betsy wrote, as 1843 opened with an invitation to France. For a moment it seemed that age and ill-health were no barrier and despite opposition from her family, she was determined to go. In March, she met someone at her son William's house who inspired her even further. He was Lord Ashley, who one day would inherit his father's title of Lord Shaftesbury. "Much devoted to promote the good of mankind, and to suppress evil," she wrote of him, "quite a Wilberforce I think."

With a donation from Hudson, Betsy left England in April. With her went Joseph John and his wife, and Josiah Forster and Katherine. It was better to leave her own Joseph behind, she said – rather as she had done the very first time he came to court her, and on so many occasions since.

From the very beginning, however, Betsy realised that the trip was a mistake. The sea was violent, and at Bolougne the weather and the beds were cold. She was unable to sleep, and with a cloudiness sometimes enveloping her mind, she feared that she might suffer the same fate as her brother John. Yet, even as she failed to make the early morning starts, and saw herself holding the whole party back, she was determined to press on. "Forward in faith," she wrote in her journal.

At Clermont-en-Oise, at the Grand Central Prison, she felt a brief respite when she discovered that her views on solitary confinement were shared by the Mother Superior. Cautiously acknowledging their respect for each other, the two women fell into deeper conversation, and then, as Betsy prepared to leave, she was unexpectedly called back. Later, in a plain convent room, with Katherine translating, she spoke to 22 Roman Catholic nuns about her life and faith, about Newgate, and about her vision for the reformation of prisoners. *"Comme elle est bonne!"* concluded the Superior.

In Paris, however, it was too hot, the hotel was airless, and the streets seemed far noisier than before. Nevertheless, it was good to meet old friends who welcomed her with flowers, and to share in meetings that opened doors into new worlds. One of them was a large gathering of "people of colour", mostly medical or law students from Haiti and Guadaloupe, and after Betsy and Joseph John questioned them eagerly for hours, Betsy concluded the evening in prayer. She finished, Katherine recalled, "on that glorious passage in the Revelations, which tells of the company that cannot be numbered, gathered out of every nation, kindred, tongue and people."[7]

On another day Betsy met M. Guizot, the French Foreign Minister, and questioned him on his government's attitudes to slavery, to religious freedom, and to French prisons. Since her previous visit, a bill had been brought before the Chamber of Deputies that ensured that while prisoners were to be separated as much as possible, they would also receive regular visits from teachers, medical attendants and clergymen, as well as from the governor himself. A vast improvement, she thought, on the system currently being introduced into Britain.

She celebrated her sixty-third birthday in Paris, and to commemorate it, the Queen of France sent her a magnificent Bible. Yet in the end, she was glad to be going home. At the St Lazare prison, where previously the convicts had wept at her words, this time they had barely been able to hear her. "The truth did not appear to reach the hearts of many," she said sadly. During their visit to the King, it had been Eliza Gurney who had preached to him with power.

Back in England, Betsy had another brief burst of energy. At the Colonial Office she raised with Lord Stanley her concerns over conditions for female convicts arriving at Hobart.

Although her voice was at times barely audible, she spoke too at Yearly Meeting, where she rejoiced that despite continued dissention, the prophesied split had never occurred. At the annual meeting of the British Society, she heard with satisfaction that the number of prison visitors was regularly increasing, and she went with Fowell and Hannah to World Conventions on anti-slavery and on peace. Sometimes she still read the Bible on Fridays at Newgate.

In July 1843 Betsy caught a chill, and Joseph rented an isolated cottage at Sandgate near Folkstone, but she was unable to settle. "I think a place so remarkably void of objects does not suit my active mind," she said. Joseph, however, loved it, and dreamed of building a house there. In August she became aware of new symptoms. "A sort of chill creeps over my skin, itching and tingling," she said, "one side of my face feels as if flies were settling upon it."

By September she had persuaded Joseph to move to Tunbridge Wells, where for a while she felt better. However, when Sam and Elizabeth came to visit, they immediately sent for a doctor. "Many, many fears creep in," said Betsy. She was also restless and craved employment, but too ill to be moved; she became miserably depressed. "When my spirit is overwhelmed within me," she begged God, "enable me to look to the Rock that is higher than I, as a refuge from the storm." Once again, the opium and port wine were increased.

She returned to Upton Lane in the autumn and for weeks rarely left her bed. Her children and Hannah Buxton spent hours reading to her, and she often quoted passages from scripture. "He that keepeth my sayings shall never see death," she said. "He that believeth in me shall never die."

In the spring of 1844 Betsy's sister-in-law, Elizabeth Fry, died; so did another grandchild, little Gurney Reynolds, Richenda's son.

Then, as summer spread over Sam's estate, Betsy was overcome by an urge to attend her Plaistow Meeting once more. Several attempts were made, but as each one failed, she became increasingly distressed. Finally, early in August, William took her there, pushing her in her wheelchair, while one of his own boys walked at their side. As he sat beside her, holding her hand, she occasionally glanced towards him and recalled how much she still hoped he would follow his uncle Joseph John. When she finally spoke, to the surprise of everyone who had watched her entrance, and observed how frail she appeared, it was in a voice that suddenly seemed full of its old vigour and certainty. "Blessed are the dead who die in the Lord," she said, "for they cease from their labours, and their works do follow them."

Shortly afterwards William moved her to Walmer, to a house he had chosen specially. Days later his second daughter, Juliana, died of scarlet fever, and desperate to prevent the disease spreading, Betsy sent three Fry nurses to care for the household servants, who were eventually taken to Guy's Hospital. Three weeks after Juliana's death, William also died of the same infection, and later his eldest daughter, Emma, followed him.

"Sorrow upon sorrow," Betsy wrote, "the trial is almost inexpressible."

Convinced that she would crumble with the shock, the family waited apprehensively. To their astonishment, she brought Julia and William's remaining children to Walmer, as if the act of consoling them was her consolation also. Returning eventually to Upton Lane, she drove out on fine days in a pony carriage given to her by her son Joseph, visiting the poor, many of them grown as old as herself.

Fowell Buxton died in February 1845. He had been ill for years, worn out by his unremitting struggle for prison reform and against slavery. With his passing, Betsy knew she had to go home to Earlham.

She stayed there many weeks, and sometimes ministered in the new meeting house that now stood in Goat Lane. Returning home one day with Joseph John, who left her alone for a moment in her chair, a movement in the park caught her eye. As she looked she seemed to see John Pitchford again, with his seven sisters in their summer gowns flitting like shadows across the grass. Looking down, she saw how paper thin was the skin that covered her hands, and how profoundly they were marked with the brown spots of age.

In May, accompanied by her son John's daughter, also named Elizabeth Fry, she attended two sittings of Yearly Meeting in London. In June, to spare her the journey, the Annual Meeting of the British Society was held at the Friends Meeting House at Plaistow. On 26 June her youngest son Harry was married.

Later in the summer, as the air grew hot and stifling, Joseph Fry moved his wife to Ramsgate, where he often sat beside her, holding her hand. At the beginning of October, she suffered a stroke which left her unconscious.

She died in Ramsgate, surrounded by her family, at four in the morning on 13 October 1845.

Throughout her life Elizabeth Fry feared death, just as she had once feared the dark. Yet she lived her life as a beacon of hope and consistently pointed each person she met towards light and towards life, life that was meaningful and fulfilled – not only for themselves, but for all those they subsequently encountered.

As a Quaker, she was convinced that the light of God was within each individual. Influenced by her Evangelical colleagues she also believed in the power of conversion to transform. She also recognised the critical importance of environment, education and attitude in bringing about and maintaining positive change. Increasingly, she accepted the necessity of influencing others, the powerful and the less powerful alike, through her own example, through ceaseless lobbying, and through what today we call networking

Through her courage and her persistence she forced her own generation to recognise that in those most rejected by society – women condemned to imprisonment – on whom society so often projected its own fears, there was the potential for transformation and growth, both within the heart and in their lives in the world. She also pointed out how narrow is the boundary between those who are publicly convicted and those who escape such condemnation. That many of her most far-reaching recommendations for the reformation of convicts have never been fully implemented, says more about the continuing debate on the nature of crime and punishment, about the fiscal priorities of government, and about society's continuing ambivalence towards those it condemns to its gaols, than it does about Elizabeth Fry's conclusions and methods.

Her significance for women is enormous. At a time when they had no public role, by walking alone into that uncharted territory she convinced the women of her generation that they had a worth beyond the domestic sphere, and that they could play a part in shaping and transforming both their own lives and their world. To the generations that followed, she left a huge legacy. One of the first to seize it in a way that would also bring about major transformation was a young Englishwoman called Florence Nightingale, who in 1850, visited Kaisersworth, the vision of Pastor Fliedner who himself was inspired by Elizabeth Fry. She left Kaisersworth, said Miss Nightingale, "feeling so brave as if nothing could ever vex me again."[8] The hospital at Scutari and the reformation of British nursing was the result.

As an evangelist and preacher Elizabeth Fry's role has never been fully recognised. Yet she preached and spoke in public to audiences of thousands: women and men; poor and rich; Quaker and non-Quaker; British, Irish, French, Dutch, Belgian and German. Surely here is an inspiration for those women today who continue to challenge discrimination and who struggle to achieve recognition and true equality of opportunity not only in the Christian church, but also in the world's other major faith traditions – and in its secular institutions too.

Elizabeth Fry was buried at the Friends Burying Ground at Barking beside her daughter Betsy. Her brother Joseph John spoke briefly in prayer and as the body was laid to rest, over 1,000 people stood in silent tribute beside the grave. Almost immediately afterwards, using the journals already edited by Betsy herself, her daughters attempted to present their mother as a saint, removing from her memory anything that might tarnish her image as a pious and devoted Christian wife and mother who somehow combined this with an extraordinary public career. It was a myth perpetrated throughout the Victorian period, and despite more objective twentieth-century biographies, it is one that still lingers. A close reading of her journals, however, discovers a very different woman. In reality, though devout and determined, Elizabeth Fry was also tortured by doubt, torn apart by conflict, and driven by forces whose origins were complex. Yet, in the face of them, she triumphed. In the twenty-first century, this is a woman we recognise.

As such it makes Elizabeth Fry a uniquely modern hero for our time.

William Savery's letter to Betsy Gurney: 1798.*

Liverpool 13th of 4th m. 1798

Dear Frd. Elizabeth Gurney

As I left thee unwell, and without having it in my Power to take thee affectionately by the hand as I was much Inclined to do, It gave me great Pleasure to Receive thy kind Letter, which brings no Complaint of thy present want of health, for I assure thee I feel Interested in thy welfare and happiness every way – my attachment has not been more Cordial nor agreeable to any young frd. in England, and my heart leapt with Joy to find thou art willing to acknowledge, a State of *"Hunger & thirst after Righteousness"*, which if thou Cherish & dwell in, thou never need to doubt my Dear Betsy, will Eventually be Crowned with an Enjoyment of the heavenly Promise, *"thou shalt be filled"*. Thou art favoured with amiable & benevolent dispositions which I hope thou hast wisely determined shall not be Eclipsed by a Conformity to the god of this world, nor Enslaved by its Rudiments & maxims, its Philosophy & Vain Deceit – but Rather with a holy magnanimity, Regardless of the *"Worlds Dread Laugh"*, thou wilt Resolve to Implore the Omnipotent hand that formed thee for glory, Immortality & Eternal Life, to finish the Glorious Work he has begun by Creating thee anew in Christ Jesus Unto Every good word & work of bringing thee Under the Dominion of his own power

---

* British Library: EG Vol.1. 3672A. Egerton Mss.

& Spirit, the fruits of which is "Love, Joy, peace, long-suffering, gentleness, goodness, faith, meekness, temperance".

I know, my Dear, thou hast, and will have many Temptations to Combat, thou will doubtless be frequently Importuned to Continue with thy gay Acquaintance in pursuit of that Unsubstantial & false Glare of happiness which the world in too bewitching & deceitful Colours holds out to the poor young unwary Traveller, which if he be Ensnared will most Certainly end in blinding the Intellectual Eye from discerning the Uncontaminated Source of Soul felt pleasure, resulting from an humble heart, at peace with its god, its Neighbours, & itself. Thou asks my Advice my Dear Betsy, & (without any premeditation when I sat down), I find I have been attempting it, but it is very Evident thou art under the Special Care of an Infinitely better Instructor, who has already uttered his Soft & heavenly voice to teach thee, that "the first Step towards Religion is true humility". Because in that State only we Can feel the Need we have of an arm stronger than human to lean upon, to Lead us out of & keep us from those polluting things which hinder our Access & Confidence in that boundless Ocean of purity, love & mercy who amidst all the Vicissitudes of time is Disposed to be our Invisible Shepherd Guardian & friend, in whom we may trust & never be afraid. But this blessed Confidence is not, it Cannot be Enjoyed, by the gay, the giddy, the licentious, proud or abandoned Votaries of this world.

It is the peculiar privilege of those who are Sincerely Endeavouring to "wash their hands in Innocence" that they may Compass the Altar of God availingly. I have Experienced what it is to be under the Imperious & Slavish Dominion of my own uncontrolled Passions, & I know that such a State is abundantly Impregnated with the Wormwood & the Gall, and I have been, through adorable mercy Convinced there is an Infinitely more happy one to be attained, even in this Life – an Enjoyment under the perfect Law of Liberty; of that Serene State of mind wherein there is no Condemnation, as Paul Speaks, the Law of the Spirit of Life in Christ Jesus setting the Soul free from the Law of sin & Death. I do not pretend my

Dear frd. to boast myself as having attained such an Uninterrupted state, yet the transient foretastes which we partake of in proportion to our Obedience to Revealed Duty is Enough to Inspire the Soul of Every Christian Soldier, so to run through god's grace and mercy, that we may Obtain the full & Compleat Enjoyment of it. There are many formal Professors of Religion who think to Obtain Peace with god by a Critical Exactness & even Rigid Austerity in Outward Observations and Outside formality, as well as many who from Constitution or habit are always Exhibiting the Dark & Gloomy side of Religion, not having in my humble Opinion, their minds Sufficiently Expanded by Just Conceptions of the adorable Love & mercy of God – & both of these spread a discouraging report of the good Land. Or of the way which our heavenly father has appointed for us to Obtain possession of it. I speak only my own Experience, Dear E. when I say that whenever I have found my way more than usually Strewn with thorns, I have generally discovered on a Deep Scrutiny of my heart, it has been the fruit of some Open or Secret Departure from the Paths of Obedience & Virtue – so that I am Confirmed that it is in our own ways we are Corrected, "but the ways of the Lord are ways of pleasantness & all his paths peace."

I know very well that the Most Virtuous, being Children of frail humanity – & this world not designed to be the place of their undisturbed Rest, but a School of Discipline to prepare us for a better – are subject to Afflictions as well as others. Still there is this Difference in the midst of them all, that while the Votary of this world is Overwhelmed with murmuring and Repining, and agitated with that sorrow which worketh Death, under the Afflictive Dispensations that all more or Less in the Wisdom of Providence for our good, must pass through in this Life – the humble Christian, believing that even afflictions from His sovereign hand are mercies in Disguise & that all things shall work eventually for good to them that Love & fear him, are Strengthened through the Lord's mercy to say, "the Cup that my Heavenly father has blessed, shall I not drink it". "For our light affliction, which is but for a moment worketh for us a far more Exceeding & Eternal Weight of Glory while we look not at the things which are seen, but at the things which are not seen; for the things which are seen are temporal, but the things – which are not seen are Eternal." On the Other hand, all the temporal Enjoyments of this Life, being Sanctified to us by the hand that gave them, and the world used without abusing it – the peace, Comfort & rational Enjoyment of them is doubly tasted by the Religious and grateful soul –

My Dear Child, my heart is full toward thee, I have wrote a great deal more than I Expected – but I fain would take thee by the hand if I were qualified so to do, & ascend as our heavenly father may Enable us, together step by step up that ladder which Reaches from Earth to heaven. But alas, my weakness is such I Can only Recommend both myself & thee to that good hand that is able to do more abundantly for us than we can Either think Or ask – & bid thee for the present, in much Christian Affection, farewell – William Savery.

Introduction to *Observations on the Visiting, Superintendance and Government of Female Prisoners*

Chapter One: Introductory Remarks

Before, however, I endeavour to develop the system of the British Society, I wish to make a few general remarks, which have long impressed me, respecting my own sex, and the place which I believe it to be their duty and privilege to fill in the scale of society. I rejoice to see the day in which so many women of every rank, instead of spending their time in trifling and unprofitable pursuits, are engaged in works of usefulness and charity. Earnestly it is to be desired that the number of these valuable labourers in the cause of virtue and humanity may be increased, and that all of us may be made sensible of the infinite importance of redeeming the time, of turning our talents to account, and of becoming the faithful, humble, devoted, followers of a crucified Lord, who went about DOING GOOD.

Far be it from me to attempt to persuade women to forsake their rightful province. My only desire is, that they should *fill that province well*; and, although their calling, in many respects, materially differs from that of the other sex, and may not perhaps be so exalted a one – yet a minute observation will prove that, if adequately fulfilled, it has nearly, if not quite, an equal influence on society at large.

No person will deny the importance attached to the character and conduct of a woman, in all her domestic and social relations, when she is filling the station of a daughter, a sister, a wife, a mother, or a mistress of a family. But it is a dangerous error to suppose that the duties of females end here. Their gentleness, their natural sympathy with the afflicted, their quickness of discernment, their openness to religious impressions, are points of character (not unusually to be found in our sex) which evidently qualify them, within their own peculiar province, for a far more extensive field of usefulness.

In endeavouring to direct the attention of the female part of society to such objects of Christian charity as they are most calculated to benefit, I may now observe that no persons appear to me to possess so strong a claim on their compassion, and on their pious exertions, as the helpless, the ignorant, the afflicted, or the depraved, *of their own sex*. It is almost needless to remark, that a multitude of such persons may be found in many of our public institutions.

During the last ten years much attention has been successfully bestowed by women on the female inmates of our *prisons*; and many a poor prisoner, under their fostering care, has become completely changed, – rescued from a condition of depravity and wretchedness, and restored to happiness, as a useful and respectable member of the community. Most desirable is it that such efforts should be pursued with patient perseverance wherever they have been already made, and that they should be gradually extended to all the prisons in the kingdom.

But a similar care is evidently required for our hospitals, our lunatic asylums, and our workhouses. It is quite obvious, that there are departments in all such institutions which ought to be under the especial superintendence of females. Were ladies to make a practice of regularly visiting them, a most important check would be obtained on a variety of abuses, which are far too apt to creep into the management of these establishments. Such a practice would be the means, not only of essentially contributing to the welfare of the afflicted sufferers, but of materially aiding those gentlemen, on whom devolves the government or care of the institutions. The Roman Catholic ladies, in many parts of the continent of Europe, have set us, in this respect, a bright and useful example; and the result of their care and attention, especially in the hospitals, has been found, in a high degree, salutary and beneficial. Nor have similar effects failed to be produced in the comparatively solitary instances in which women, in our own country, have been in the habit of regularly visiting the public abodes of poverty or disease.

While I would direct the attention of my own sex (in whose usefulness I take a very lively interest) to the importance of their visiting and superintending the females in our public institutions, I am far indeed from desiring to discourage them in other and more private walks of Christian charity. Among the most interesting exertions of female benevolence, will ever be numbered the visiting of the poor in their own habitations, the necessary attention to the supply of their temporal and spiritual wants, and, above all, the diligent promotion of the education of their children; but the economical arrangement of time, and more especially a suitable division of labour, will enable the benevolent females of any place or district to accomplish, without material difficulty, *all* their charitable objects. Regard ought always to be had to the age and circumstances of individuals. For example, a young lady may be well employed in attending to a school, or in visiting a sick neighbour, who would be very far less suitable than the more elderly and experienced for the care of the hospital, the workhouse, the asylum, or the prison; and yet, the one service will in time form an admirable preparation for the other.

Much may be accomplished by the *union of forces*. – If, in every parish or district, such ladies, as desire to make the best use of their time, would occasionally meet together, in order to consider the condition of their neighbourhood, and would then divide themselves and allot the labours of Christian love to the several parties respectively, according to their suitability for different objects, the employment of but a small portion of their time would enable them to effect more extensive good than could previously have been thought possible; and, instead of being incapacitated for their domestic duties, they would often return to those duties, refreshed in spirit, and stimulated to perform them with increased cheerfulness, propriety, and diligence.

To revert, for a short time, to the subject of our public institutions, although I feel it a delicate matter so earnestly to insist on the point, I must now express my conviction, that few persons are aware of the *degree* in which the female departments of them stand in need of the superintending care of judicious ladies. So great are the abuses which exist in some of those establishments, that *modest* women dare not run the risk to which they would be exposed, did they attempt to derive from them the relief which they require. I would have this subject occupy the serious consideration of the benevolent part of the community. All reflecting persons will surely unite in the sentiment, that the female, placed in the prison for her crimes, in the hospital for her sickness, in the asylum for her insanity, or in the workhouse for her poverty, possesses no light or common claim on the pity and attention of those of her own sex, who, through the bounty of a kind Providence, are able "*to do good, and to communicate.*"

May the attention of *women* be more and more directed to these labours of love; and may the time quickly arrive, when there shall not exist, in this realm, a single public institution of the kind, in which the degraded or afflicted females who may happen to be its inmates shall not enjoy the *efficacious superintendence* of the pious and benevolent of THEIR OWN SEX!

Having expressed my general views respecting the importance and right application of the benevolent exertions of women in aid of the unfortunate of their own sex, I may now proceed to offer to the reader a few remarks respecting the system pursued and recommended by the members of the British Ladies' Society *in visiting and superintending the female inmates of our prisons*. My observations, and the advice which

I shall venture to offer, will be found to relate to the following successive points. *First*, the formation of Ladies' Committees. *Secondly*, the proper deportment of the visitors towards the prisoners and towards the officers of the prison. *Thirdly*, the necessity of employing female officers in gaols, and their proper character. *Fourthly*, classification and inspection. *Fifthly*, instruction. *Sixthly*, employment. *Seventhly*, medical aid, food, clothing, and bedding. And, lastly, the attention required in the care of criminals after their dismissal from prison.

Items provided by the British Ladies' Association for each female transport bound for Australia

One Bible;
One Hessian apron;
One black stuff ditto;
One black cotton cap;
One large Hessian bag (to keep her clothes in);
One small bag containing:
    One piece tape;
    One ounce of pins;
    One hundred needles;
    Four balls of white sewing cotton;
    One ditto black;
    One ditto blue;
    One ditto red;
    Two balls of black worsted, half an ounce each;
    Twenty-four hanks of coloured thread;
One of cloth, with eight darning needles, one small bodkin fastened on it;
Two stay-laces;

---

* Katherine Fry and Rachel Cresswell, *Memoir of the Life of Elizabeth Fry*

One thimble;
One pair of scissors;
One pair of spectacles, when required;
Two pounds of patchwork pieces;
One comb;
One small ditto;
Knife and fork to each mess;
Ball of string.

Notes to the text

Several of the letters quoted, which appear in the text of *A Memoir of the Life of Elizabeth Fry* by Katherine Fry and Rachel Cresswell, or *The Gurneys of Earlham* by Augustus Hare, also exist in their original form either at the Library of the Religious Society of Friends, London (LSF), or at the Department of Manuscripts, British Library, London.

Chapter 1. The child at Earlham

1. Fry and Cresswell, 1847, Volume I, pp. 7–11.
2. A letter held in the archives of the Library of the Religious Society of Friends, London, dated London 7 10th 1774, describes John Gurney as "the handsome Quaker".
3. Fry and Cresswell, 1847, Volume I, Chapter 1. (Plus all subsequent quotations from Catherine Gurney's journal.)
4. See Punshon, 1984, pp. 17, 22.
5. See Fry and Cresswell, 1847, Volume I, p. 13. Also O'Gorman, 1997, pp. 142, 242–3, 283, 336.
6. Hare, 1895, Volume I, p. 25
7. Fry and Cresswell, 1847, Volume I, chapter 1. (Plus all subsequent quotations from Betsy's brief sketch.)
8. Rachel Cresswell [*née* Fry] describes the old-fashioned Quaker costume on p. 43 of her book, *A Memoir of Elizabeth Fry*.

Chapter 2. The briary thorny wilderness

1. Hare, 1895, Volume 1, p. 34. Other quotations by Kitty Gurney, unless otherwise stated, are also taken from Volumes I and II of this work.
2. A reference to the dream appears in the notes Betsy added to her earliest remaining journals in 1828, the year in which she destroyed much else. References also appear in the later journals, especially at the time of her conversion and before her marriage.
3. References to these symptoms appear in the notes Betsy added to her earliest remaining journals, and also in her later journals.
4. Daniel Gurney's reminiscences are contained in Hare, 1895, Volumes I and II.
5. John Crome 1768–1821. English painter and etcher, born in Norwich, Norfolk. A painter of landscapes who earned his living by giving drawing lessons and selling an occasional picture. Often called Old Crome to distinguish him from his son, John Bernay Crome (1794–1842), known as Young Crome, who was also a painter.
6. Hare, 1895, Volume I, p. 45. Other quotations by Priscilla Gurney, unless otherwise stated, are also taken from Volumes I and II of this work.
7. See O'Gorman, 1997, p. 242.
8. The origin of the bank dates from 1765, when John Taylor and Sampson Lloyd set up a private banking business in Birmingham. In 1865 the partnership changed its status to a joint-stock company, naming itself Lloyds Banking Company Limited. Two sons of the original partners also followed in their fathers' footsteps by establishing their own bank: Barnetts Hoares Hanbury and Lloyds, in Lombard Street, London. In 1884 this was absorbed into the growing Lloyds Banking Company. The company eventually became the high-street bank now known as Lloyds TSB.

9. Hare, 1895, Volume I, p. 52. Other quotations by Louisa Gurney (later Louisa Hoare), unless otherwise stated, are also taken from Volumes I and II of this work.

10. John Gurney's brother, Richard "Uncle" Gurney, had a country property at Northrepps, near Cromer. He also had a shooting-box at Hampstead, near Holt.

11. Hare, 1895, Volume I, p. 74. Other quotations by Richenda Gurney (later Richenda Cunningham), unless otherwise stated, are also taken from Volumes I and II of this work.

12. Fry and Cresswell, 1847, Volume I, p. 9 (Betsy's brief sketch).

13. Hare, 1895, Volume I, p. 11.

14. *ibid.*, p. 41.

15. See Punshon, 1984, pp. 42–43.

16. *ibid.*, p. 103.

17. Hare, 1895, Volume I, p. 96.

18. Epithalamium: a poem written on the occasion of a marriage.

19. Hare, 1895, Volume I, pp. 83–86.

20. Henceforward, unless otherwise stated, all quotations by Elizabeth Gurney (later Elizabeth Fry) are taken from her original journals, or very occasionally, when original writing is indecipherable or very faded, from the *Memoir* compiled by her daughters in 1847.

Chapter 3. The light

1. William Crotch was a minister at Goat Lane Quaker Meeting, Norwich, who befriended the newly converted Betsy Gurney.

2. Quoted in Whitney, 1937, p. 43.

3. The petition to which William Savery appended his name was presented by American Friends to the United States Congress on 4 October 1783. Details are listed at www.rootsweb.com. The original as cited there is to be found on microfilm M247, Papers of the Continental Congress 1774–1783, roll 57, p. 337, item 43, National Archives, Seattle, USA.

4. See Jemison and Schein (eds), 2000.
5. See Taylor, 1925.
6. See Punshon, 1984.
7. See Fry and Cresswell, 1847, Volume I, p. 35. William Savery himself also refers to this in his letter to Betsy dated Liverpool 13th of 4th m. 1798. See Appendix 1.
8. William Savery at this time was 48 years old.
9. Fry and Cresswell, 1847, Volume I, p. 34.
10. Whitney, 1937, p. 44 quotes William Savery's journal: "... at length believed it most for my peace to stand up with 'Your Fathers, where are they, and the Prophets, do they Live Forever?'" (I have taken the liberty of enlarging briefly, based on my understanding of the Quaker message and Elizabeth Gurney's reaction. JH.)
11. Fry and Cresswell, 1847, Volume I, p. 33.
12. Quoted in Whitney, 1937, p. 47.
13. Quoted in Fry and Cresswell, 1847, Volume I, p. 33.
14. John Wesley, "The new birth", in A.C. Outler (ed.), *The Works of John Wesley*, Volume 2 (Nashville, 1985), p. 187. Quoted in Bebbington, 1993, p. 3.
15. See Punshon, 1984, p. 166.
16. Hare, 1895, Volume I, p. 98.
17. In October 1797, the British naval defeat of France's Dutch ally at the Battle of Camperdown, which cleared the Channel temporarily of hostile fleets, led to national rejoicing and thanksgiving in churches.
18. Quoted in Whitney, 1937, p. 46.
19. Castle Hill in the centre of Norwich, site of the ancient Norman keep of Norwich Castle. Now a museum.

Chapter 4. A minister of Christ

1. Hibbert, 1969, p. 184.
2. The eldest son of George III who would become Prince Regent in 1811 and George IV in 1820.
3. It was customary in the London theatres of this period to perform two plays each night: a main feature, plus

another, possibly abbreviated, as a shorter support. See Hibbert, 1969, p. 176.

4. Quoted by Betsy in her journal.

5. The spelling of the Savory surname had evidently changed earlier in its journey across the Atlantic.

6. John Opie, 1761–1807. Born at St Agnes near Truro, Opie quickly gained local recognition as a painter of portraits. In 1780 he arrived in London, where he was introduced as "The Cornish Wonder", a self-taught genius, and proved almost instantly popular. Opie worked hard, however, at improving his painting technique, as well as rectifying his early deficient education and polishing his provincial manners by mixing in cultivated and learned circles. In 1786 he exhibited his first major historical work, "The Assassination of James 1", and in 1787 he was elected an associate of the Royal Academy. He became a full member in 1788 and concentrated thereafter on historical works and portraits. After his death, a memoir of his life was produced by his widow, Amelia Opie.

7. Robert Barclay (1648–1690) originally wrote his book in Latin. It was published in 1676 as *Theologiæ Vere Christianæ Apologia*. Two years later it was published in English as *An Apology for the True Christian Divinity*.

8. 1 Corinthians 14: 34, 35.

9. Betsy's own journal entry at this point, presumably made soon after the event, is (perhaps not surprisingly), somewhat rambling. For the sake of the flow of the text I have amended it slightly. JH.

Chapter 5. Joseph Fry

1. Fry and Cresswell, 1847, Volume I, pp. 62–63.

2. Founded in 1799, Ackworth School is still in existence today at Pontefract. www.ackworthschool.com

3. Founded in 1796 by the Quaker, Joseph Tuke, the Retreat Hospital is still in existence today at York. www.retreat-hospital.org

4. Mary Anne Galton (1778–1856) was the daughter of Samuel Galton, a Quaker and member of the Lunar Society of Birmingham. Father and daughter both campaigned against slavery. Later, as Mrs Lambert Schimmelpenninck, Mary Anne wrote several books on the subject of female education.

5. Hare, 1895, Volume I, p. 106.

Chapter 6. I appear to have taken my flight from spiritual things

1. Animal magnetism was a procedure developed in the 1770s by Franz Mesmer. It was based on his theory of a "universal fluid" and relied on a combination of water, magnetised iron filings, iron rods and hypnotism. Also see Veith, 1993, pp. 221–223.

2. As Quakers, neither Frys nor Gurneys acknowledged saints; therefore they referred to the London address as Mildred's Court.

3. Due to the Quaker habit of marrying within their own relatively small society, almost all Quakers at this period were related to some extent. Relevant family pedigrees kept at the Library of the Religious Society of Friends, London, provide details of some of these complex relationships.

4. Dr Sims was witness to the births of several of the Fry children, designating himself J. Sims MD.

5. The original London headquarters of the Society of Friends was at the Bull and Mouth Tavern in Aldersgate. When it was destroyed by the Great Fire in 1666, Friends acquired Devonshire House, an old mansion in Bishopsgate. In 1925 the headquarters was moved to its current location at Friends House, Euston Road.

6. Joseph Lancaster's School was at Borough Road, Southwark. He was one of the founders, together with Dr Andrew Bell of Madras, of the monitorial system. Later, the Lancastrian Society became the British & Foreign Schools Society, which ran schools, trained teachers and

spread to many parts of the world, both within and outside the British Empire. For 50 years it was the mainstay of non-denominational educational provision in England, It finally became obsolete when public elementary education followed the Education Act of 1870.

7. The Treaty of Amiens was finally signed on 25 March 1802.

8. The procedure against smallpox was developed in Britain by Edward Jenner (1749–1823), a doctor in Berkeley, Gloucestershire. His first experiment was carried out in 1796 and a paper submitted to the Royal Society the following year. Many people remained unconvinced, however, and the clergy in particular were hostile. In 1801, when baby Katherine was inoculated, the procedure was still controversial and perhaps indicates progressive thinking by both Betsy and her physicians.

9. With the growing popularity of the Romantic Poets, most notably William Wordsworth, Robert Southey and Samuel Taylor Coleridge, who were themselves inspired by the rugged beauty of the Cumbrian lakes and mountains, the region became an increasingly popular destination for wealthy and fashionable tourists.

Chapter 7. Now there is an opening made

1. See Chapter 2 of this work.
2. Hare, 1895, Volume I, p. 157. Other quotations by Rachel Gurney, unless otherwise stated, are also taken from Volumes I and II of this work.

Chapter 8. The theatre of action

1. Fry and Cresswell, 1847, Volume I, pp. 176–177.
2. Referring to Dr Willan and the practice of inoculation against smallpox, Katherine and Rachel describe him in their *Memoir* (Volume I, p. 172) as "one of its earliest advocates and most skilful practitioners".
3. Fry and Cresswell, 1847, Volume I, p. 170.

4. See Hare, 1895, pp. 221, 222.
5. William Wilberforce, *A Practical View of the Prevailing Religious System of Professed Christians in the Higher and Middle Classes in This Country Contrasted with Real Christianity* (London: T. Cadell, jun. & W. Davies, 1797). The book sold 7,500 copies in the first six months. By 1826, some 15 editions had been printed in Britain, and 25 in the United States. Translations were also printed in French, Dutch, Italian, Spanish and German.
6. Hare, 1895, Volume I, p. 235.
7. *ibid.*, p. 147.
8. See Punshon, 1984, pp. 195–197.
9. Hare, 1895, Volume I, p. 230.
10. See Bebbington, 1993, pp. 50–74.
11. Hannah More, *An Estimate of the Religion of the Fashionable World* (London, 1808 edn), p. 146. Quoted in Bebbington, 1993, p. 12.
12. See O'Gorman, 1997, p. 237.
13. See Whitney, 1937, pp. 177–178.
14. Anna Buxton married William Forster two years after their separate visits to Newgate Prison.
15. "Traversing sundry vaulted passages (which being lighted with gas have a very gloomy appearance)." Benjamin Seebohm (ed.), *Memoirs of the Life of Stephen Grellet* (London, 1862). Quoted in Whitney, 1937, p. 187.

Chapter 9. Newgate

1. Luke 8: 43–48.
2. Gurney Correspondence, LSF.
3. There appears to be no record relating to the Gurneys indicating whether Prince William Frederick's support for the cause of penal reform was due to his early friendship with the family.
4. Fowell Buxton, quoted in Babington 1971, p. 154.
5. Gurney Correspondence, LSF.
6. Fry and Cresswell, 1847, Volume I, p. 266.
7. *ibid.*

8. *ibid.*, pp. 269–270.
9. Hare, 1895, Volume I, p. 283.

Chapter 10. Too much divided

1. Hare, 1895, Volume I, pp. 283–286.
2. Babington, 1971, p. 167.
3. The Millbank Penitentiary was finally completed in 1821. It was demolished in 1902. The site is now occupied by the Tate Gallery.
4. Babington, 1971, p. 171.
5. See O'Gorman, 1997, p. 335.
6. Babington, 1971, p. 173.
7. *ibid.*
8. *Report from the Committee of the Prisons within the City of London and Borough of Southwark, House of Commons, 1818.*
9. *ibid.*
10. *ibid.*
11. Fry and Cresswell, 1847, Volume I, p. 311.
12. *ibid.*, pp. 309–310.
13. *ibid.*, p. 305.
14. Hare, 1895, Volume I, pp. 313–314.

Chapter 11. A sweet united band

1. Hare, 1895, Volume I, pp. 308–309.
2. Fry and Cresswell, 1847, Volume I, p. 342.
3. At several times during his reign, King George III was unable to rule owing to sickness: between 1788 and 1789, again in 1801 and after 1810. His eldest son, later George IV, acted as Prince Regent from 1811 onwards.
4. Consumption (tuberculosis) causes a breakdown of the normal lung tissue. In the early nineteenth century, when its causes were not understood, it was responsible for about 25 per cent of all deaths in Britain.

5. The practice of suttee – widows dying on their husband's funeral pyre – was finally banned in British India in 1830, after a long campaign by Fowell Buxton.
6. Hare, 1895, Volume I, p. 318.
7. See Timpson, 1847, pp. 61–65.
8. Fry and Cresswell, 1847, Volume I, p. 363.
9. *ibid.*, pp. 367–371.
10. Hare, 1895, Volume I, pp. 332–333.
11. Quoted in Fry and Cresswell, 1847, Volume I, p. 402.
12. Lord John Russell (1792–1878) was a member of the House of Commons from 1812 and a campaigner for parliamentary reform. He was also Home Secretary 1835–39; Secretary for War and the Colonies 1839–1841; Prime Minister 1846–1852 and 1865–1866; Foreign Secretary 1859–1865.
13. *The Times* 4 June 1821. Quoted in Fry and Cresswell, 1847, Volume I, p. 404.

Chapter 12. It is not of our own ordering

1. Bebbington, 1993, p. 129.
2. *ibid.*
3. Fry and Cresswell, 1847, Volume I, p. 401.
4. Comptroller of the Royal Navy – a position which subsequently disappeared.
5. Hughes, 1987, p. 151.
6. Fry & Cressell, 1847, Volume I, p. 447.
7. *ibid.*, p. 449.
8. *ibid.*, p. 450.
9. *ibid.*, pp. 444–445.
10. *ibid.*, p. 445.
11. Charles Robert Leslie RA (1794–1859) was born in London to an American family. After spending his childhood in Philadelphia, Leslie returned to London in 1811 to begin a course of study at the Royal Academy Schools. There he rapidly achieved recognition as a history and portrait painter and became Professor of Painting at the Academy in 1848. He also produced a handbook for young painters,

based on his own lectures, as well as a biography of his friend, John Constable. His son, George Dunlop Leslie RA, was also a painter.

12. In *Lavengro*, George Borrow's tale of gypsy life published in 1851, the Quaker who opposes fishing is based on Joseph John Gurney at Earlham. See also Hare, 1895, Volume II, pp. 17–21.

13. Prison Act 1821.

14. See Babington, 1971, p. 178.

15. Thomas Chalmers (1780–1847) entered St Andrew's University at the age of twelve to study mathematics. At 15 he began training for the ministry and was licensed to preach at the age of 19. After further studies at Edinburgh he was ordained, and twelve years later was appointed by Glasgow Town Council to the Tron Church where he became famous as a preacher and also began a massive programme of social reform. He attracted the attention and friendship of leading British clergy and statesmen, including William Wilberforce. He became Professor of Moral Philosophy at St Andrews in 1824 and in 1828 accepted the chair of Theology at Edinburgh. After 1843, and the Disruption which split the Scottish church, and in which he played a major role, he became the first Moderator of the Free Church of Scotland and Principal of Divinity at New College, Edinburgh. See also Fry and Cresswell, 1847, Volume I, pp. 468–469.

16. The Coast Blockade Service was founded in 1816, amalgamating three separate organisations founded earlier to patrol the land, the shore and British coastal waters on behalf of the Revenue Service. In 1831 it was absorbed into the Coastguard Service.

17. Fry and Cresswell, 1847, Volume I, p. 473.

18. *ibid.*, pp. 475–476.

Chapter 13. The storm

1. Christopher Wordsworth (1774–1846) was Master of Trinity College, Cambridge, from 1820 to 1841. He was

married to Priscilla Lloyd, a close friend of Kitty and Rachel Gurney, and sister to James Lloyd.

2. Amelia Opie became a Quaker in August 1825, following the death of John Opie.

3. The Jews' Society. Originally the London Society for Promoting Christianity among the Jews, it was established in 1809 as an interdenominational body and reconstituted in 1815 as an Anglican organisation.

4. Legh Richmond (1772–1827) was an English clergyman educated at Trinity College, Cambridge. He was powerfully influenced by William Wilberforce and took a prominent interest in the British and Foreign Bible Society, the Church Missionary Society and other similar organisations. The best-known of his writings is *The Dairyman's Daughter*, which sold approximately four million copies in 19 languages before 1849.

5. Hare, 1895, Volume II, pp. 22–23.

6. See "The Financial Crisis of 1825 and the Restructuring of the British Financial System" by Michael D. Bordo, in *The Federal Reserve Bank of St Louis Review*, May/June 1998.

7. Hare, 1895, Volume II, pp. 31–32.

8. Fry and Cresswell, 1847, Volume I, pp. 380–390.

9. Fry and Cresswell, 1847, Volume II, pp. 69.

10. *ibid.*, pp. 59–70.

11. Gurney and Fry Correspondence, LSF.

12. Fry and Cresswell, 1847, Volume II, p. 78.

Chapter 14. Absolute duty

1. Fry and Cresswell, 1847, Volume II, p. 87.

2. Hannah Gurney, who married Jonathan Backhouse of Darlington, was a daughter of Joseph Gurney of Lakenham Grove.

3. Sydney Smith (1771–1845). Although Smith's early ambition had been to read for the Bar, family pressure compelled him to enter the church, and after receiving an MA at Oxford in 1796, he was ordained the same year. He went on to study moral philosophy, medicine and chemistry at

Edinburgh, where as well as gaining fame as a preacher, he was instrumental in setting up the *Edinburgh Review*. He was also its first editor and remained a contributor for many years. Intensely practical by nature, as a clergyman he concentrated on social issues, and in his various parishes he worked to improve conditions for the poor, focussing especially on education. After moving to London, where his preaching regularly drew huge crowds, he increasingly became a commentator on social affairs, particularly in the cause of reform.

4. Babington, 1971, pp. 175–176.

5. *Report from the Select Committee on Secondary Punishments, House of Commons, 22 June, 1832.*

6. *ibid.*

7. *ibid.*

8. *ibid.*

9. Fry and Cresswell, 1847, Volume II, p. 147.

10. Sir John Henry Pelly (1777–1852) was Governor of the Hudson Bay Company 1822–1852, and Governor of the Bank of England 1841–1842.

11. Fry and Cresswell, 1847, Volume II, p. 159.

12. *ibid.*, p. 183.

13. *Report from the Select Committee of the House of Lords on the Present State of the Gaols and Houses of Correction in England and Wales, House of Commons, 28 July 1835.*

14. *ibid.*

15. *ibid.*

16. Work on a new Houses of Parliament, designed by Charles Barry in collaboration with Augustus Pugin, began in 1840. The House of Lords was completed seven years later, and the rest of the building was ready for use five years after that. The clock tower, "Big Ben" was completed in 1858, and the Victoria Tower in 1860.

Chapter 15. Duty calls me that way

1. *Prison Inspectors' Report on Newgate, 1836.*

2. Appendix to *Twenty-fifth Report of Inspectors-General of Prisons in Ireland, 1847*. Quoted in Fry and Cresswell, 1847, Volume II, p. 225.

3. Mrs Rawlings, 1 September 1847. Fry and Cresswell, 1847, Volume II, pp. 225–226.

4. The Factory. The female penitentiary at Paramatta near Sydney, from which Timpson maintained that the more orderly and well-behaved prisoners were assigned positions as servants on the recommendations of clergymen or magistrates. See Timpson, 1847, p. 147.

5. Fry and Cresswell, 1847, Volume II, p. 260.

Chapter 16. A city set on a hill that cannot be hid

1. 1 Corinthians 14:34–35.

2. Tractarians. The Oxford Movement emerged in the early 1830s with the aim of highlighting the Catholic heritage of the Church of England. The campaign began with a series of publications called tracts which attacked what the movement regarded as prevailing weaknesses in the church, especially what it termed "liberalism". The most well-known of the movement's leaders were John Henry Newman, John Keble and Edward Pusey.

3. Gurney and Fry Correspondence, LSF.

4. Fry and Cresswell, 1847, Volume II, p. 354.

5. *ibid.*, p. 358.

6. Hare, 1895, Volume II, pp. 114–115.

7. Fry and Cresswell, 1847, Volume II, p. 370.

8. *ibid.*

9. Fry Papers, British Library, Department of Manuscripts: Egerton Mss EG 3672–3675.

10. *ibid.*

Chapter 17. My dear love to all our sisters

1. "The movement for women's suffrage, both in England and America, may be dated from the World's Anti-Slavery

Convention." *Lucretia Mott's Diary*, Introduction, p. 2. In Tolles (ed.), 1952.

2. "Harriet Elizabeth Georgiana Leveson-Gower, Duchess of Sutherland (1806–1868) was interested in many philanthropic causes; it was at Stafford House, her London residence, that a group of English women were to frame a protest against American slavery in 1853." *Lucretia Mott's Diary*, footnote to page 45. In Tolles (ed.) 1952.

3. Fry and Cresswell, 1847, Volume II, p. 395.

4. Bevan Braithwaite, 1854, p. 265.

5. Timpson, 1847, p. 13.

6. The new Royal Exchange replaced a predecessor destroyed by fire in 1838.

7. Gurney of the Arctic. While serving as a lieutenant on board HMS Agincourt, Samuel Gurney Cresswell distinguished himself in several actions against pirates in Borneo and Brunei. In 1848 he volunteered for Arctic service, in order to assist in the search for Sir John Franklin, lost in a search for the North-West passage. After almost five years, when the ship, *Investigator*, became trapped in ice, Lieut. Cresswell led a sledging party across the frozen ocean with dispatches for the Admiralty. By good fortune they eventually encountered a ship which returned them to Scotland. Thus Lieut. Cresswell's party were credited with being the first to traverse the North-West passage. Although he became something of a hero on his return to Norfolk, and later rose to the rank of captain, Gurney's health was broken by his Arctic experiences, and he died in 1867 at Bank House, his mother's home, aged only 39.

7. Fry and Cresswell, 1847, Volume II, p. 452.

8. Woodham-Smith, 1951, p. 66.

Bibliography

Babington, Anthony. *The English Bastille: A History of Newgate Gaol and Prison Conditions in Britain 1188–1902*. London: Macdonald, 1971

Bartholomew, M., Hall, D. and Lentin, A. (eds). *The Enlightenment: Studies, 1*. Milton Keynes: The Open University, 1992

Bartholomew, M., Hall, D. and Lentin, A. (eds). *The Enlightenment: Studies, 2*. Milton Keynes: The Open University, 1992

Bebbington, D.W. *Evangelicalism in Modern Britain: A History from the 1730s to the 1980s*. Unwin Hyman, 1989

Bevan Braithwaite, Joseph (ed.). *Memoirs of Joseph John Gurney*. Norwich: Fletcher & Alexander, 1854

Bordo, M.D. "The Financial Crisis of 1825 and the Restructuring of the British Financial System" in *The Federal Reserve Bank of St Louis Review*, May/June 1998

Brewer, John. *The Pleasures of the Imagination: English Culture in the Eighteenth Century*. London: HarperCollins, 1997

Cresswell, Rachel. *A Memoir of Elizabeth Fry*. London: Piper, Stephenson & Spence, 1856

Defoe, Daniel. *Moll Flanders*. (With introduction and notes by David Blewett.) London: Penguin, 1989

Ehrenreich, B. & English, D. *Complaints and Disorders: The Sexual Politics of Sickness*. New York: The Feminist Press at The City University of New York, 1973

Eliot, S. and Whitlock, K. (eds). *The Enlightenment: Texts, 1*. Milton Keynes: The Open University, 1992

Fowell Buxton, T. *An Inquiry whether Crime and Misery are produced or prevented by our present system of Prison Discipline*. London: John & Arthur Arch, Cornhill;

Butterworth and Sons, Fleet Street; and John Hatchard, Piccadilly, 1818.

Fry, K. and Cresswell, R. *Memoir of the Life of Elizabeth Fry with Extracts from her Journal and Letters*. (2 Volumes) London: John Hatchard, 1847

Fry, Elizabeth. *Observations on the Visiting, Superintendence and Government of Female Prisoners*. London: John & Arthur Arch, Cornhill; Hatchard & Son, Piccadilly; Norwich: S. Wilkin, 1827

Gurney, J.J. and Fry, E. *Report addressed to the Marquess Wellesley, Lord Lieutenant of Ireland*. London: 1827

Hare, Augustus. *The Gurneys of Earlham*. (2 Volumes) London: George Allen, 1895

Hibbert, Christopher. *London: The Biography of a City*. Great Britain: Longmans, Green, 1969

Hughes, Robert. *The Fatal Shore: A History of the Transportation of Convicts to Australia, 1787–1868*. Great Britain: Collins Harvill, 1987

Jemison, G.P. and Schein, A.M. (eds). *Treaty of Canandaigua 1794*. Sante Fé, New Mexico: Clear Light Publishers, 2000 (Contains as appendix: "The Savery Journal: The Canandaigua Treaty". Excerpt reprinted from *A Journal of the Life, Travels and Religious Labours of William Savery, a Minister of the Gospel of Christ, of the Society of Friends, Late of Philadelphia. Compiled from his original memoranda by Jonathan Edwards*.)

Kent, John. *Elizabeth Fry*. London: B.T. Batsford, 1962

O'Gorman, Frank. *The Long Eighteenth Century: British Political & Social History 1688–1832*. London: Arnold, 1997

Porter, Roy. *The Enlightenment* (Series: Studies in European History). Basingstoke & New York: Palgrave, 2001

Prison Inspectors' Report on Newgate, 1836. Microfiche Edition, Chadwyck-Healey Microform Publishing Services, 1980 (Original Volumes: The Library of the Department of Trade and Industry, London)

Punshon, John. *Portrait in Grey: A Short History of the Quakers*. London: Quaker Home Service, 1984

Report from the Committee of the Prisons within the City of London and Borough of Southwark. House of Commons, 1818 (Also called: *Prisons of the Metropolis. Committee Report with Minutes of Evidence and Appendix, 1818*; Irish University Press Series of British Parliamentary Papers). Shannon, Ireland: Irish University Press, 1970

Report from the Select Committee of the House of the Lords on The Present State of Gaols and Houses of Correction in England and Wales. House of Commons, 28 July 1835 (Irish University Press Series of British Parliamentary Papers). Shannon, Ireland: IUP, 1968. Reprinted, London: Routledge, 1993

Report from the Select Committee on Secondary Punishments. House of Commons, 22 June 1832 (Irish University Press Series of British Parliamentary Papers). Shannon, Ireland: IUP, 1969

Rose, June. *Elizabeth Fry*. London: Macmillan, 1980

Taylor, Frances R. *Life of William Savery*. Pub. New York: The Macmillan Company, 1925.

Thomas, Emyr. *Coalbrookdale and the Darbys*. Ironbridge Gorge Museum Trust, 1999

Timpson, Revd Thomas. *Memoirs of Elizabeth Fry*. London: Aylott & Jones, 1847.

Tolles, F.B. PhD (ed.) "Slavery and the 'Woman Question': Lucretia Mott's Diary of Her Visit to Great Britain to Attend the World's Anti-Slavery Convention of 1840" Supp. No. 23, *Journal of the Friends' Historical Society*. Haverford, USA: Friends' Historical Association; London: Friends' Historical Society, 1952

van Drenth, A. and de Haan, F. *The Rise of Caring Power: Elizabeth Fry and Josephine Baker in Britain and the Netherlands*. Amsterdam: Amsterdam University Press, 1999

Veith, Ilza. *Hysteria: the History of a Disease*. Northvale, New Jersey: Jason Aronson, 1993. Originally published Chicago: University of Chicago Press, 1965

White, R.J. *Life in Regency England*. London: B.T. Batsford, 1963

Whitney, Janet. *Elizabeth Fry: Quaker Heroine*. London: George
   G. Harrap, 1937
Woodham-Smith, Cecil. *Florence Nightingale*. London:
   Penguin Books, 1951

Unpublished sources

Bright, Simon. Joseph John Gurney (1788–1847): A Study in
   Evangelical Quaker Biography. Unpublished Master of Arts
   Thesis, 1992. LSF
Extracts from the Minutes and Advices of the Yearly Meeting
   of Friends held in London. Printed by James Phillips, 1783.
   LSF
Fry Papers. Gurney and Fry Correspondence 1700–1872.
   British Library, Department of Manuscripts. Egerton Mss
   3672–3675
Fry, Elizabeth. Manuscript Journals 1797–1845. Library of the
   Religious Society of Friends, London (LSF)
Fry, Elizabeth. Manuscript Journals 1816–1818 and 1821–1822
   Norwich Record Office, Norfolk
Fry, Elizabeth. Manuscript Journals 1830–1836. Johnson
   Matthey plc, London
Fry, Joseph. Manuscript Journal. LSF
Gurney and Fry Correspondence. LSF

Internet resources

The Peel Web: www.historyhome.co.uk

Index